Dickensian Affects

In *Dickensian Affects: Charles Dickens and Feelings of Precarity*, Joshua Gooch argues that Dickens's novels offer models of feeling that illuminate the dissensions that accompany life's precariousness under capitalism. By examining the role of violence, anxiety, surprise, and suspense in Dickens's novels, Gooch explores the representation and shaping of emotions to create rhythms specific to their historical moment. To unearth Dickensian affects, Gooch examines how Dickens's novels yoke elements in their difference to signal different kinds and ways of feeling, what he terms affective form. This patterning of elements links a text's ways of feeling to its conjuncture and locates lines of flight that allow its representations of emotion to become something more. The violence of *Oliver Twist* links its satire of the New Poor Law to the post-abolition period of apprenticeship in the West Indies. The pervasive anxiety of *The Old Curiosity Shop* links Nell's journey to arguments about inheritance and land reform. The surprise of *David Copperfield* binds its interests in questions of character and trust to Britain's professional world and credit markets. And the suspense of *Great Expectations* relies on a sense of shame that sends Victorians on a search for new models of masculine character exemplified by the Volunteer rifle militias of the 1860s. *Dickensian Affects* argues that questions of feeling reveal the precarity of feeling itself. For Dickens, to feel is to know the possibility of feeling otherwise.

Joshua Gooch is an Associate Professor of English at D'Youville College in Buffalo, New York. His research focuses on intersections of work, power, and aesthetics in literature and film, particularly in relation to cultures with financialized economies. His first monograph *The Victorian Novel, Service Work, and the Nineteenth-Century Economy* (New York: Palgrave Macmillan, 2015) examines the Victorian novel's role in representing and shaping the service sector's emergence.

Routledge Studies in Nineteenth-Century Literature

For more information about this series, please visit: https://www.routledge.com

Contents

Dickensian Affects
Charles Dickens and Feelings
of Precarity

Joshua Gooch

Routledge
Taylor & Francis Group

NEW YORK AND LONDON

First published 2020
by Routledge
52 Vanderbilt Avenue, New York, NY 10017

and by Routledge
2 Park Square, Milton Park, Abingdon, Oxon, OX14 4RN

*Routledge is an imprint of the Taylor & Francis Group, an
informa business*

Library of Congress Cataloging-in-Publication Data
A catalog record for this title has been requested

ISBN: 978-0-367-41609-6 (hbk)
ISBN: 978-0-367-81541-7 (ebk)

Typeset in Sabon
by codeMantra

For Brodie.

Preface

When I am in a room full of educated people, I am always surprised to learn their most transformative moments occurred in some institutional setting. A classroom, an internship, a professional mentor. Mine was a house party one late fall when I was perhaps seventeen. A sweaty room full of people and drums, amplifiers, and guitars, and a lot of what was likely quite awful noise. Yet for me it was an affective event, a loss of self and a discovery of something else, something that brought others and made it difficult to know where or if that distinction of self or other mattered in the first place. What a thing it is to have power, Dickens said. What a thing. It is not a thing that ever belonged to me or, truth to tell, that I have ever been especially good at. I chased it anyway, dropping in and out of college until I finally fell out with a PhD. That power, though, never left my thoughts. There is something necessary and generative in becoming other, of feeling and working and shaping with others and of not becoming attached to a self and whatever that self might mean. To embrace happening and doing with. In 2015, one of those I had happened and done with the most died. A something doing isn't much of a doing at all if it's just doing something alone. Yet doing together, as potent as it is, is something that seems out of bounds in modern life, including in intellectual life. We're done together all the time but doing together almost never. My argument here is an attempt to think about doing with. Doing with as what a novel does, as what readers do, as what critics do. These aren't apolitical doings, of course. They're real doings with real divergences and dissonances and arrhythmias. This is my attempt to think about thinking with and without too much concern about the priority of that with-ness.

This work on doing with would not have been done without the intellectual support and encouragement of friends and colleagues. Douglas Dowland was a source of guidance and encouragement throughout the project, reading the manuscript in varying degrees of disarray and doing his best to help me find structure in disorganization. He and Anni Pullagura also gave me the opportunity to expand the ideas that undergird this project in its effects and affects on contemporary cinema. Richard Adelman and Catherine Packham provided me with an initial forum to approach thinking about Dickens and inequality and their help in shaping that early work into publishable form gave me the impetus to expand and explore the ideas you find here. Neil David Ramsay generously included me in an amazing project of scholarship about the development of war, media, and contingency in the Romantic era that reshaped my understanding of war and warfare and affected the argument of the end of the project. Many of the initial insights that guided the work in this book were the result of a brilliant NEH summer seminar organized by Sharon Aronofsky Weltman and the Dickens Universe at the University of California at Santa Cruz. Iain Crawford, Lillian Nayder, and Joyce Wexler gave me the good fortune to be able to develop these insights for conferences. I also gained immeasurably from the panelists who presented on panels I organized for the Northeast Modern Language. The opportunity to write brief provocations about the discipline and its pedagogy from Rachel Ablow and Daniel Hack, and Jen Cadwallader and Laurence Mazzeno were important to the project's development as well. Though I am largely a lurker in online academic communities, discussions on the VICTORIA list-serv and academic Twitter have proven valuable sources of insight. I am obliged to the many students who have thought through these ideas with me and forced me to think always of the research process as a search for better ideas and better ways of thinking that can matter for others. Most of all, I am grateful for the love and forbearance of my family, especially my partner Sara and my son, who at three years old carts around stacks of books and shouts, "Look, I'm daddy!"

An earlier version of Chapter 3 appeared in *Political Economy, Literature, and the Formation of Knowledge, 1720–1850*, edited by Richard Adelman and Catherine Packham (Routledge, 2018) as "The Anxiety of Inheritance: Work and the Impasses of Accumulation in Dickens's *The Old Curiosity Shop*."

Introduction
What a Thing It Is to Have Power

In 1844, Charles Dickens finished his second Christmas book, *The Chimes*. Exhilarated, he wrote from Italy to his friend Thomas Mitton, "I believe I have written a tremendous Book and knocked the Carol out of the field" (*Letters* 4, 211–12). His confidant John Forster gave Dickens more reason to believe in the success of his tale after circulating it amongst their friends. Dickens bragged to his wife, Catherine:

> Anybody who has heard it, has been moved in the most extraordinary manner. Forster read it (for dramatic purposes) to A Beckett—not a man of very quiet feeling. He cried so much, and so painfully, that Forster didn't know whether to go on or stop; and he called next day to say that any expression of his feeling was beyond his power. (*Letters* 4, 234)

He added a postscript to include the reaction of William Macready, the renowned Victorian actor, to his own reading: "if you had seen Macready last night undisguisedly sobbing, and crying on the sofa as I read—you would have felt, as I did, what a thing it is to have Power" (*Letters* 4, 235). Dickens will chase after this experience for the rest of his life, not only in his amateur theatricals, his famed public readings, and his secret life with Ellen Ternan but also in his novel's tighter and tighter interweaving of formal innovation and social critique. In his life and his writing, Dickens was an affect junkie.

Dickens's insistence on the lasting power of *The Chimes*, however, was somewhat misplaced.[1] A dour tour through working-class poverty, the story means like the *Carol* to foster Christian charitableness, but its central vision—a mother driven by poverty to drown her infant daughter out of fear she will become a prostitute—is more graphic and bleak than the *Carol* and its implication of Tiny Tim's death. One might say the dreariness reflects the despair of the hungry forties. Friedrich Engels's observations of working-class poverty in *The Conditions of the Working Class in England* were written nearly simultaneous with *The Chimes* and underscore the increasingly widespread sense that workers' conditions were unmoored from the economic success of industry. This hopelessness affects even the language of *The Chimes*. Gone is the *Carol*'s terse irony which evokes with little detail. *The Chimes* relies instead on lengthy descriptive passages and harsh narratorial invective, a difference that may help us grasp how and why Dickens would think or his readers would feel as they did at this moment in 1844. Its images and its moral—that people are not as bad as political economists imagine them to be—capture the horrors of poverty and the indifference of a middle class inculcated by political economic common sense at a particular moment in time. This historical embeddedness of the affective likely indicates why *The Chimes*, though its initial run successfully netted Dickens £1,500 (see Ackroyd 459), did not supplant the *Carol* in popularity. Indeed, Dickens's next Christmas tale, *The Cricket on the Hearth*, sold twice as many copies in its first run as *The Chimes* (see Ackroyd 485) and remained popular into the early twentieth century, including a 1909 film adaptation by D.W. Griffith. By contrast, *The Chimes* had and lost its moment much more quickly. Dickens included it in his initial repertoire of professional performances beginning in April 1858 but had dropped it by September. In a letter from November 1858, he describes the tale as "*very* dramatic, but very melancholy on the whole" (*Letters* 8, 483).[2] He performs *The Chimes* just one more time in greatly edited form on his farewell tour on 19 January 1869.[3] The story that had so moved its initial auditors with expressions beyond their control had become, in Dickens's words, "a little dismal," he explained in a letter written the day of this final reading, and so he had "shortened and brightened it as much as possible" (*Letters* 12, 277).[4] Such brightening meant excising nearly a third of the text, including the narrator's harsh social commentary mouthed through the embittered worker Will Fern and revising the text's winding sentences into shorter, more conversational form. These alterations indicate that what had been central to the tale's affective power—the material deprivations of the 1840s—had become less pressing for Dickens fourteen years later. Even given the 1866 Hyde Park demonstration for political reform, Dickens's final reading text reflects a perspective embedded in the midst of the so-called age of equipoise and before the long economic downturn of the 1870s. The tale's concerns about material living conditions—starvation, short wages, and lack of work—may have also been less present for his auditors in this relatively quiet period between Chartism's peak in 1848 and the rise of socialist organizing in the 1880s. As a result of these changed conditions, Dickens found it necessary to alter the tale's affects and style lest its drama and dismalness overwhelm its performability.

Although *The Chimes* did not knock *A Christmas Carol* from the field, the rush of Dickens's initial claims for it indicates the degree to which the power of the affective—that is, the ability to affect and be affected—is central to the writing of fictional narratives and to which its reception is deeply embedded in the conjunctural—that is, the political, economic, material, and affective environment beyond a writer's control. For Dickens, *The Chimes* reveals the contingency with which a work of narrative fiction may achieve its desired affective ends through timely or topical contents and that such ends themselves end as history moves on. What resonates is far from certain, and if something does resonate, whether it will continue to resonate is even less certain. The representation of a materially present concern may be highly freighted for a contemporaneous audience without any guarantee of resonance over time. It may be too much. It may be too little. As Dick Hebdige writes in another context, "forms cannot be permanently normalized" (16). Temporal lags affect a text's ability to signal particular emotions or ways of feeling and thus reveal the ways in which narrative fiction produces what I call here affective forms—discussed in more detail below—as well as the ways in which readers may act as historically embedded Goldilockses in search of texts at just the right affective temperature. Fredric Jameson describes fiction's drive for affect as one of realism's central antinomies, an unresolved tension between the narration of plot events and the affective unfolding of experience in scenes—in short, a tension between telling and showing with telling bound to a sense of temporal finality and showing to an affective present. For Jameson's dialectical approach, there is an "irrevocable antagonism between the twin (and entwined) forces in question" (*Antinomies* 11). For Dickens, however, the seeming antagonism between affective description and narrativized plotting is far less clear. On the one hand, his style would seem nearly empty of the affective because of its style of narration and its use of the preterite. Barring a few exceptions—for instance, the reflective sense of presentness in *David Copperfield* when David narrates events like his drunken revelry with Steerfield or his marriage to Dora—one would be hard pressed to locate passages that suggest in Dickens the protomodernist descriptions of affect that Jameson locates in scene. On the other hand, however, Dickens's reliance on melodramatic plotting means to evoke feelings for characters and readers—for instance, Little Nell's journey and decline in *The Old Curiosity Shop*—that make his narratives often nothing less than a series of signals for different feelings.[5] In Dickens, a reciprocal pressure between narrative and affect suggests they are not as antagonistic as one might believe. Dickens's tales yoke and conjoin story and discourse, showing and telling, and affect and cognition, to produce intensities for readers that are conjuncturally embedded formal signals of emotions in textual form. It is this formal and conjunctural work of Dickens's novels that *Dickensian Affects* explores.

Consider the formal and affective qualities of the climactic sequence of *The Chimes*. Trotty Veck, after viewing his daughter Margaret's descent into poverty, her husband's turn to drunken despair, and her friend's seduction into prostitution, enters the room as his daughter finishes watching over her husband's deathbed. The spirits of the chimes tell Trotty that he will learn a lesson here "from the creature dearest to your heart!" (*Christmas* 150). The narration of this instruction, however, is not didactic:

> It was over. It was over. And this was she, her father's pride and joy! This haggard, wretched woman, weeping by the bed, if it deserved that name, and pressing to her breast, and hanging down her head upon, an infant. Who can tell how spare, how sickly, and how poor an infant! Who can tell how dear?
>
> "Thank God!," cried Trotty, holding up his folded hands. "O, God be thanked! She loves her child!" (*Christmas* 150–51)

The sentimentality of this passage resides in Trotty's cry, a turn to God and celebration of domestic love, but its affective punch resides in its clipped sentences, its repetitions, and its refusals of specificity. "It was over" may have meant to denote Richard's life but its distance from Richard's death obscures the reference and allows ambiguity to creep in. Margaret's experience watching is as plausibly "it" as Richard's life, and this reference would bind her wretchedness to the passage's equivocation of despair and finality. Yet this is not the end of the ambiguity. "It was over" also allows for an indetermination of character and narratorial voice. At first, it suggests Trotty's perspective but as the next sentence winds and extends its description of Margaret's state, the description of her weeping by a bed "if it deserved that name" seems to belong to the narrator rather than Trotty. The penultimate sentence's anaphora further marks the narrator's presence—and what is Dickensian narration without anaphora?—and thus the closing question "Who can tell how dear?" seems to come from the narrator until Trotty breaks in with an answer.

Dickens plays with this problem of character and narratorial voice earlier in *The Chimes*. An Alderman threatens to jail the poor for attempting suicide yet describes his friend's suicide as "a lamentable instance" (*Christmas* 134). A voice that seems to belong to the narrator then castigates him:

> What, Alderman! No word of Putting Down? Remember, Justice, your high moral boast and pride. Come, Alderman! Balance those scales. Throw me into this, the empty one, no dinner, and Nature's founts in some poor woman, dried by starving misery and rendered obdurate to claims for which her offspring *has* authority in holy mother Eve. Weigh me the two, you Daniel, going to judgment, when your day shall come! Weigh them, in the eyes of suffering thousands, audience (not unmindful) of the grim farce you play. Or supposing that you strayed from your five wits – it's not so far to go, but that it might be – and laid hands upon that throat of yours, warning your

fellows (if you have a fellow) how they croak their comfortable wickedness to raving heads and stricken hearts. What then?

The words rose up in Trotty's breast, as if they had been spoken by some other voice within him. (*Christmas* 134–35)

The recognizably Dickensian invective is suddenly and rather shockingly located in the "breast" of the heretofore deferential Trotty. This reframes its succinct language as that closest to Trotty himself but stripped of its deference: "What, Alderman?" "Come, Alderman! Balance those scales." "What then?" To attribute these words to Trotty Veck—as out of keeping with his character as they may be—makes the sentimental Trotty sound like one of the heckling voices in a working-class demonstration. While Sloppy will later "do the police in different voices" (*Our Mutual Friend* 1.16:198), the narrator of *The Chimes* does the poor first.

Trotty/the narrator's outburst captures a stylistic forcefulness and conveys an anger and despair that pervades the text. Elsewhere, Will Fern enacts these feelings by denouncing the gentry's attempts at charity:

when work won't maintain me like a human creetur; when my living is so bad, that I am Hungry, out of doors and in; when I see a whole working life begin that way, go on that way, and end that way, without a chance or change, then I say to gentlefolks, 'Keep away from me!' (*Christmas* 116–17)

Fern captures the particulars of the text's conjuncture: not poverty as such but *working* poverty; not hunger as such, but hunger *regardless of relief* (hence "Hungry, out of doors and in"); and not stretches of difficulty in working life but *working life as such made an unchanging, inescapable hell.* Anger and despair are organized by an intensity of the feeling of class schism signalled by Fern's demand that the gentry "Keep away from me!" Affective form here dissolves subjective distinctions as a contrast to its angry and despairing class divisions, an enfolding of narrator, character, and reader in opposition to an oppressor.

This indetermination of voices indicates form's role in articulating Dickensian affects as a question of the intertwining of content, style, and feeling. These formal concerns run throughout Dickens's work but have been particularly noted in his Christmas books. Claire Pettitt writes of Dickens's Christmas tales that he is often "not trying to dispense with tenses altogether so much as to break the grammar of oppression by their temporary confusion" (120). As a result, one might imagine that the use of free indirect discourse in *The Chimes* suits the overcoming of divisions rather than their deepening. After all, it brings narrator, character, and reader together in unmediated, non-visual experience. The piece's climactic scene has Trotty save Margaret and his granddaughter from drowning using the same abrupt rhythm but for gestures of physical connection: "She was in his arms. He held her now. His strength was like a giant's" (*Christmas* 157). Punctive rhythm reinforces a narrative of relief—Margaret does not drown her baby!—and increases the narrator's proximity to Trotty's consciousness. The narrator holds Margaret as much as Trotty does. Yet this terseness also obscures important narrative information. Until this passage, Trotty's ghost-like form could not affect anyone in his vision. Only at this critical juncture can he intercede. The narration captures his doing and his being able to do while conveying little about how it is done—he *does*, just as the narrator does—and the simile further compresses the doing done to a feeling of mythological and monumental strength.[6] This moment of Trotty-becoming-narrator presages his enunciation of the tale's moral; in Trotty's words, "we must trust and hope, and neither doubt ourselves, nor doubt the good in one another" (*Christmas* 157). In terms of purposive sentiment, then, the tale's dance of free indirect discourse seems to reinforce a sense of shared moral good.

There is a problem with this attempt to recode the tale's affective form through sentimentality, however. That the poor may be good, the narrative shows; that the poor may reach out to save one another, it enacts; that it offers a way past class separation, it merely asserts. The denouement of the *Carol* offers a similar moral lesson but illustrates its cross-class charitableness with Scrooge providing a Christmas feast and performing good acts. In *The Chimes*, by contrast, Trotty's lower middle-class landlady brings a small breakfast the morning of Margaret and Richard's wedding and everyone dances. The poor remain poor, albeit together, and the Aldermen and gentry keep away. Futurity is out of consideration. In this respect, *The Chimes* is undoubtedly an affecting tale but of a different sort than the *Carol*. It is, as Dickens said, "a little dismal." When Dickens revised the tale for his last reading, he excised Fern's speech, its denunciation of the Alderman, and its self-reflexive use of free indirect discourse. Instead, after the repetitions of "It was over," Dickens added to an otherwise unchanged paragraph one clarifying sentence: "The ruins of Richard [her husband] cumbered this earth no more" (*Sikes and Nancy* 54). The terse rhythms and indeterminations of Trotty's hold on Margaret at the river become more narratorial and anaphoric in the reading text: "*He could touch her, now. He could hold her, now. His strength was like a giant's*" (*Sikes and Nancy* 56). The narrator's voice, written for Dickens's now-practiced performance voice, insists on its difference from Trotty's and speaks to tell his audience what "he could" do rather than what he did. Separate voices, changed rhythms, different intensities—a new affective form for a new conjuncture.

In *The Chimes* and its revisions, one begins to see the work of affective form in Dickens's writing, the work of a conjunction of formal strategies, story events, and economic, social, historical, and political context.

out assumptions in older criticism that such issues are feminine and unworthy of examination.[2] Yet much as the affective turn has made feeling worthy of study, the underlying theoretical problem that affect poses for literary studies remains.

Consider the role of experience and affect in narrative theory. Narratology routinely notes the centrality of experience to narrative but focuses on modes of telling rather than the relation of narrative to qualities of experience. Even versions of narratology most engaged with experience and embodiment—for example, Monika Fludernik's account of "natural narrative"—tend to focus on cognition and the textual embedding and transmission of ideas.[3] Affects, such theorists argue, are more readily tracked in the temporal arts—that is, dance, music, theater, and audio-visual texts—because they operate nonconsciously and directly on spectators. A close-up of a face or a montage rhythmically bound to music affects viewers without mediation, whereas a reader confronts a temporal and cognitive hiatus that allows for conscious reflection and thus limits the possibility of direct affects. Yet this hiatus does not make affect in texts impossible so much as multiple. Affects in texts are the likely or potential result of the formal mechanisms they use to signal feelings through their representations and of the cultural and historical embeddedness of the texts and their readers. To say that any individual reader may not be affected by a text is not to eliminate affective experience so much as to underscore the necessity of attention to the ways in which texts mean to signal affects and are embedded in historically specific structures of feeling that bear different possible positions for singular persons to occupy. Here, then, affect is no longer simply eruptive but something in part *crafted*—by a creator, by a reader, by a situation.

Hence the analytic method most closely aligned to my work here is what cultural studies scholars call conjunctural analysis. A conjuncture, as Stuart Hall explains, "is a period during which the different social, political, economic and ideological contradictions that are at work in society come together to give it a specific and distinctive shape" ("Interpreting" 57). Conjunctural analysis brings these differences to bear on a text, in practice pressing outward from cultural texts to new contextual sources of difference and contradiction in an effort to "produce better conjunctural stories" (Grossberg, *Cultural Studies* 101). For cultural studies scholars, such analysis is inseparable from affect. As Lawrence Grossberg and Bryan G. Behrenhausen note, conjunctural analysis allows one to "[take] the contingency of affect seriously" by considering the many hybrid assemblages of a conjuncture (1019)—that is, it allows us to grapple with the different ways affects are produced by cultural texts, their situations, and their readers. In practice, however, it can be difficult to explain the operations of conjunctural analysis in literary studies. What does such an analysis do? Close read, certainly. But what

The intensities that a form signals are a result of its use of the narrated, the felt, and the conjunctural to signal an overdetermination, a nexus of stacked and related concepts and feelings. In affect studies, the word *intensity* describes the efficient expression of a multiplicity of relations, what Brian Massumi explains as the way that intensity "culminates the playing out of the tensions inherent in their qualitative differentials" (*99 Theses*, 40). Dickens's work relies on these kinds of differential intensities and signals them through a mixture of story, discourse, and conjunctural resonance. One of the central aspects of the affective qualities of *The Chimes*, its too-muchness, is its focus on the signaling of intensities by yoking form to content and context. It suggests a multiplicity without reducing it and can thus overwhelm with an excess of relations in too brief a space (though it also may not hit its mark at all). This is not unique to *The Chimes* so much as more readily located there. Intensities mark all of Dickens's work and operate in a variety of forms in the search for efficient expressions of relations between plots, characters, emotions, and historical experiences. The conjunction of Dickens's narrative strategies, construction of emotions, and sentimentality alongside his unremitting focus on poverty and precarity are the basis of his affects. In a word, their forms.

In the following pages, I analyze some of Dickens's most affectively freighted and personal novels, exploring their forms to locate affective lines of flight that open their representations of emotion to otherness. The form of *Oliver Twist*, in its relentless focus on the violence of personal domination, reveals the text as not simply about the new Poor Law or Dickens's feelings of maternal abandonment but also the end of slavery and the so-called apprenticeship system in the British Empire, the use of race to distinguish workers in England from those in the West Indies and Jews from the English, and the oppression of women. The affective form of *The Old Curiosity Shop*, often the subject of analyses that highlight sentimentality and grief, underscores anxiety as part of its understanding of love, and this conjunction of emotion and affect indicates the economic turmoil represented in the text and role of inheritance law and land reform to the discussion of inequality in the 1840s. *David Copperfield*, seemingly Dickens's least historically and socially engaged text, grapples with questions of character and character formation that are bound to the history of credit and professional character, both of which rely upon relations of trust and the feeling of surprise at its abrogation or confirmation. In this way, the novel engages with the disorganized credit landscape of bill-brokering, a system that arose in the aftermath of the crisis of 1825 and reaches its crisis-point in 1857. The affective form of *David Copperfield* reveals the recalcitrance of character, always holding out the possibility of another character and another way of feeling. David's success is haunted by a shame that is so inexpressible it appears in the text only as a feeling of surprise. By contrast, the affective form of *Great Expectations* subjects this recalcitrance to askesis, an attempt to suspend character's feelings of vulnerability and shame for an aggressive, masculine model of character formation. Its narrative construction of a character meant to protect masculine subjects from the threat of foreign affective forces connects *Great Expectations* with the creation of the Volunteer riflemen militias in the early 1860s and suggests a more affectively nuanced suspension of this masculine urge toward violence.

One might understand the work of affective form as similar to the constellations of text and history of Walter Benjamin's dialectical images. Benjamin's concept, though, perhaps too readily suggests a homology between text and history, an aesthetic resolution of historical problems. Affective form insists on the singularity and irreducibility of its parts. Pip's shame in *Great Expectations* does not merely reflect a vulnerability felt by white British men which found expression in the new Volunteer forces but instead explores vulnerability as such, a feeling that informs text and conjuncture but that finds its own trajectory of development in Dickens's text. The singularity and openness of affective form—the machinic qualities that allow it to connect disparate pieces, to denude them of prior feelings and meanings, and to produce new ones instead— allows the feelings represented by a text like *Great Expectations* and the manner in which they are signaled and performed to resonate with the rise of the Volunteer forces. It also reveals variegations in the ways a tale may be shaped and adapted to suit new conjunctures. As the conclusion argues, this reshaping draws on a novel's affective form yet demands important alterations to engage with changes in conjuncture, medium, and industry. Film adaptations of *Great Expectations* reveal this in their engagements with the end of the Second World War, the rise of the neoliberal creative economy, and the mass insecurity of the twenty-first century. Affective forms provide a way to describe how texts articulate themselves to produce feelings within and across historical moments.

It is this attention to form as a material and (trans)historical process that separates my argument from prior scholarship on Dickens. Critics have discussed affective aspects of Dickens through the lens of Victorian sentimentality and taken such sentimentality as a way of navigating the desires and rivalries created by changes in social hierarchy, including new experiences of social mobility in the nineteenth century. Scholarship focused on sentimentality emphasizes the ways that affect serves an instrumental purpose in Dickens's work. Without a doubt, sentimental motifs and appeals—the lost angelic mother, the appeal to domestic life, the cleansing power of tears—are part of the humane and humanizing sympathies that Dickens means to activate in his fiction. Whether one insists on the eighteenth-century roots of this sentimentality, as Fred Kaplan does, or on the specificity of nineteenth-century sentimentality, as Miriam Bailin and Michael Bell do, scholars have understood sentimentality in Dickens's work to serve a pedagogical purpose. They are incitements to feel with others. There is no doubt that this need to *feel with* undergirds much of Dickens's affective project and must inform any engagement with affect in his work. Yet sentimentality's purposiveness should not obscure a text's other affective potentials, most especially since sentimentality and sympathy render its subjects as objects and limit who or what seem fit objects for sympathy. Sentimentality provides a point of entry into the affective work of Dickens's novels but too tight a focus may reduce our understanding of their affective work to a set of seemingly coherent emotions and thus evacuate it of possibilities and conflicts. It is in the suggestive evocation of affects that one discovers in Dickens's novels histories of the nineteenth century that his works seem to exclude, histories of racial animus, imperial violence, and the invisible industries of finance, insurance, and real estate. To treat feeling in Dickens as purposive and potential is to discover an impersonal and asubjective openness and range of potentialities beyond his desired sentimentality or sympathy for the poor.

By contrast, most critical studies of Dickens which suggest the affective rely on the purposive and the subjective, and operate in one of three modes: examinations of the historical and philosophical mechanisms that undergird sentimentality, often grounded in Adam Smith's theory of the moral sentiments[7]; attempts to reclaim the affectivity of the sentimental as such[8]; and investigations of the historical contexts which inform different literary modes of sentimentality.[9] When Miriam Bailin and Audrey Jaffe engage with Victorian sentimentality as distinct from eighteenth-century or Romantic sentimentality, they rely on the use of visual identification and the staging of scenes found in Smith's work to describe this sentimentality, in effect, trusting the presence of a scene to bring spectators, either as characters or readers, into moral alignment with an imagined unitary moral code. Scholarly reclamations of the sentimental focus on the need to feel with a text and reflect upon those feelings, an approach that presages Rita Felski's encouragement to critics to consider their own affects. In this line of scholarship, the affective needs a subject, even if that subject is simply the critic. For example, in tracking the power of the affective, Emma Mason argues that to approach the sentimental one should bracket the historical—in essence, claiming that historical detail creates blocks to affective experience that can be overcome only by focusing on the experiential relation between readers and texts. Eugenie Brinkema rightly argues against this approach to affect, describing it as a variant of the New Critical affective fallacy that one begins from the instrumentality of the sentimental to arrive at the truthfulness of a critic's affective experience.[10] The seeming ease with which sentimentality allows a blurring of personal experience and affect, an ease encouraged by treating affects as contagious, poses a problem for literary critics by suggesting—however unfairly—a return of the subjective as the basis for criticism. One need not be a proponent of Northrop

Frye to endorse his arguments against such a method. I would argue that critics must attend to textual form and its affective incitements in order to discover the potential for affective difference. To focus solely on the effectiveness of sentimentality threatens to elide this problem. For this reason, we must also throw into question the centrality of visuality and cognition to sentimentality and sympathy. As I discuss in Chapter 1, sentimentality, most especially in Smith's theory of moral sentiments, begins from a viewing subject and demands a cognitive process of reflection and judgment. This approach to sentimentality asks: What would it be to suffer like the sufferer that I see before me? Affect, by contrast, is not an affair of subjects, cognition, or reflection. Whether it is found in the most sentimental of scenes or the least, affect simply *occurs*. All else comes after.

Yet this focus on the occurrent is not to suggest that affect can be understood as anything other than contextual, conjunctural, and situational. To suffer is an event, a happening embedded in a time and place. Prior explorations of affect and form thus find their strongest ground in scholarly work on the contexts that inform different literary modes of sentimentality as Sally Ledger's work exemplifies. Ledger identifies Dickens's use of "sharp affective juxtapositions"—typically between tears and laughter—as the basis for what she terms "a species of Brechtian alienation effect avant la lettre" (7). For Ledger, Dickens's sentimental scenes reveal the importance of melodrama to his fiction—also explored by scholars such as Martin Meisel, Juliet John, Elaine Hadley, and others—and that his project is in essence "a realism of affect, rather than representational realism" (12). In this way, Ledger begins to unravel the form and historical basis of the affective in Dickens even as she remains focused on the intentionality of his affective solicitations. My argument builds from Ledger's important insights while pressing questions of instrumentality and control raised by affect studies. Dickens's "affective juxtapositions" are part of what makes his affective forms distinct. As Malcolm Andrews rightly argues, the basis of Dickens's comedy results from the "friction" between "his high formal style" and "his ventriloquized vernacular speech styles" (*Dickensian Laughter* 8). Dickens's affective forms are not focused on the production of a single affect or way of feeling but of sets of emotions and feelings given a particular kind of affective cast or coherence. Dickens's novels are never simply happy or sad, after all. His forms mean to—need to—signal different kinds of feelings and to articulate these feelings to their conjuncture. Attention to the multiplicity of feeling in Dickens thus highlights what is unique about his affective forms, their textual historicity. As controlled and produced as Dickens's signals to affect may be, their success lies in factors beyond his control.

Current work on affect provides theoretical scaffolding to explain why. At the most fundamental level, affects are neither personal nor

Chapter 4 turns to *David Copperfield*. No novel of Dickens' is as fraught with sentiment and suffering as *David Copperfield*, or as caught in the meshes of autobiography. As Dickens's biographers note, his early experiences of poverty and lost social position mark nearly all of his fictional texts, and one may suspect that these gave him the lived experience necessary to produce the affective textures of economic precarity that mark each of my chapters: class domination, racial threats, and economic anxiety. In *David Copperfield*, precarity becomes the basis for a positive project that grounds scene, which tends toward the affectively dense, and narrative, which tends toward the evocation of emotion, in a shared problematic, one that blossoms into what we now recognize as thematic coherence. This shared problematic, I argue, is trust, a relation deeply bound to mid-Victorian notions of character and the making of the self. In his *Logic*, John Stuart Mill highlights the way in which personal character is grounded in the feeling that one has the possibility of autonomy from total determination, even if such autonomy is never actually achieved. David's character is deeply embedded in this understanding of character and its feeling of a potentially notional autonomy. Throughout the novel, the people David meets try to form his character, to make him suitably "firm," yet also threaten to undermine the qualities that David imagines to be intrinsically his. The novel's focus on character, determination, and autonomy resonates with the development of the call loan system in the British money market from the 1820s through 1860, a system that underwrote financial risk taking at all levels of society and relied upon notions of character that began with the person and ended with institutions. One needed the proper character to obtain a bill as an individual—a problem about which Mr. Micawber comments at length—and the call loan system relied upon the Bank of England's insistence that only bill brokers had the proper institutional character to discount bills with the Bank itself. This system was grounded in the personal character of key actors, yet it led to an expansion of the credit markets and the development of more and more impersonal credit systems. It is the surprise that inhabits the tension between the personal and impersonal trust which constitutes the affective form of *David Copperfield*, at once suggesting the centrality of David as a commanding narrator whose personal character guarantees our trust and of David as an impersonal and permeable figure that allows others to come into view through his narration. David's impersonality allows the novel to suggest the "davidual," the production of impersonal affects within and beyond narrative determination, a kind of blooming of present affect that can cause the narrative to stutter.

Where *Copperfield* emphasizes character's role in the cultivation of trust, *Great Expectations* underscores its role in the mediation and modification of one's own vulnerabilities. What matters to *Copperfield* entirely transmissible but rather the transindividual stuff of sociality. For this reason, much as individuals, groups, institutions, or states solicit and attempt to regulate affect as emotion, affect is at once prepersonal or impersonal and connects those impersonal singularities in ways that allow it to slip free of regulation. In short, affect signals a spectrum of possibilities rather than determining a particular response. Dickens's belief in the likely historical success of *The Chimes* over *A Christmas Carol* offers one instance of the historical trials of affect in narrative fiction, a snapshot of the distance between the ability to construct affective forms and to regulate them. Out of such incommensurability, one may discern the inherence of affective form within a text, a form related to the historical contents and affects a text may intend to signal and what any one reader experiences, a form that remains irreducible to intentionality or subjectivity. From the perspective of structuralism, form suggests matrices of elements and their permutations and transformations. Form in this sense is the possibility of patterns using these elements, the *langue* of structuralism. Attention to affect might thus seem attention to *parole* and thus outside formalist concern. Yet affect also indicates the stylization of abstract forms, inflections of structural organization that articulate their elements and their organization to particular ways of feeling and acting in the world. In its abstraction, structural form has distinct limits, clearly defined bounds and rules that cannot be superseded. Affective form, however, does not. Its affectivity is an event, a happening that is also an event to come. This is why affect studies treat the affective as an event, an enfolding and unfolding of its situation that includes and excludes other beings and exceeds them.[11] If the affective is something doing, as Brian Massumi likes to say, that is because it is an event of affecting and being affected.[12] For affect studies, all art aspires to the creation of such events. As Gilles Deleuze and Felix Guattari write, "artists are presenters of affects... they not only create them in their work, they give them to us and make us become with them, they draw us into the compound" (*What is Philosophy* 175).[13] Much as this suggests that artists produce works that would seem unchanging in their affective qualities, it also indicates the necessity of the situational. When narrative fiction presents affects, it does so in ways that are conjuncturally embedded, and what is outside and beyond an author's control is part of what makes a text capable of becoming part of an affective event. Critics of Dickens have intuited this interaction between the affective and the historical at the level of the personal or biographical. Nicola Brown notes the effect of Nell's death on William Macready and John Forster, both of whom had recently lost children. It is important to emphasize that such states extend beyond the personal or biographical, however. Affective form helps us see these events as becomings, situations in which the apparent tension between what seems objective (e.g., history) and subjective (e.g., feeling) operates, in Massumi's words, as "a dynamic mutual inclusion of phases of process in each other" (*Semblance and Event* 9). Affective forms in texts exist as potentials or signals waiting for readers in resonant situations. The transhistorical nature of texts relies on this interaction of impersonal affective forms and resonant situations.

This is not to discount the difficulties that the language and discourse of affect—a twentieth-century turn—raises for scholarship engaged with nineteenth-century literature. Much of the scholarship that approaches issues of affectivity in nineteenth-century literature relies on the language of *feeling*, a term capacious enough to capture the many ways that Victorians engaged with problems of physical receptivity, the passions, emotions, moods, and other modes of shared feeling. Yet attention to feeling and language in literary scholarship tends to focus on the interface between body and text, an approach that conjures questions of *style*. Perhaps the foremost proponent for a return to analyses of style in literary studies is Garrett Stewart, whose work traces links between style and embodied response to illuminate what literature and art may do to bodies. Stewart defends style as a line of scholarly inquiry, and argues that "style ... is a name for the reader's *passage through* [form], narrative's only *way forward*" (*Value* 15).[14] It is, he suggests, "not the last refinement of [narrative] meaning but its articulating energy" (17). Stewart's approach suggests much for work in affect yet is deconstructive and bears a substantial debt to the open structuralism of theorists such as Gérard Genette and Michael Riffaterre. His analyses of style attend to the letter of the text and bring out matrices of meaning which map the slide of the signifier and the drift of the embodied voice against axes of meaning and significance. Stewart's work moves fluidly between how signification allows for a disembedding and sliding of the textual (what he terms "the phonotext" [*Reading* 28]) and the narrative mechanisms by which texts emplot readers. (This approach recalls work in film studies that examines the construction of an ideal viewer and its potential destabilizations in contrast to work on a historically particular set of viewers.) Stewart's recent work on Dickens's style underscores this dualism. He describes Dickens as essentially two-sided: on the one hand, the Inimitable Boz of Dickens's plots and, on the other hand, a stylistic deterritorializing of language that Stewart presents as the result of "a continuous three-way interference across political oratory, poetic theatre, and the stenographic antithesis of each" (*The One* xxv). These influences, however, eventually reveal for Stewart his titular *Other Dickens*—not Catherine, as in the title of Lillian Naydler's biography—a Dickens much like the phonotext, and which he describes as "an impersonal function of textual encounter" (173).[15]

My work here means to redress a problem that Stewart confronts in his engagement with form and style. When one approaches the affective as the interface between bodies and texts, the social and prepersonal threaten to become relations between texts while bodies remain the inert bodies of already existing readers. Who reads? You read, it would seem, and you read as you are. Stewart confronts this problem in his closing discussion of the textual drift found in his Other Dickens and explains reading itself as an encounter with difference:

> Incurred here is no identificatory finding of *myself* in or when reading, through narrative involvement and recognition, ethical, psychological, or otherwise. Rather, in reading this thickly layered Dickens, not just reeled off in serviceable decoding but more deeply peeled away at, I *find myself a reader*, steeped in linguistic action, soaked through by the rippling surge of words, not bested by the madcap play of syllables but invested in it, embroiled. (173)

I agree altogether that it is in the process of encounter and reading that we enter into a process of becoming. The affective, however, is as important an aspect of this process as the discursive. Notice how even for Stewart, the literary critic fascinated by style, his response is more affective than cognitive: he is steeped, soaked, embroiled in the visceral act and gustatory metaphors that constitute his affects of reading. He is "moved in the most extraordinary manner," and in this enthusiasm finds himself as a reader and a critic. Stewart's responses show us how the affective pushes us to question the function of a preconstituted reading subject or subject of discourse, a knowing reader who interprets and feels, and to imagine instead a reader who operates in prepersonal and social registers, feeling before knowing and connecting those feelings with other forms of experience to become whatever subject.[16]

To attend to affective form is to treat the reader as a multiplicity of *dividuals*, a term that captures the plurality of social functions which traverse any one person. Reading does not so much unify a reader as ramify a surfeit of possible readers, a continual rhizomatic signaling of affective and connotative experience. Indeed, as Stewart readily admits, Stewart the reader may seem the same but is not synonymous with Stewart the critic. For much of literary criticism, the division and plurality of the dividual has been treated as the corrosive effects of postmodernity on what we imagine to be the truth of subjectivity, an idealized notion of the unified individual whose passage we should mourn and whose death should be attributed to the rise of capital and its divisions and alienations of the social world through the commodity form.[17] That this process of mourning seems to take place time and time again and across different modes of production—the appearance of the commodity form in early modernity, the rise of industrial capitalism in the nineteenth century, the consolidation of finance capital in the late nineteenth century, the hyper-financialization of the late twentieth century—seems to me to indicate a story too vague to be of much service. This is not to dismiss the importance of material economic factors but to question whether the story of an organic society fractured by commodification and the rise of *homo economicus* or the bourgeois individual is too simple to capture the complexities of historical and human experience, a variant of the "organisms plus environment" model of science that Donna Haraway argues has now become "unthinkable" in the sciences (30). We need a more supple way of *thinking with*. The dividual offers a way to engage with the singularities of a person and to treat one's relationships with the social world as more fragmentary than western accounts of subjectivity would accept. When anthropologists first used the term, they did so to describe societies in which the categories of *society* and *individual* are not so clearly counterpoised and thus in which the maintenance of those terms was more likely to mislead investigators than to help their analyses.[18] In her study of Melanesia, Marilyn Strathern writes,

> Far from being regarded as unique entities, Melanesian persons are as dividually as they are individually conceived. They contain a generalized sociality within. Indeed, persons are frequently constructed as the plural and composite site of the relationships that produced them. The singular person can be imagined as a social microcosm. (13)

As we will see in Chapter 1, affect studies allow us to conceive of the singular person as the site of multiple forms of sociality and subjectivity. For literary critics, the dividual can reframe the work of narrative fiction not as transindividual but as the trans-dividual, an articulation of discrete affects and socialities that produces manifold kinds of readers. The dividual escapes the drive to find expression in a particular subject and directs our attention to readers as singular individuals, situated sites where different articulations of affect and experience meet in an event. This singularity underscores the precarity of any feeling as it may or may not be shared. One singularity may or may not converge with another in this event and thus the event is a situation traversed by difference. It is this precarity of shared affective experience, I argue, that one finds in Dickens—albeit a precarity largely focused on the human experience of precarity—and that guides my discussion of affect. In this way, Dickens's novels offer something more real than realism. Where George Eliot or George Gissing present us with a realism in which characters aspire to coherent subjectivity, Dickens offers a realism of the dividual, one in which characters are social functions and feelings impersonal and always potentially different. The feeling of life's precarity in Victorian Britain in Dickens includes an insistence that no matter how one may feel, one might soon feel otherwise. It is this precarity of feeling—most obvious but by no means limited to his quick turns from laughter to tears—that affects most in Dickens's novels even as their plots and tropes suggest other forms of precarity, from the physical, economic, and political, to the gendered, sexual, and racial.

It is for this reason that although much of my discussion begins from the perspective of economic vulnerability, I have preferred the language of precarity to that of class. Precarity more fully captures an array of vulnerabilities and possible positions without insisting on one's inscription as a subject by that precarity. Judith Butler usefully distinguishes precariousness, an operative fact of all life, from precarity, the distribution of precariousness through political, social, and economic segmentation and differentiation. For Butler, precarity highlights the social embeddedness of an individual's physical insecurity: our shared precariousness has been divided unequally into hierarchies of secure, grievable lives and insecure, ungrievable ones. Dickens understood this at an intuitive level in his focus on the child. As a figure, the child in Dickens approaches Butler's sense of precarity as physical and social vulnerability, the embodied experience of being what others see as readily discarded, ungrievable life. Yet Dickens's novels engage with precarity not simply as physical vulnerability but also as structural and situational. In other words, unlike Butler, Dickens's sense of precarity also understands it to be a result of economic, social, and political conflicts. Yet such conflicts should not obscure that precarity for Dickens is something that is first and foremost *felt*. His work insists on the tight interweaving of affect and precarity in the emotional, economic, and political textures of his conjuncture. As we will see, the use of precarity as felt, situational, and antagonistic is crucial to Dickens's affective forms. Dickensian affects are bound to precarity, a yoking of emotions, sentiments, and feelings to experiences of insecurity, exclusion, and ungrievability. Dickens's affective realism may have had intentional goals as social reform but his texts and their forms exceed these goals. In their exploration of precarity, they do not so much teach individual readers how or what to feel as produce new dividuals. His forms thus provide fictive events of affective encounter that exceed the staging of visual scenes with existing subjects and subject positions, unitary moral codes, or even the rhythmic alternation of scenes of laughter and tears. They unfold instead as events to be traversed by singularities and to produce readers, characters, and narratives.

To examine the event of an affective form, then, one must analyze how a text signals feelings and the particularities of its conjuncture. Our goal is to locate intensities, impacted sites of too much relation, of dividual pluralities that allow for conjunctions of the sociological and the fictive, the felt and the linguistic. As one might sense, this is to grapple with something much like Raymond Williams's structures of feeling. As Williams writes,

we need, on the one hand, to acknowledge (and welcome) the specificity of these [aesthetic and affective] elements—specific feelings,

———. *Reading Voices: Literature and the Phonotext.* Berkeley: University of California Press, 1990.

———. *The Value of Style in Fiction.* Cambridge: Cambridge University Press, 2018.

Strathern, Marilyn. *The Gender of the Gift: Problems with Women and Problems with Society in Melanesia.* Berkley: University of California Press, 1984.

Tilley, Audrey. "Sentiment and Vision in Charles Dickens's *A Christmas Carol,* and *The Cricket on the Hearth,*" *19: Interdisciplinary Studies in the Long Nineteenth Century,* vol. 4 (2007). www.19.bbk.ac.uk/articles/abstract/10.16995/ntn.457/

Tyler, Daniel, editor. *Dickens's Style.* Cambridge: Cambridge University Press, 2013.

Wachman, Richard, "Pawnbrokers' Efforts to Shed Dickensian Image Suffers Setback as OFT Moves In." *The Guardian,* 25 February 2012. www.theguardian.com/money/2012/feb/26/pawnbrokers-payday-loans-oft-inquiry

Williams, Raymond. *Marxism and Literature.* Oxford: Oxford University Press, 1977.

to explain why those suffering need to attune their sentiments with those of spectators. He writes:

> the emotions of the spectator will still be very apt to fall short of the violence of what is felt by the sufferer. Mankind, though naturally sympathetic, never conceive, for what has befallen another, that degree of passion which naturally animates the person principally concerned. That imaginary change of situation, upon which their sympathy is founded, is but momentary. The thought of their own safety, the thought that they themselves are not really the sufferers, continually intrudes itself upon them; and though it does not hinder them from conceiving a passion somewhat analogous to what is felt by the sufferer, hinders them from conceiving any thing that approaches to the same degree of violence. The person principally concerned is sensible of this, and at the same time passionately desires a more complete sympathy. He longs for that relief which nothing can afford him but the entire concord of the affections of the spectators with his own. To see the emotions of their hearts, in every respect, beat time to his own, in the violent and disagreeable passions, constitutes his sole consolation. But he can only hope to obtain this by lowering his passion to that pitch, in which the spectators are capable of going along with him. He must flatten, if I may be allowed to say so, the sharpness of its natural tone, in order to reduce it to harmony and concord with the emotions of those who are about him. What they feel, will, indeed, always be, in some respects, different from what he feels, and compassion can never be exactly the same with original sorrow; because the secret consciousness that the change of situations, from which the sympathetic sentiment arises, is but imaginary, not only lowers it in degree, but, in some measure, varies it in kind, and gives it a quite different modification. These two sentiments, however, may, it is evident, have such a correspondence with one another, as is sufficient for the harmony of society. Though they will never be unisons, they may be concords, and this is all that is wanted or required. (*Theory* 1.4.7:26–7)

Smith's musical metaphors and use of harmony at first seem to reference the Pythagorean harmony of the spheres and Plato's subsequent deployment of that harmony in the *Republic* to describe social harmony. Yet what Smith highlights here are the mechanics of harmony, a set of operations that he maps to sympathy. In short, Smith describes how feeling may be shared in a situation not as a discursive or reflective event based on the spectator's imaginative visual displacement but as a musical event.

Smith's use of the musical and auditory highlights the situation itself as a concept. Much as Smith privileges the specular in his theory of sympathy, he also notes in passing that "sympathy... does not arise so much constitutive of a capitalist world-ecology, and thus makes capitalism itself "an ecological regime" ("Transcending" 2). See Moore, "Transcending the Metabolic Rift," and *Capitalism and the Web of Life*. See also Wark, *Molecular Red*, esp. xiii–xiv, and 216. WS Jevons, another nineteenth-century thinker, addressed this issue in *The Coal Question*.

8 On novels as subject-producing, see Armstrong.

9 On the connections between analytic psychology and associationist psychology, see Dames, *Amnesiac Selves*; on phrenology and mesmerism, see Kaplan, *Dickens and Mesmerism* 3–33.

10 See Dames, *Amnesiac Selves* 133–34.

11 Important early work in this affective turn includes Berlant, *Female Complaint*, and Williams, *Playing the Race Card*. A more detailed survey of crucial insights into nineteenth-century sentimentality and melodrama can be found in the introduction.

12 Discussions of specularity and sentimentality in work on literature follows decades of psychoanalytic feminist work on specularity in film. See Silverman, Williams, *Playing*, and Williams, "When the Woman Looks," Doane, and as well as collections such as *Home is Where the Heart Is* and *Women in Film Noir*. See also Chandler, *An Archaeology of Sympathy*.

13 To a degree, this notion of yoking appears in the language of some affect-based studies, such as Sedgwick's analysis of nineteenth-century narrative. See Sedgwick 44, 77, 78, 79, and 81.

14 See Chandler, *An Archeology of Sympathy* 1–36.

15 See also Stewart, "Ethical Tempo of Narrative Syntax."

16 This pluralization of sympathy may suggest the reflective sentimentalism advocated by Michael L. Frazer. Nonetheless, Frazer's pluralism does not retain affect studies' focus on difference but rather suggests a plural set of human norms that contain "a single overlapping consensus supporting basic principles of justice and reciprocity" (13).

17 For cognitive work in literary studies, see Zunshine, Keen, and Turner; for studies of the sentiment and feeling, see Kaplan, Jaffe, Gallagher, and Chandler.

18 See Ablow and Hughes.

19 See Bailin 1027.

20 As Eagleton notes, Kant similarly suggests a "mutual harmony" (*Ideology* 96) between the world and humanity's cognitive capacities and thus imagines "the cultural domain... [to be] one of non-coercive consensus" (*Ideology* 97).

21 See Marshall 55–70, 167–92.

22 In *Treatise IV* of his *Moral Philosophy*, Hutcheson uses the spectator to argue that we bear "some standard of moral good antecedent to any sense" (4.1:134), though he means any sense other than the moral one. Specifically, "*every spectator*, or he himself upon reflection, *must approve* his action, and disapprove his omitting it, if he considers fully all its circumstances" (4.1:134). See also Hutcheson 132–38.

23 See Boltanski 37–39.

24 Sade, Nietzsche, Bataille, and others will later raise similar counter-argument to notions of a moral sense. See Boltanski 131–46.

25 See Hobbes 42, 48, and 50.

26 For discussion of this concept in Smith in relation to the case, see Chandler, *England in 1819*, 229.

27 See Gallagher 236. Khalip presses this concept to argue "performances of the self are evidence of its nothingness" (891).

precarity were left untouched. This shared understanding of a worker's dependence or independence in terms of their availability to physical abuse allowed British society to reject slavery while it simultaneously, as Davis notes, "approved experiments in labor discipline [such as the workhouse] which appeared to gravitate toward the plantation system" (*Age of Revolution* 458).

The abolitionist understanding of free labor came largely from political economy. British abolitionists often restated Adam Smith's view of slave labor as "in the end the dearest of any" (*Wealth* i.412). For Smith, work premised in service and servility placed workers in a state of dependence that made it difficult if not impossible to assert their interests and thus to act as a corrective to the interests of others. Menial servants, imperial bureaucrats, and the enslaved were essentially socially and economically corrosive. Enterprises in which the interests of workers, managers, and owners were not aligned were inefficient and corrupt in Smith's view. Heavily reliant on managerial labor and slavery, colonial ventures were his key examples. Slaves, Smith argued, were more expensive than free men not only because they must be fed, clothed, housed, but because they must be forced to work. By contrast, Smith argued that free laborers were naturally more parsimonious because they had to support themselves—that is, they had to eat—and they were thus more inclined to work. Although later economists proved that slavery was in fact profitable, Smith's claim became a foundational principle for abolitionists. During the abolition debate, it led some to insist that the end of slavery would *increase* sugar production by replacing less productive slave labor with more productive free labor.[8]

If the difference between a free man and a slave was simply that between hunger and the whip, then it should be no surprise that abolitionists hoped hunger would serve a similar function in the West Indies after slavery ended. Nevertheless, the situations of free labor in Britain and in the West Indies fundamentally differed. In Britain, given its continuing if unfinished history of enclosure as well as its eighteenth-century assault on the customary rights of working people, free laborers had little choice but to work for wages as they had no access to land.[9] (As I discuss in Chapter 3, Chartists would make land reform a key demand in the 1840s in an attempt to imagine ways out of the trap of wage labor). By contrast, in the West Indies, former slaves faced no such constraints. Indeed, the Colonial Office and planters worried abolition would lead to an exodus of labor fatal to the plantation economy. In an 1833 memo for the Colonial Office, Henry Taylor wrote discouragingly: "[the former slave] must be expected in general to prefer working on grounds of his own, if that be his choice, to hiring himself out for the harder labour of sugar cultivation" (qtd. in Engerman 306). From the perspective of plantation owners and the Colonial Office, it was imperative that the formerly enslaved embrace wage labor. High wages were imagined to be specific rhythms—and yet to find ways of recognizing their specific kinds of sociality, thus preventing their extraction from social experience. (133)

Attention to affect and form in Dickens encourages us to track the lines of flight in his texts from their immediate context to our present. Each of the four novels in this study suggest particular dispositions or emotions—domination, love, trust, and shame—but it is their textual form and historical embeddedness that reveals their affective forms and Dickensian qualities. I argue that we can connect the dynamic forms of feeling in these texts to underexplored historical experiences of social inequality and marginality: *Oliver Twist* with a violence that connects to the abolition of slavery and shifts in British racism; *The Old Curiosity Shop* with an anxiety that connects to Chartist agitation for land reform; *David Copperfield* with a surprise that articulates to tensions in the credit markets' forms of credit and trust; and *Great Expectations* with a suspension of feeling that recalls the attempted suspension of feelings of vulnerability raised by the Indian uprising of 1857 and a threatened invasion by France. As Dickens scholars know, Dickens's biography deeply marks each of these texts, from his feelings of abandonment in *Oliver Twist* and the loss of Mary Hogarth in *The Old Curiosity Shop* to the autobiographical elements of *David Copperfield* and *Great Expectations*. The purpose of choosing these personal and affect-laden texts is to reveal how feelings that may derive from personal experience become in fiction affectively open structures that reveal antagonisms in their contexts and resonate in ways beyond biographical control, including, as I show in the conclusion, in twentieth- and twenty-first-century film adaptations of his works. Affective form traces the mechanisms by which a text signals feelings—its use of narrative, genre, rhetoric, and style—and the situations in which these feelings may resonate, an analysis that allows us to discover how parts of the past persist in the partial selves that may be produced reading Dickens in our continued and varied states of precarity.

Affects and Presentism

Dickensian Affects is part of a theoretical intervention in the continuing discussion in literary scholarship of what Anna Kornbluh has polemically called "strategic presentism"—that is to say, a clearer and stronger engagement between scholarship and contemporary political, social, and cultural events. Kornbluh describes strategic presentism as "an alternative to positivist historicism [.... that] might invigorate our scholarship with consequence, [and] might therefore first of all be understood as a historically specific commitment, an intimacy with the nineteenth century" (99). Although Kornbluh promulgates this vision through her work with the V21 Collective, her explanation here predicates this intimacy upon a theory of spatialization, a concept that seems modelled on Fredric Jameson's cognitive mapping and thus straddles "Victorian structures that overdetermine contemporary experience" and "other structures, other spaces" (99). In response to such calls, Andrew H. Miller replies that the history of Victorian Studies has been and continues to be marked by engagements with present concerns. Miller suggests that the call for presentism reflects a desire for deeper engagement with cultural theory than with Victorian studies and highlights two key questions: "Why study the nineteenth century? And why Britain?" (123). Miller argues that the importance of Victorian Studies in the years following the Second World War came from an understanding of the Victorian era as one of peaceful modernization. Victorian Studies was thus engaged with questions of the future and ripe for political interventions about the shape of that future. As this role for the Victorians recedes, Miller notes, so too does the seeming relevance of Victorian studies. Calls for strategic presentism tend to leave this fundamental problem—why study the nineteenth century in Britain?—unanswered.

Proponents of presentism would likely respond that the roots of the present moment are in the past. Only by unravelling those links can we fully understand our present and ponder our future. This claim is undoubtedly true but it is not a compelling case for the study of the nineteenth century in Britain—Why not early modernity? Why not the medieval period? Why not elsewhere in the world?—nor does it explain why presentism has become increasingly important to humanities scholars in the 2010s. Presentism cannot be extricated from the ever greater institutional threats to the humanities in the academy and thus to humanities scholars search for their relevance, due either to administrative insistence or professional self-preservation. We must become public intellectuals for our own good and use our cultural, historical, and theoretical specialization to be part of a larger cultural conversation. This insistence is not new to literary studies where it is as much a desire as a demand. We have knowledge! literature professors cry, Listen! Perhaps nowhere is this frustration more apparent than in work on literature and economics. Leading scholars freely admit that their work on the discursive and historical construction of economics may hope to achieve a wider audience but is primarily for other literary scholars, and that economists, even at shared institutions, have no interest in work on the history of economic thought.[19] Even when we wish to have a public conversation, we wind up speaking to one another.[20] This is no doubt in part a result of credentialism. Those in other fields see no reason to listen to interdisciplinary scholars let alone interdisciplinary *literary* scholars. Consider anthropologist Arjun Appadurai. In his recent book on financialization and language, *Banking on Words*, Appadurai cites key works by Mary Poovey and Marc Shell that could helpfully inform his argument only to breeze past them with the insistence that his work is entirely unrelated to theirs—it isn't—and thus merits no engagement—it does. These feelings of intellectual exclusion may be exacerbated by the fact that economists can freely draw from literary examples as one may find in the unlikely international bestseller by Thomas Piketty, *Capital in the Twenty-First Century*. Literary scholarship and discursive histories of economics can and should add to public intellectual discussion, but our culture's increasing focus on areas of specialization has made it unclear to those outside our field what literary scholars can offer. One might also excuse those searching for historical context for turning first to historians. I would hazard this is why literary scholars are perhaps most able to act as public intellectuals when they serve as literary historians. Given the existential threats to literary studies, though, it seems unlikely that a literary study which exists solely as a history of literature will survive.

The desire for relevance and standing has led literary scholars rightly to a renewed focus on the specificity of literary studies as something that can and should matter to everyone beyond the limits of a history of .... This is why the demands for presentism and the rise of a new formalism are inextricable and why discussions of form tend to echo the theoretical models of the linguistic turn. The linguistic turn of high structuralism gave literary studies a seeming purchase on all forms of knowledge and the ability to speak about everything. Miller is thus right to argue that theory holds a deep sway over demands for presentism and we should be conscious of the ways this bridging of interest in relevance and form may lead to a problematic revival of structuralism. I am most especially concerned that it has revived the notion that individuals are determined by social structures or forms, mapped onto grids of various kinds. Affect studies offers a way out of this dead end of social analysis. As Brian Massumi neatly describes it,

> The aim of [structuralism's] positionality model was to open a window on local resistance in the name of change. But the problem of change returned with a vengeance. Because every body-subject was so determinately local, it was boxed into its site on the culture map. Gridlock. (*Parables* 3)

We can see this difficulty in one of the decade's most influential books on form, Caroline Levine's *Forms: Whole, Rhythm, Hierarchy, Network*. Levine insists that forms do political work and argues that "attending to the affordances of form opens up a *generalizable understanding of political power*" (7). For Levine, this is because the confrontation between different forms will be "constrained" or "unsettled" by other forms—in short, forms operate in reciprocal yet unexpected ways upon one another. This is the positionality model as literary form, the interference of one discourse with another or the overlaying of social analysis grids. It is a model in which change occurs more or less through slippage between forms. This approach may lead to suggestive literary analyses because it pays close attention to what a text *does*, but the model itself can produce blindspots because it subordinates conjunctural analyses and what escapes a form to confrontations between forms. Take an early instance from Levine as a politics of form. Women in academia, she writes, confront two different forms, the so-called biological clock and the tenure clock. She writes: "these consequences [women in academia working as adjuncts or part-timers] do not flow from any particular patriarchal intention or ideology other than the assumption of an uninterrupted adult life" (8). A beautiful confrontation of forms that at once absolves academia of patriarchy and of adjunctification by disconnecting analysis from a conjuncture in which the vast majority of women (and men) in American academia work as adjuncts. Is there not a certain patriarchal affect in the treatment of these workers, most of whom are not covered by union bargaining contracts, as either vulnerable dependents, inscribed by their structural position as part-time workers who must be either protected (we are the great protectors of labor!) or submitted to the discipline of the market (you should have made better life choices!)? By focusing attention on two forms in conflict, this analysis elides other possibilities and subjectivities as women in academia come to seem mere figures caught helpless between structures. Efforts to unionize, extend job protections, or agitate for working conditions in which social reproduction is not an unspeakable onus placed upon women seem like fantasies given the immovable reality of capitalism's impersonal forms steadily grinding its subjects into subjection. This is why it is important to engage with form without returning to structuralism's blinkered social analysis. Affect underscores the multiplicity of situations and the ways in which singular persons affect, are affected, and may change. We are formed and forming. In recognizing the reciprocity of this becoming, we cease to view change as something simply done to a person—an analysis that encourages feelings of vulnerability and helplessness—and instead a doing and a done that admits of resistance even in the face of likely defeat.

Affect, then, can give us reasons to study literature or cultural texts more broadly. It can help illuminate how cultures signal particular ways of feeling with some and to not feel with others. Nineteenth-century British literature grapples with these dissensions of feeling as it confronts a modernity predicated on the material production and distribution of precariousness. This is not to claim that the nineteenth century in Britain was the only period in which state and non-state agents discovered new mechanisms for the production and distribution of precarity but that it is perhaps the period most engaged with that production and distribution in its cultural texts. It is no mistake that this focus on the feelings of precarity in literary texts occurred alongside the emergence of the different sciences of society such as political economy, sociology, and anthropology. The nineteenth century is the period that taught us to think of ourselves as individuals inscribed by our social world. Victorian literature reinforces our sense of structural social inscription even as its persistent interest in feeling suggests that subjection and inscription are not all encompassing, perhaps most especially texts that give shape to feelings of precarity. This is why we would be ill-served to treat feelings and their dissensions as belonging to existing subjects. Affects are not personal but impersonal and can reveal our dividual-ness, the many social roles that traverse us and reveal us to be more or less than one. Attention to affective form opens presentism to the shaping and unshaping of the present, of the production of particular ways of feeling precarity. And by suggesting that affect surpasses and outpaces our singular existence, it also provides us with the urge to act.

In Chapter 1, "Toward a Theory of Affective Form: Sentimentality, Resonance, Rhythm," I argue that affect's plural, impersonal, dividual-ness, central to the study of affect, allows us to rethink one of the central hurdles of formalism, the plurality and ambiguity of textual meaning. The purpose of such theoretical work is to find a path from theory to practice. As critics, we are used to arguing that texts may reflect their discursive contexts, produce their own complex logical or rhetorical effects, reveal under explored histories, or model particular ways of thinking, but we accept the idea of a sharable experiences only as the result of ideological projects. Confronting what stories do—and the plurality of those doings—and their situations in doing, I argue, can give work in literary studies meaning beyond our discipline. To a degree, this is to engage in what Stuart Hall calls conjunctural analysis, examining cultural texts and their contexts to find contradictions and dissensions and thus to produce more compelling accounts of their being. Affective form, the textual yoking of signifying and asignifying elements in their difference to produce signals of manifold intensities and historical meanings, means to ground this work in formal textual analysis. To read for affective form is to sift texts for signals by attending to their couplings and uncouplings at the level of the text and to bind these processes to historical, social, and political discourses. A text creates intensities, resonances, and rhythms through its yoking of form and content, its embedded- and disembedded-ness of its conjuncture, and its readers' relations to these elements. This has particular usefulness for literary studies prior to the twentieth century. By examining how texts produce situations for feeling with and their refusals of and resistances to feeling with, analyses of affective form reveal affect is not an innately modernist or postmodern cultural concern. I build the notion of affective form from work in eighteenth-century moral sense philosophy, which precedes the emergence of the affective as a central aesthetic and theoretical concern, and in contemporary affect studies. I begin by examining sentimentality in order to draw a line of flight from Adam Smith's theory of sympathy to contemporary accounts of the plural affective situation. Smith's work initially suggests a convergence of feeling between spectator and sufferer, but close attention reveals a buried scenario in *The Theory of Moral Sentiments* in which sufferer and spectator engage in a musical conflict that plays out in the registers of tonality and rhythm. I connect this conflictual musical metaphor to psychologist Daniel N. Stern's notion of vitality forms. Unlike emotions, Stern argues that vitality affects are based in form and "correspond to characteristic patterned changes... [that take place] over time" (*Interpersonal* 57). These forms affect the singular person, drawing one into or out of attunement the feelings of another through the dynamics of experience. Stern's concept is important for the work in affect studies by Felix Guattari, Brian Massumi, and Sara Ahmed because it reveals the permeability of subjectivity and the ways that feelings are formed and performed in ways that are prepersonal and readily if not directly transmitted between persons. Affect studies's subsequent attention to the dynamic conflicts that make up an affective event focuses our attention on the forms that produce these experiences, the ways in which a situation may or may not enfold its participants in a shared feeling, and the ways in which a text signals the possibility of feelings that may be shared.

Chapter 2 puts theory into practice by examining the generative situation produced by *Oliver Twist*. Dickens's first social reform novel is marked by its use of divergent narrative modes, including melodrama, the comedic grotesque, and the sentimental, a series of shifts that the narrator describes as narrative's "streaky, well-cured bacon" (17:129). This streakiness is central to the novel's affective form, one that coheres a multiplicity of experiences of abuse and violence around situations of domination. The novel's affective solicitations persistently revolve around violence against dependents, a situation that resonates with the abolition of slavery in the West Indies at the time of the novel's drafting and publication. As a result, *Oliver Twist* raises questions about slavery and race that have been underexplored in criticism. Although the novel has often and rightly been read in light of the aftermath of the 1832 Reform Act and resonates with prior and subsequent Parliamentary acts, including Catholic emancipation, Poor Law reform, and the failed push for Jewish emancipation, my argument does not focus on the Slavery Abolition Act of 1833, but on the abolitionist agitation in 1837–38 to repeal the transitional period of what was euphemistically termed apprenticeship. By tracing the underlying connections between the ideas organizing the administration of the New Poor Law and post-abolition apprenticeship, I argue that the novel's focus on violence against dependents enacts an ambivalence if not outright antagonism to the formerly enslaved. Such feelings were already present in the late 1830s between the so-called "white slaves" of the English working class and the newly freed slaves in the West Indies. As a result, the novel racializes its villains in order to reverse the violence of coerced and dominated labor its narrative and affects solicit. The novel's use of "violent" and "violence" throughout illustrate a dominator's use of force when attempts to coerce work fail—a theme that also marks contemporary discussions of slavery and abolition. Although *Oliver Twist* is not a formally coherent work like later Dickens's novels, it nonetheless suggests a form for feeling the problems of a conjuncture in its stylistic multiplicity.

Chapter 3, "Anxiety, *The Old Curiosity Shop*, and Failed Inheritances," articulates a different kind of generative situation, one more tightly bound to the economic situation of the 1840s. The novel draws on discourses about inheritance and land reform in its response to economic inequality. By tracing the importance of legal rights of bequest and inheritance to post-1789 political arguments, I uncover the ways that discussions of inequality and inheritance in British political economy relied upon arguments about land reform. At the time of Dickens's novel, the Saint-Simonians had memorably framed inheritance as a disincentive to work and industry. Their arguments greatly affected John Stuart Mill, who in *Principles of Political Economy* connects their position with Jeremy Bentham's argument that the state should receive the estates of the childless wealthy. Mill too argues in favor of work, suggesting that the state should pose limits to inheritance that allow children to remain members of their original class. Chartist agitation for land reform during this period held similar positions about the need to limit disincentives to work. This sense that inheritance was at once a discouragement to industry yet a legal necessity for the maintenance of a stable class-based society informs *The Old Curiosity Shop*'s plots of failed, frustrated, and partial inheritances. The novel's two divergent narrative trajectories—Nell's journey from work toward death and Dick Swiveller's narrative rise—map the limits of respectable escapes from the corruptions of work, either through death or acceptably modified inheritances. The novel's engagement with inheritance highlights the novel's affective form, yoking together its two most prominent affects, love and anxiety, as a tale not of the passes and impasses of economic circulation but of the trials of capital accumulation. The passage of money and objects between characters and across generations and the transfers of emotions between characters and the novel's readers reveals a complex interweaving of the political and economic with the affective and the sentimental. By examining the passage of affects rather than money while drawing on discourses about land reform and inheritance, Dickens's novel reveals an affective form organized by anxiety as a constant push-pull between the anxiety generated by the need for money to survive, and the love of a world that exists in an imagined spiritual world free of material goods.

is to bring one's presentation of self into agreement with one's interiority. By contrast, *Great Expectations* focuses on the raw experience of being seen. In Chapter 5, I examine the ways in which the novel signals shame and contempt, emotions suggested by David's experience in *Copperfield* yet there of limited effect. In *Great Expectations*, shame and contempt reveal a persistent exposure that precedes the self and gives it shape. This feeling of vulnerability links the novel to a widespread feeling of white British masculine vulnerability in the late 1850s, in part a result of the 1857 Uprising, an event that crystallized Dickens's later racism. Global instability at this moment led the upper-middle class to organize a new Volunteer rifle corps for domestic defense, an event that fascinated the British press during the period immediately prior to and during the publication of *Great Expectations*. Importantly, the volunteer corps were portrayed at the time as both comically inept and the valiant protectors of Britain. I argue that this ambivalence marks Pip's ironic presentation and the novel's interleaving of irony, shame, and contempt. The affective form of the novel captures this crisis in masculinity as suspense, a drive to escape the emotional sense of vulnerability, whether to foreign threats or to social and economic precarity. By searching out suspensions of feeling and exploring what the feeling of such suspensions may be, the novel's ambivalent conclusion becomes a culmination of suspended emotion, an openness that I argue suggests both manifold possibilities and yet reserves those possibilities to Pip as a man.

The conclusion examines the openness and creative richness of Dickens's affective forms in film adaptations. Questions of presentism come to the fore as I consider three adaptations of *Great Expectations*, that of David Lean (1946), Alfonso Cuarón (1998), and Mike Newell (2012), and situate their differences within their historical and filmic contexts. The articulation of shame and contempt to precarity in the original text threads through each film and generates unexpected resonances between their narratives and different conjunctures: a postwar British film made with limited resources and a desire to reclaim lost British military and economic power as cultural power; a 1990s Hollywood film that transforms the plot into a teen popcorn flick and gives it an ideological twist suitable for a service economy premised on creative and intellectual production; and a British heritage film that grapples with the affective landscape of the 2010s by presenting Pip as character without reflection or sense of futurity.

This attention to the formal properties of the affective and their transhistorical dimensions illuminates the *Dickensian* as a term that now conjures a past that should be past. Late Victorians coined it to describe the specifics of Dickens's prose, but the word now carries two disjunct ideas that the OED has entwined in a single definition: "Of or pertaining to Dickens or his style; marked by conditions or features resembling those described by Dickens."[21] When one looks at contemporary usage, writers tend to make explicit the links between Dickensian social reality and modern economic travails, often with explicit borrowings from Dickens's work. Headlines such as "A Dickensian Tale at J.P. Morgan," "Dhaka's Dickensian Workhouses Should Shame Us All," "Pawnbrokers' Efforts to Shed Dickensian Image Suffer Setback as OFT Moves in" introduce essays that make explicit reference to Dickens's engagement with Victorian social conditions.[22] In the United States, the Dickensian is often simply Dickens as such. Headlines about attacks on social welfare policies adumbrate the man, the period, and the feeling: "Trump's America Goes Full Charles Dickens" or "Charles Dickens Could Teach Trump a Thing or Two about How to 'Keep Christmas Well.'" As imprecise as these headlines may be, they suggest a certain durability of Dickens's affective forms with their unique imbrication of style and historical material conditions. Dickens captured ways of experiencing precarity that persist in our world, experiences of domination, anxiety, trust, and shame that allow the Dickensian to continue to resonate.

Notes

1 Robert L. Patten documents the difference in sales between *The Chimes* and *A Christmas Carol*, and notes that records begin, unfortunately, after the initial publications of both pieces. For 1846, the first documented year, the records show Bradbury and Evans's 5s. editions of the two works show the *Carol* already outpacing *The Chimes*: the *Carol* sold 1,057 copies and *The Chimes* 793. For context, the new Christmas book for that year, *The Cricket on the Hearth*, sold 3,541 copies of the 5s. edition in 1846. Although the collected cheap edition of the Christmas books sold astronomically more copies of both works—total sales for the years spanning 1853–1858 exceeds 300,000—sales of the individual works mark a divergence of fortunes. Records for the first year of Bradbury and Evans's 1s. editions of each reveals further decline: where *The Chimes* sold 4,216 copies, the *Carol* sells 6,898. *The Chimes* did sell more in subsequent years than *Cricket*. Later sales are difficult to track once the works were folded into the sales for Chapman and Hall's People's Edition. See Patten 368–77.
2 To HG Adams, 30 November 1858; *Letters, Vol. 8*.
3 See Andrews 287.
4 To WP Frith, [19] January 1869, in *Letters, Vol. 12*.
5 Sally Ledger and Fred Kaplan both tell the story of the initial reception of *The Chimes* but ignore Dickens's extraordinary claims for the story's longevity, his later sense that its affective form was no longer suited to its moment, if not perhaps slipping from his control, and his stylistic revision to bring its affectivity into alignment with the great moderation of the late 1860s. See Kaplan, *Dickens* 177–81, and Ledger, "'Don't Be So Melodramatic!'"
6 This suggests a distinction that Bethan Carney identifies in Dickens's early and late critics: early critics found his work to be humane not sentimental where later ones found sentimentality. See Carney.
7 See Jaffe 2–23 and Tilley.
8 See Brown.
9 On Victorian notions of the sentimental, see Carney, Ledger, Bell.
10 See Brinkema 33.
11 See Massumi, *What Animals* 31–32; and Massumi, *Semblance and Event* 19–20.
12 For example, see Massumi, *Politics* 52 and Massumi, *Semblance and Event* 1.

13 I bracket here Deleuze and Guattari's focus on an artist's greatness in creating new affects (cf. *What is Philosophy?* 174). For them, Dickens would likely be an artist of affects only for the obsessive love for and horror of bureaucracy that he creates in *Bleak House*, an affect that Kafka identified as unique to the novel before creating it anew in his work.

14 To a degree, Stewart aligns his notion of style with that of Stanley Fish and his affective stylistics. Although I similarly appreciate Fish's emphasis on the temporal and experiential as an unfolding within the text, his approach places truth in the reading subject via linguistic competence in ways that I believe block the transtemporal and plural experiences that affect studies underscores. For more on the difficulties raised by Fish's concept, see Belsey 33–36.

15 Two recent collections illustrate how scholars of the nineteenth century have taken up Stewart's focus on prose stylistics. Daniel Tyler's edited collection, *Dickens's Style*, shows scholars examining the nuances of Dickens's style, drawing on Stewart's uniquely detailed textual analysis of Dickens for analyses of individual texts and historical contexts. Rachel Ablow's edited collection, *The Feelings of Reading*, similarly builds on Stewart's textual emphases while offering detailed historicizations of the nature and relationship to reading and feeling, whether this is to conjure feelings in readers or to allow readers to block unpleasant or unwanted feelings. Both volumes also end with essays from Stewart himself.

16 I share this approach with John Hughes, whose *Affective Worlds* is both deeply Deleuzian and Stewartian. There are, however, limitations to the ideas of this line in affect studies, perhaps most especially, as critics such as Jonathan Flatley and Sara Ahmed note, its insistence on fine-grained distinctions between affect, emotion, mood, and such.

17 For example, see Deleuze, "Postscript," and Massumi, *Power* 13. Although Deleuze's use of the dividual focuses on it as a regressive concept, the discussion of segmentarity in *A Thousand Plateaus* suggests a similar understanding of the singular person as consisting of discrete segments in which different forms of sociality may communicate in a variety of forms. See Deleuze and Guattari, *A Thousand Plateaus* 208–10.

18 See Strathern 11–15, and Appurdai 100–23.

19 See Poovey, "Some Lessons of History" and Elaine Hadley, "Human Labor, Human Capital and the Education Premium."

20 See Felski 14–51.

21 See "Dickensian," OED, sv1.

22 For example, see Wachman, Elliott, and John Carney.

References

Ablow, Rachel, editor. *The Feeling of Reading: Affective Experience and Victorian Literature*. Ann Arbor: University of Michigan Press, 2010.

Ackroyd, Peter. *Dickens*. New York: Harper Perennial, 1990.

Ahmed, Sara. *The Cultural Politics of Emotion*. Edinburgh: Edinburgh University Press, 2014.

Andrews, Malcolm. *Dickens and His Performing Selves: Dickens and the Public Readings*. Oxford: Oxford University Press, 2008.

Appadurai, Arjun. *Banking on Words: The Failure of Language in the Age of Derivative Finance*. Chicago: University of Chicago Press, 2016.

Attridge, Derek. *The Singularity of Literature*. London: Routledge, 2017.

Bailin, Miriam. "Dismal Pleasure": Victorian Sentimentality and the Pathos of the Parvenu," *ELH*, vol. 66, no. 4 (Winter 1999), pp. 1015–32.

Barthes, Roland. *Writing Degree Zero*. Translated by Annette Lavers and Colin Smith. New York: Farrar, Straus and Giroux, 1968.

Bell, Michael. *Sentimentalism, Ethics, and the Culture of Feeling*. New York: Palgrave Macmillan, 2000.

Belsey, Catherine. *Critical Practice*. London: Routledge, 1980.

Brinkema, Eugenie. *The Form of the Affects*. Durham, NC: Duke University Press, 2014.

Brown, Nicola. "Introduction: Crying Over Little Nell," *19: Interdisciplinary Studies in the Long Nineteenth Century*, vol. 4 (2007). www.19.bbk.ac.uk/articles/abstract/10.16995/ntn.453/

Butler, Judith. *Frames of War*. London: Verso, 2010.

Carney, Bethan. "Introduction: Mr Popular Sentiment: Dickens and Feeling," *19: Interdisciplinary Studies in the Long Nineteenth Century*, vol. 14 (2012). www.19.bbk.ac.uk/articles/10.16995/ntn.644/

Carney, John. "A Dickensian Tale at J.P. Morgan," *Wall Street Journal*, 15 January 2015.

Deleuze, Gilles. "Postscript on Societies of Control," *October*, vol. 59 (Winter 1992), pp. 3–7.

Deleuze, Gilles, and Felix Guattari. *A Thousand Plateaus*. Translated by Brian Massumi. Minneapolis: University of Minnesota Press, 1987.

———. *What is Philosophy?* Translated by Hugh Tomlinson and Graham Burchell. New York: Columbia University Press, 1994.

Dickens, Charles. *A Christmas Carol and Other Christmas Books*. Edited by Robert Douglas-Fairhurst. Oxford: Oxford University Press, 2006.

———. *Our Mutual Friend*. Oxford: Oxford University Press, 2008.

———. *Sikes and Nancy and Other Public Readings*. Oxford: Oxford University Press, 1983.

Elliott, Larry. "Dhaka's Dickensian Workhouses Should Shame Us All." *The Guardian*, 18 December 2016. www.theguardian.com/business/2016/dec/18/dhaka-dickensian-workhouses-should-shame-us-all

Fish, Stanley. "Literature in the Reader: Affective Stylistics," *New Literary History*, vol. 2, no. 1 (Autumn 1970), pp. 123–62.

Felski, Rita. *The Limits of Critique*. Chicago: University of Chicago Press, 2015.

Flatley, Jonathan. *Affective Mapping: Melancholia and the Politics of Modernity*. Cambridge, MA: Harvard University Press, 2009.

Hadley, Elaine. "Human Labor, Human Capital and the Education Premium." Annual Conference for the North American Victorian Studies Association, November 3–6, 2016. Presented 4 November 2016.

Harraway, Donna J. *Staying with the Trouble*. Durham, NC: Duke University Press, 2016.

Hebdige, Dick. *Subculture: The Meaning of Style*. London: Routledge, 1979.

Hughes, John. *Affective Worlds: Writing, Feeling, and Nineteenth-Century Literature*. Eastborne: Sussex Academic Press, 2011.

Jaffe, Audrey. *Scenes of Sympathy: Identity and Representation in Victorian Fiction*. Ithaca, NY, and London: Cornell University Press, 2000.

Jameson, Fredric. *The Antinomies of Realism*. London: Verso, 2013.

Kaplan, Fred. *Dickens, A Biography*. Baltimore, MD: Johns Hopkins University Press, 1988.

——. *Sacred Tears: Sentimentality in Victorian Literature*. Princeton, NJ: Princeton University Press, 1987.

Kornbluh, Anna. "Present Tense Futures of the Past," *Victorian Studies*, vol. 59, no. 1 (September 2016), pp. 98–101.

Ledger, Sally. "'Don't Be So Melodramatic!': Dickens and the Affective Mode," *19: Interdisciplinary Studies in the Long Nineteenth Century*, vol. 4 (2007). http://19.bbk.ac.uk/index.php/19/article/viewFile/456/316

The Letters of Charles Dickens, Vol. 4, 1844–1846, The Pilgrim Edition. Edited by Kathleen Tillotson. Oxford: Oxford University Press, 1977.

The Letters of Charles Dickens, Vol. 8, 1856–1858, The Pilgrim Edition. Edited by Kathleen Tillotson. Oxford: Oxford University Press, 1995.

The Letters of Charles Dickens, Vol. 12, 1868–1870, The Pilgrim Edition. Edited by Kathleen Tillotson. Oxford: Oxford University Press, 2002.

Levine, Caroline. *Forms: Whole, Rhythm, Hierarchy, Network*. Princeton, NJ: Princeton University Press, 2015.

Mason, Emma. "Feeling Dickensian Feeling," *19: Interdisciplinary Studies in the Long Nineteenth Century*, vol. 4 (2007). www.19.bbk.ac.uk/articles/abstract/10.16995/ntn.454/

Massumi, Brian. *99 Theses on the Revaluation of Value*. Minneapolis: University of Minnesota Press, 2018.

——. *Parables for the Virtual*. Durham, NC: Duke University Press, 2003.

——. *The Politics of Affect*. Malden, MA: Polity, 2012.

——. *Power at the End of the Economy*. Durham, NC: Duke University Press, 2014.

——. *Semblance and Event: Activist Philosophy and the Occupant Arts*. Cambridge, MA: MIT Press, 2011.

——. *What Animals Teach Us About Politics*. Durham, NC: Duke University Press, 2014.

Millbank, Dana. "Trump's America Goes Full Charles Dickens." *The Washington Post*, 13 June 2018. https://wapo.st/2lc47KB?tid=ss_tw&utm_term=.382840fb71fc

Miller, Andrew. "Response: Responsibility to the Present," *Victorian Studies*, vol. 59, no. 1 (September 2016), pp. 122–26.

Nichols, John. "Charles Dickens Could Teach Trump a Thing or Two About how to 'Keep Christmas Well.'" *The Nation*, 24 December 2018. www.thenation.com/article/charles-dickens-donald-trump-christmas/.

Patten, Robert L. *Charles Dickens and His Publishers*. Oxford: Oxford University Press, 1978.

Pettitt, Claire. "Dickens and the Historical Present." *Dickens's Style*, edited by Daniel Tyler. Cambridge: Cambridge University Press, 2013, pp. 110–36.

Poovey, Mary. "Some Lessons of History: Why Economists Failed to Anticipate the Great Recession." Presentation, Writing Political Economy Conference, University of Sussex, January 16, 2016.

Stewart, Garrett. *The One, Other, and Only Dickens*. Ithaca, NY: Cornell University Press, 2018.

1 Toward a Theory of Affective Form

Sentimentality, Resonance, Rhythm

For many, the word *affect* conjures only the uncontrolled, the knotted, and the eruptive. To speak of affect is to speak of the disruption of order and signification rather than the construction of forms. The disordered and slippery embedded narratives of Emily Brontë's *Wuthering Heights* with its violent turns and eruptions of characters' emotions would seem more suited to an analysis of its affects than the more sentimental work of Charles Dickens. My choice of subjects, then, means to expand our understanding of affect. Affects may indeed oppose signification and order yet they may also become part of signifying processes and patternings in texts. Dickens proves a useful case study because his novels make questions of feeling central to their narrative structures even as their incitements to feel escape the bounds of their signifying purposes. Of course, this is not unique to Dickens but perhaps more readily locatable in his texts due to their sentimental appeals. Dickens forces us to confront narratives as machines that signal emotive and affective experience. We read, we listen, we tell to affect and to be affected.

This insight is hardly new, yet it is one that we seem to have theoretical difficulty defending. We need affect to explain what culture does yet as critics we are more used to arguing that texts reflect their discursive contexts, reveal underexplored histories, or model particular ways of thinking than create experiences.[1] To say that literature may produce or signal shared experiences seems naïve. I.A. Richards's arguments for the centrality of sharable experience in literary form may be suggestive, but the ambiguities of language and reference make shared experience difficult if not impossible to achieve. To discuss affect and form as shared experience would seem to forget what Paul de Man called "the dead-end of formalist criticism" (*Blindness* 229). The sliding of the signifier makes the possibility of shared experience through texts contingent if not altogether improbable. To make matters worse, discussions of affective experience are themselves likely to suggest the New Critics' affective fallacy, a mistaking of my experience for a text's affective truth. The work of feminist, gender studies, and queer scholars have addressed this critical suspicion of emotion, feeling, and affect, insisting on the differences of affective experience and throwing

grounds its social analysis and how is that articulated to a practice of close reading?

Because cultural studies scholars draw on the work of Marxist social theory, a conjunctural analysis can suggest something akin to Marxist literary theory and its reliance on the notion of social totality. Kathi Weeks usefully describes the totality as a way "to conceive the social systematically as a complex process of relationships" (*Constituting* 5). In essence, the totality attempts to replace the functional expression of material economic relations in the cultural superstructure with a more rich description of social relations. This rich description nonetheless intuits a certain consistency which allows critics to treat society as an analyzable whole and thus to read closely in light of that whole. At its most theoretically insightful, as in the work of Louis Althusser, the totality can suggest an irreducibly complex structure and many different relations in a particular form of capitalism. Yet even in Althusser, the totality's complexity tends to encourage discussion in abstraction and to obscure the particulars and complexities at work in the processes of overdetermination that the concept of the totality means to help uncover.[4] Totality-based analyses tend toward a certain reductiveness that privileges abstraction and propose a simplistic account of material relations and causality that subordinates a multiplicity of relations to the economic determinism of capitalism and the commodity form. This problem may be inextricable from the line of subjectivist Western Marxism that grounds Marxist literary criticism. For Georg Lukács, for instance, society's domination by the commodity form produces an ineluctable diminution of subjective experience and particularity (see *History* 99). Analyses that rely on the social totality may aim for Althusserian complexity, but often end with a Marxist simplicity: to read in light of the totality becomes a process of close reading in search of increasing abstraction and decreasing particularity.

Formal analysis is especially open to this concern since formalism reduces complexities to abstraction. In terms of narrative analysis, formalism solicits not totality but totalization, the process by which one treats a text as a given whole. The homology between textual totalizations and social totality informs Marxist literary theory, the articulation of one complex whole to another as the revelation of a political unconscious, a dominant ideology, or a construction of hegemony. In literary studies, this is perhaps best seen in the work of Fredric Jameson, where the complexity of Althusser's totality leads Jameson to grapple with the persistence of master narratives and levels of interpretation and to deduce the abstractions and complexities of the social totality from processes of textual totalization, a process that yields Jameson's political unconscious.[5] The most prominent recent literary analysis of form, that of Caroline Levine, operates from a related premise and treats the social as a realm of many forms that operate one

against another. Levine's definition of form, however, is fairly simple: "*an arrangement of elements—an ordering, patterning, or shaping*" (*Forms* 3). Levine thus brackets the problem of the totality's abstractions and complexities to focus instead on the operation of forms in particular. Everything has a form, she suggests, but form is merely one aspect of that thing.

Although my version of conjunctural analysis here is informed by Marxist literary and social theory, it means to step back from the abstractions that lurk in Althusserian assumptions of totalities and forms. It underscores instead the affective particularities of textual modes of ordering and arranging and the articulation—local, contingent, and historical—of those particulars and their patterning in their conjunctures. In this way, it shifts emphasis from textual processes that suggest totalization to those that Althusser would describe as overdeterminations, but which affect studies leads me to term more simply *intensities*. This is to move from analyses that infer a textual whole and thus reveal the ideologically obscured to those that couple and uncouple disparate pieces and link different and potentially contradictory aspects of a conjuncture to signal particular affects and effects. From this perspective, forms matter less as abstract patterns—which can too readily become metonyms for the commodity form—than as the particular patterning of specific elements and the ways these patterns may signal ways of feeling or understanding. This shift to intensities which are by their nature partial allows us to engage theoretically with differences that may not yield to distinct or all-encompassing divisions or antagonisms, though they may be implicated in either or both.[6] Rather, it begins from a position of plurality and maintains that pluralism as it traces unifying forms and closes with an insistence on the openness of its findings.

These patterned yet open articulations of text and context to signal feeling I call *affective form*. The return of formalism in literary studies may have made *form* seem both overused and undertheorized. My use here indicates simply a nontotalizing patterning or ordering. An affective form, then, is an arrangement of elements, signifying and asignifying, to signal ways of feeling that may or may not be realized by any singular reader. To read for affective form is to read for patterns that signal intensities and thus open onto larger contexts that may themselves feed back into and signal new intensities. Such a project follows a different trajectory from the subjective inflection of Western Marxism, that of the neglected ecological and scientific aspects of Marx's work. As John Bellamy Foster shows in *Marx's Ecology*, Marx's thought offers a scientific ecologically minded critique of capitalism informed by developments in soil science and evolutionary theory. Ecological readings of Marx have led some scholars to shift their focus from the totality—though they retain the concept itself—to

what escapes. When the world is understood as a metabolism in which humanity and nature engage in shared processes of creation and exchange, capitalism's key feature becomes the break-flows it introduces between humans and nature, production and exchange, and so forth. Foster calls these break-flows *metabolic rifts* and highlights the ways in which rifts in capitalism drain an ecology of its resources and contribute to modernity's fundamental alterations and deformations of the world. In sociological terms, metabolic rifts mark historically specific and materially determined human intercessions that articulate society and the natural world.[7] Literary theorists may intuit a certain rhyme between Foster's metabolic rift and Jameson's political unconscious: the metabolic rift suggests that history must be read in its absence, a concept that echoes Jameson's description of history as a kind of Lacanian "Real... [that] necessarily passes through its prior textualization, its narrativization in the political unconscious" (*Political* 35). Yet as McKenzie Wark argues, metabolic rift does not so much reveal a lost history, totality, or unifying metabolism as a plural set of happenings. A rift in one system unleashes another in a different system and so on, a process that Wark describes as a "tragedy of the totality, a vast yet molecular process that only reveals its contours when something goes wrong" (*Molecular Red* 135). For this reason, Wark argues that our current predicament of a world of metabolic rifts demands new forms of knowledge, social organization, and action to trace its many divergent paths.

Affective form engages with this problem of a world of rifts by treating form as an arrangement of elements that do and undo, that mean to signal certain feelings and affects but that also may signal something else. The focus falls on what is doing in a system and what can be done when that something doing starts doing something else. This is an engagement with form that does not turn to the social totality or the closure of textual totalization for explanatory power precisely because their conceptualizations of causation too often tell us what a form or a text is or does before we know much about its doings. Although my deployment of affective form is not part of an ecological project as such, it takes seriously that forms are systems that open, interact, and reshape themselves. That means paying attention to the specificities of what surrounds a form to understand its expected and unexpected interactions with other social, cultural, political, and economic forms. These specificities provide elements that may yoke one form to another, like a narrative to a molar socioeconomic form such as industrial capitalism, or that may yoke disparate elements to produce new intensities. This is why affective form does not treat readers as subjects or novels as focused on the creation of subjectivity.[8] Elements yoked to produce sensations may indeed produce subjects bound to preexisting forms, but they may also produce other forms of becoming.

Excavating Affect from the Nineteenth Century and Sentimentality

It would be fair to object that such a project has little reason to focus on Dickens. Affect, after all, is not a Victorian concept. Its theoretical roots lie in William James's reversal of Victorian analytic psychology's view of emotion. In *Principles of Psychology* (1890), James explains:

> Our natural way of thinking about these coarser emotions is that the mental perception of some fact excites the mental affection called the emotion, and that this latter state of mind gives rise to the bodily expression. My theory, on the contrary, is that *the bodily changes follow directly the perception of the exciting fact, and that our feeling of the same changes as they occur IS the emotion.* (449)

Affect studies contains a diversity of approaches but James's understanding of emotion as the psychic capture of feeling is their necessary precondition. Here we see a strong distinction between emotion—what someone expresses—and affect—what builds to expression. By contrast, the discourses of feeling and emotion available to a Victorian writer like Dickens would come from dominant mid-century discourses like analytic psychology, fading discourses like phrenology, physiognomy, and mesmerism, and a residual discourse like sentimentality.[9] Scholarship on Victorian psychology thus tends to rule out affect as a term. Nicholas Dames argues that mid-nineteenth-century literature relied on analytic psychology's understanding of memory as willed recollections that create a self, a process that makes all recollection purposeful, symbolic, and linear rather than open to affective incitement.[10] Yet the differences between James's view of emotion and that of analytic psychology are perhaps overstated. In 1859, Alexander Bain, a key figure in mid-century analytic psychology, wrote that "no emotion, however tranquil, is possible without a full participation of the physical system" (*Emotions* 8). Of course, Bain begins from the expression of an emotion—to his empirical mind, the first observable moment—and only subsequently maps the body's participation. By contrast, James follows bodily change and feeling in the run up to the expression itself. A central line of affect studies tends to follow James in this focus on the unformed physicality of affect. Brian Massumi explains that affect studies "asserts that bodies think as they feel" (211) and that "there is an expansive mental aspect... to every bodily event" (212). To the degree that one insists on a strong distinction between affect and emotion and expects to encounter such distinctions in contemporary aesthetics, Jamesian affect would seem of little interest for mid-Victorian literary criticism. One should begin instead, as Carolyn Burdett demonstrates, with Vernon Lee. Affect, it would seem, belongs to modernism.

Yet if we take seriously the ways that literature signals different forms of *feeling with*—as scholars engaged with melodrama, sentimentality, and sensation fiction have—we find that scholars of the nineteenth century are quite comfortable talking about the affective as long as the term is held in abeyance.[11] Scholarship examining sentimentality is of particular importance because it highlights questions of feeling with and its failures. Nevertheless, discussions of the moral sentiments tend to privilege analyses of specular relations over other forms of affectivity. In part, this is a result of Adam Smith's theory of the moral sentiments—of which more below—and of the insights of feminist scholarship regarding the ways in which gendered and racialized constructions of spectacle implicate spectators and reveal fractures in seemingly closed texts.[12] Yet critical engagement with affect must go beyond the specular relations at the heart of the sentimental since the affective is not subjective. Specular relations tend to reinforce a sense that affect involves a stable or unitary subject, a position from which one sees or is seen. If affect is understood to be disruptive, it is because it disrupts the apparent stability of a subject where one was not presupposed. Moreover, it is necessary to go beyond the specular because the affective operates in nineteenth-century texts not only through the sentimental but against it.

An analysis of Dickens, then, needs to understand what the sentimental does and the ways in which that doing may breakdown or do otherwise. In what follows, I examine how moral sense philosophy theorizes *feeling with* first as a visual relation between subjects and then as a more supple auditory coupling of elements. This focus on a yoking of singularities without reducing the one to the other not only matters to unearthing affective relations in moral sense philosophy but also to unearthing the affective in literature prior to its conceptualization. In both, parts are irreducible yet coupled, held together in a skein of generative tensions.[13] A number of critics have approached this yoking of elements through the rhetorical figure of *syllepsis*, the yoking of the figurative and the literal that Michael Riffaterre argues is "the literary sign par excellence" (638). For James Chandler, syllepsis is a key feature of sentimental texts but in a specular and speculative way. By blurring the actual and the virtual, syllepsis demands that readers of sentimental cultural texts speculate about the cases on offer, a rhetorical turn that begins with Sterne's *A Sentimental Journey* and continues through sentimentality's cinematic forms.[14] In sentimental terms, this suggests a coming together of subjects. Syllepsis's potential for more open asubjective yoking appears in Garrett Stewart's reading of Dickens's style, where "the variety of this trope allows for effects as tender or melancholic there as they are more often farcical elsewhere" ("Lived Death" 233).[15] This way of doing—a rhetorical yoking of singularities that retains their differences while producing something new—allows a text to capture rhetorically the pluralization of positions and experiences that affect studies takes up more broadly in response to the exclusions that make up the sentimental. To think of affect as a yoking is to redress the problematic histories of sentimentality and sympathy as the basis for different forms of exclusion.[16] As Seth Lobis demonstrates, the early history of sympathy marks a shift from a broad sense of the magical connection of things within the world to an individual moral sense, a shift that limited how humanity understood its capacities to feel with the natural world. Manu Samriti Chander further traces the effects of sympathy in its promotion of white settler colonialism (See 67–90). By examining the limits of sympathy as a visual construct and its potential retheorization as affects bound up with rhythm and harmony, we encounter situations that allow for experiences of different singularities rather than images of a universal subject or impartial spectator. In this way, we may begin to trace how affect in texts may work in tension with the sentimental to produce situations that make other modes of *feeling with* possible, if always uncertain.

Our problem, then, becomes what it means to *feel* in literature.[17] Historical studies of the eighteenth- and nineteenth-century novel rightly underscore the question of feeling with others as bound up with the sentimental and its aesthetics, a line of inquiry most often traced via Adam Smith's rigorous account of the moral sentiments.[18] Yet as Miriam Bailin and Michael Bell demonstrate, different periods approach the sentimental in different ways. Eighteenth-century texts tend to dramatize the spectatorial encounter of the sentimental and its resulting feelings while nineteenth-century texts displace these narrated character sentiments onto a reader.[19] It would be a mistake to apply eighteenth-century moral philosophy, most especially of the Scottish variety, directly to Victorian texts, yet it is necessary to return to moral sense philosophy to understand the origins of the ambiguities that run through nineteenth-century literature and our own understanding of feeling as individual or social. This division of the world into an order of specifically human sympathy, one in which individuals encounter one another and interact as part of a social rather than natural whole is, as Lobis notes, a historically locatable displacement of "the idea of universal sympathy by a heightened confidence in human sympathy as an ordering principle" (283). Eighteenth-century moral sense philosophy marks the emergence of this principle and thus provides the bases by which questions of feeling came to seem at once wholly personal, deeply social, and radically limiting in their constructions of communities of feeling. In other words, moral sense philosophy helps to reveal the implicit politics of feeling that we need to unravel in order to attend to affective form in literature.

Ideology critique rightly notes that eighteenth-century moral sense philosophy's notions of sociability and sympathy can be read as soothing responses to political, economic, and cultural disturbances. Terry Eagleton notes, "if the moral values which govern society are as self-evident as the taste of peaches, a good deal of disruptive wrangling can be dispensed with" (*Ideology* 34). This unification does not operate through an enlightenment reliance upon rationality but rather through a focus on sense and affect, a move that reaches its apex in the apparent displacement of reason by custom and habit in Hume. Such a project relies upon a unitary set of values and an implicit universal subject able to embody those values. The subject, then, is at once the solution to and the result of a world divided into individual and society with the natural and inhuman left out. Astute critical readings of the moral sense philosophies attempt to extricate the subject from this quandary by attending to its interior divisions. Discussions of Smith's "man within" (3.3.5:159) by critics such as David Marshall or Luc Boltanski suggest that he is something akin to Jacques Lacan's split subject, what McKenzie Wark aptly describes as "a definition of the bourgeois: those for whom there appears to be a gap in the natural order" (*General Intellects* 131). Smith's man within thus posits and attempts to overcome a fundamental contradiction in moral sense philosophy, namely that humans are innately social beings yet live atomized lives. For moral sense philosophers, a person is at once never and always alone. Lacan's split subject resolves this problem by internalizing this insurmountable gap between the social and the individual. The unitary subject of eighteenth-century moral philosophy similarly solves this riddle insofar as it operates as a kind of aesthetic creation. As Boltanski notes, eighteenth-century sentimental novels construct an "authentic self ... which, in the manifestation of *sentiments*, carries out the synthesis of the divided selves" (89). This synthesis of the divided self through the manifestation of the sentiments allows moral sense philosophers, in Eagleton's words, "to oil the wheels of political hegemony... [and] also provide, contradictorily, what can be read as a discourse of utopian critique" (*Ideology* 38). Perhaps no eighteenth-century passage bears witness to this simultaneous construction of hegemony and critique in an aesthetic subject than Adam Smith's well-known argument in *The Wealth of Nations* that workers should be educated to combat the moral stagnation and political unrest produced by the division of labor. For Smith, education encourages workers to "feel themselves, each individually, more respectable and more likely to obtain the respect of their lawful superiors, and they are therefore more disposed to respect those superiors" (*Wealth of Nations* ii.309). A division within the political and economic, then, can be reshaped through an education of subjective feeling to produce a unified moral and political sense. In effect, British moral sense philosophy imagines a subject who embodies an aesthetic community of a shared sense of moral and political judgment, a position that suggests Kant's later *sensus communis* of aesthetic judgment without its attendant focus on reason and the faculties of cognition.[20]

This conjunction of a subject and an aesthetics indicates the specular focus of moral sense philosophy. As David Marshall convincingly argues, the theater is a central metaphor to the operations of the moral sense in Shaftesbury and Smith.[21] The specular also informs the work of Francis Hutcheson, albeit in less theatrical form.[22] The visual relation thus serves as the relation par excellence in moral sense philosophy for theorizing intersubjectivity and underscores a distinction between spectating subjects and subjects of the spectacle. After all, spectators sit in the audience while the spectacle occurs on stage. For Smith, theatricality provides the solution to the problem of humanity's simultaneous atomization and sociality by providing a way to understand "the relation which [the affections] stand in to the cause which excites them" (1.3.8:23). While Shaftesbury and Hutcheson treated shared sentiments as spontaneously transmitted infections, Smith relies instead on the theatrical situation of multiple spectators viewing an event or an object to coordinate their sentiments.[23] The sociality of feeling is for Smith a similarity of felt reaction. The individual remains individual and the social is merely the serial.

This spectating subject reveals Smith's notion of sympathy to be essentially reflective. This is most apparent when Smith describes self-judgment. To evaluate one's own conduct, Smith argues, one must treat oneself as spectacle and spectator. In the sympathetic relation, the subject ports himself into the image of the sufferer, sees out from it, and contrasts the experience with his judgment of proper reaction. When a subject must evaluate his own sentiments, the process is reversed. As Smith writes, one must "view [one's own sentiments] with the eyes of other people, or as other people are likely to view them" (*Theory* 3.1.2:128). Indeed, Smith describes the social itself as a reflective surface, a "mirror" that reveals to a subject whether others will approve or disapprove of his passions (*Theory* 3.1.3:129). Smith's argument thus recalls and rejects Hutcheson's claim that the moral sense was a unique intrinsic faculty. For Hutcheson, the moral sense may be similar to reason and reflection but it is intuitive, noncognitive, and embedded in the social. In *Treatise II* of his *Moral Philosophy*, he writes,

Notwithstanding the mighty *reason* we boast of above other animals, its processes are too slow, too full of doubt and hesitation, to serve us in every exigency, either for our own preservation, without the *external senses*, or to influence our actions for the good of the whole, without this *moral sense*. (*Moral Philosophy* in *Philosophical Writings*, 2.7.3:109)

In other words, for Hutcheson, the moral sense is affective. By contrast, the specularity of Smith's moral sense demands a near-constant insertion of distance and reflection and thus a certain amount of cognition, a process that guarantees the subject as stable, coherent, and at a persistent imaginative distance from itself and from others.

Smith's reflectiveness poses a problem, however, as it suggests a near convergence with Thomas Hobbes's selfish materialism. For Scottish moral sense philosophers, Hobbes's arguments were the subject of constant denigration, most especially his account of pity as the "imagination or fiction of future calamity to ourselves, proceeding from the sense of another man's present calamity" (53).[24] Hutcheson rejected Hobbes's argument because he maintained it "will never explain how the sensation [of pity] increases, according to the apprehended worth of the sufferer, or according to the affection we formerly had to him" (2.1.3:73). A theory that privileges a spectator's evaluation of his own imagined response to a situation cannot account for the interaction between one's feelings about the sufferer and his imagined response. In other words, what if the sufferer is a jerk? Smith's focus on the spectator takes him dangerously close to Hobbes's argument by similarly locating knowledge and sentiment in the subject alone.[25] Smith avoids Hobbes's argument by insisting that the spectator does not imagine how *he* would respond if placed in a similar circumstance but rather how *the sufferer* should feel in this circumstance. The spectator's capacity for imaginative displacement—the first suggestion of subjectivity's malleability—reflects him into a situation to see "with [the sufferer's] eyes and from his station" (*Theory* 3.1.2:128).[26] Thus Smith insists that when a person comforts a friend, his expressions of grief are "entirely upon [his friend's] account and not in the least upon [his] own" (7.3.1:374). Smith's notion of the cognitive work of reflection, then, at times seems to fade into a pure transparency of self that allows one to feel simply as another rather than as oneself.

The specularity of Smith's unitary subject, however, poses a problem for this transparent transference of feeling. By making feeling the feeling of an individual, Hobbes can examine how the senses may alter, distort, or otherwise mislead identifications and feelings. Smith's approach, by contrast, has little room for perspectival distortion. For Smith, the process of self-judgment makes us "the spectators of our own behavior" and our reflection on this behavior "is the only looking-glass by which we can, in some measure, with the eyes of other people, scrutinize the propriety of our own conduct" (3.1.5:131). Transparency is a necessity for Smith's judgment, a problem underlined by his discussion of the man within. This figure of judgment lacks any defining qualities other than a Shaftesburian sociality, which Smith describes as "an original desire to please, and an original aversion to offend his brethren" (3.2.6:135). What matters to Smith about the man within is that he sees "from the place and with the eyes of a third person, who has no particular connection with either [one's own misfortune or that of another person], and who judges with impartiality between us" (3.3.3:157). As Catherine Gallagher notes, Smith's man is no one and everyone.[27] A transparent figure of pure spectatorship, he allows the sentimental's "embodied sensorium," in James Chandler's words, to become "embedded in a text ... [as] the spectator turns virtual" (*Archaeology* 17). To see is thus to be sentimental.

Yet in the first edition, Smith includes a passage immediately following his discussion of the looking-glass that throws into question the possibility of the man within's imagined impartiality. Extending his looking-glass metaphor, Smith writes:

> Unfortunately, this moral looking-glass is not always a very good one. Common looking-glasses, it is said, are extremely deceitful, and by the glare which they throw over the face, conceal from the partial eyes of the person many deformities which are obvious to every body besides. But there is not in the world such a smoother of wrinkles as is every man's imagination, with regard to the blemishes of his own character. (*Theory* 3.1.5:131)

Smith's use of the looking-glass as the vehicle for imaginative distortion in this metaphor raises fundamental problems for his theory. If the specular provides an image so full that a spectator may "change persons and characters" (7.3.1:374) with the observed, then how could images of the self be distorted? Further, if the imagination mitigates "the blemishes of [one's] character," how could it also allow one to feel accurately in the place of another? Scant surprise he deleted it.

Yet one can see in the sections that immediately follow this discussion how Smith tries to mitigate the threat of visual distortion by introducing other rhetorical figures to imagine the problem of feeling with. These new figures take us closer to the affective. First, Smith shifts from metaphors of reflection to those of scale and distance, describing how "the eye of the body" and "the natural eye of the mind" both have difficulty evaluating distant objects (3.3.2:156). For Smith, if the bodily eye learns a proper sense of scale through "habit and experience" (3.3.2:156), then so too does the mind's eye with moral judgments. Smith's example is an elaboration of Hume's claim that while one may "give the same approbation to the same moral qualities in *China* as in *England*" (*Treatise* 371), physical contiguity affects one's sympathies. Smith offers an account of a European man's response to reports of a disastrous earthquake in China. This bourgeois subject reflects on "the precariousness of human life" and "the effects which this disaster might produce upon the commerce of Europe" but continues his life "as if no such accident had happened" and Smith notes that "the most frivolous disaster which could befall himself would occasion a more real disturbance" (3.3.4:157). At this point, Smith deploys a new auditory metaphor to describe how the man within retrains the mind's eye. The man within, he writes, "calls to us, with a voice capable of astonishing the most presumptuous of our passions, that we are but one of the multitude, in no respect better than any other in it" (3.3.4:158). In the section that follows, Smith reiterates that "the man within immediately calls to us, that we value ourselves too much and other people too little, and that, by doing so, we render ourselves the proper object of the contempt and indignation of our brethren" (3.3.5:159). This shift to the auditory means that Smith does not try to return to the visual register and bring distant moral objects forward for closer examination by the mind's eye. Instead, a voice *overtakes* and *astonishes* the self. It is this amplification of astonishment that precipitates a moral rendering of scale. The man within becomes a physical affect—a sound—and only later a source of cognition.

Smith's turn to an auditory metaphor and affective mechanism for conscience usefully distinguishes his work from other auditory incitements to moral conduct such as Martin Heidegger's call of conscience or Louis Althusser's interpellation. First and foremost, Smith's call brings forward sound's physicality. For Heidegger, the call is also "an alien voice" but it "reports from the uncanniness of [Da-sein's] thrown being" (255), meaning that it "speaks in the uncanny mode of silence" (255) because it uncovers an absence at the heart of Da-sein. The call to conscience in effect is a call that emphasizes a lack of sound. Althusser's description of interpellation as being hailed by a policeman more closely resembles Smith's metaphor, though Althusser's cry of interpellation turns the subject toward the voice of interpellation in recognition not astonishment. For Althusser, like Smith, the voice is a reinforcing supplement to ideology's underlying specular structure and Althusser's account appears immediately before he describes ideology as "a mirror-structure" in which individuals are interpellated by an "Absolute Subject" and recognize themselves through this subject's recognition (122). Much like the auditory in Smith, the voice in Althusser also offers a point of potential divergence and resistance from the apparently all-encompassing power of ideology's recognition.[28] Judith Butler notes that the temporality and immediacy of the voice in Althusser's discussion provide a narrative distantiation that his theory otherwise lacks when presented as a specular structure. The result, Butler argues, suggests a duality in Althusser. On the one hand, "the subject's existence cannot be linguistically guaranteed without passionate attachment to the law," and on the other hand, "the discursive possibilities for existence exceed the reprimand voiced by the law" (*Psychic Life* 129). The difference between Althusser and Smith, then, is that resistance in Althusser seems to be discursive rather than affective. The voice provides a metaphor that allows resistance to emerge, but it is a discursive resistance against a more inchoate set of passionate attachments.

Smith's shift to the auditory inaugurates a line of flight beyond the limits of his otherwise specular theory. Consider his focus on sound when he takes on the problem of the spectator's subject, the sufferer. Smith describes the sufferer's desire to receive sympathy from spectators

from the view of the passion, as from that of the situation which excites it" (*Theory* 1.1.10:15). The situation affords a spectator an engagement with the feelings of another, one that encompasses but is not limited to a visual encounter. The problem of the subject dissipates, then, as Smith imagines the situation to be a catching up of spectators in an interior imaginative process of affections:

> By imagination we place ourselves in his situation, we conceive our-selves enduring all the same torments, we enter as it were into his body, and become in some measure the same person with him, and thence form some idea of his sensations, and even feel something which, though weaker in degree, is not altogether unlike them. (1.1.2:12)

Imaginative situating emphasizes the particularities of physical sensation—the affective—but at one remove from direct bodily encounter. For Smith, the situation remains largely something to be seen, but the ex-tended metaphor of the musical situation reveals it can also suggest a more inchoate set of shifting affects and their relations. A situation does not in and of itself conjure emotions with "the same degree of violence" but instead generates a series of actions and reactions that *may* create a musical "concord of the affections" between sufferer and spectator. The musical metaphor shifts Smith's account of otherwise distinct agents to offer a more gnarled set of entanglements that are at least in part the result of craft. Smith advises sufferers to bring their passions more in line with the affections of their spectators but neither predominates in the movement of intensities in this metaphor. The sufferer sets the pace and rhythm of the encounter in order to get "the emotions of [spectators'] hearts ... [to] beat time to his." The spectator sets the tonal center, so the sufferer "must flatten ... the sharpness of its natural tone, in order to reduce it to harmony and concord with the emotions of those who are about him." Together, they produce "the harmony of society," a com-position crafted by the sufferer's modulation to the spectator's domi-nant tonality but given its performative specificity and rhythmic urgency by the sufferer's direct emotive experience. In this way, one might say that Smith's sympathy catches the sufferer and spectator up in a creative event. Smith's initial definition of sympathy as situated comes to indicate the possibility of an imaginative encounter with a situation, a creative event marked by a constant push-pull for domination between tonality and rhythm.[29]

Smith's account, then, suggests how the sentimental may allow us to open texts that precede modernism to the insights of affect studies and provides us with a model for thinking the affective in Dickens's work. As Bell notes, Dickens's novels operate in two converse directions through their use of sentimentality, the one toward an individual premised on sentiment, the other outward toward a social psyche constituted by the novel's minor characters which express variations on a psychic theme (see 131–32). Smith's discussion provides a way to understand these dual forms. On the one hand, the musical relation between spectator and sufferer describes a kind of sentimental becoming, an aesthetic unification that operates outside vision which one can note in David Copperfield's account of Agnes's angelic influence upon him:

> With the unerring instinct of her noble heart, she touched the chords of my memory so softly and harmoniously, that not one jarred within me; I could listen to the sorrowful, distant music, and desire to shrink from nothing it awoke. How could I, when, blended with it all, was her dear self, the better angel of my life? (60:844)

Here the musical situation retunes to bring together, a unification that produces social and personal harmony. On the other hand, it also suggests that situations may be riven by differences even as they produce affective events. One can find a scene of affect's differences and impersonalities when Rosa Dartle performs for David and Steerforth:

> I don't know what it was, in her touch or voice, that made that song the most unearthly I have ever heard in my life, or can imagine. There was something fearful in the reality of it. It was as if it had never been written, or set to music, but sprung out of passion within her; which found imperfect utterance in the low sounds of her voice, and crouched again when all was still. (29:442)

The "unearthly" here is also a "fearful... reality," a "passion" that Rosa enacts but does not exhaust. This is a situation in which differences remain irreducible—Rosa's love for Steerforth, Steerforth's indifference toward her, and David's sense of these differences only in the strangeness of the event itself—even as an event of feeling occurs that connects them. Affective form draws out the patterns and inflections which organize the use of these modes in Dickens's novel, the ways in which they deploy the sentimental and the unearthly yet fearfully real.

The Muiscality of Affective Form

This line of flight in Smith connects the sentimental to twenty-first century affect studies without reducing affect to sympathy or the sentimental or maintaining categories such as the individual, society, the human, and the in- or nonhuman. By focusing on the musicality of affective form, we discern an intimation of affect in moral sense philosophy and sentimentality, one that does not rely upon the metaphorics of the visual. Instead, we discover what we might call an affective musicology, one that opens an analysis of situations as political soundscapes where conflicts can be felt. Social harmony is built upon the exclusion of tonalities and rhythms that the dominant tonality would insist are in fact atonalities and asynchronous rhythms. Smith's discussion of the situation and its affectivity suggests that sympathies do not simply erupt but are also the subject of craft and thus takes us beyond a view of affect as mere violence, disruption, or asignification, though it may be that too. The musicality of the situation, its creation of a space of feeling with and its exclusion of other ways and forms of feeling, indicate what I call affective form. In it, form and content are inextricable, situated elements engaged in a temporal negotiation that continually suggests, includes, and excludes tonalities, harmonies, and rhythms, a process that cannot but approach in different ways the potential of tonal and rhythmic collapse. If it is a form at all, it is a form defined by its rifts, not as absent presences or the production of differences through repetition and drift, but as ways of doing through pattern, tone, and rhythm that may become other ways of doing through the introduction or elision of one part or another, signifying or not.

In this way, we return to the question of how texts may produce experiences that exceed individual apperception. Affect studies provides some answers to the question of feeling's sociality but they are fraught. Much of contemporary affect studies draws on modern psychological research, yet as Teresa Brennan notes psychology has undertaken only limited research on this aspect of the affects.[30] Of most influence is the work of Daniel N. Stern, who explores intersubjective experience through what he calls the attunement of infant and caregiver. Here we see not so much a sociality of affect as an affective experience in which the boundaries between one singular individual and another are permeable. The operation of attunement in Stern reveals a distinction between what he calls "the traditional or Darwinian *categorical affects* of anger, joy, sadness, and so on" and "vitality affects" (*Interpersonal* 55).[31] In Stern's early work, vitality affects are "elusive qualities ... better captured by dynamic, kinetic terms" (*Interpersonal* 54) and "correspond to characteristic patterned changes... [that take place] over time" (*Interpersonal* 57). He later renames these *vitality forms* and offers a more concise definition as "the temporally contoured feelings that accompany all experience" ("Introduction" 13).[32] Vitality forms, in short, are dynamic patterns of feeling. Such patterns are the basis for the affective permeability between infant and caregiver, what allows one to show that one shares an affect without replicating someone else's experience. As Stern writes, "the exact performance of the behavior, in terms of timing, intensity, and shape, can render multiple 'stylistic' versions or vitality affects of the same sign, signal, or action" (*Interpersonal* 159). A caregiver may repeat an infant's "ooohahhoooh" with inflections, facial reactions, or other intensities to indicate a sharing of the infant's affect.[33] Vitality forms, then, are a style of doing that allow for the sharing and shaping of affective experience. Indeed, through what Stern calls misattunement, emotional experience may be reshaped by stylistic modulation as dynamic form dampens or intensifies an affective experience.

If all this sounds a bit like Smith's musical situation, it should. The negotiations that Smith highlights between spectator and sufferer become in Stern's language questions of attunement. Stern's work, however, underscores the implication in Smith that attunements can be the result of form and craft. Here we approach formalism in a non-Kantian vein. Roger Mathew Grant rightly suggests that aesthetic work drawing on affect studies should understand affect not as intentionally or unintentionally produced but rather as creating signals, signs without intention.[34] From this perspective, art is no longer disinterested and of limited purposiveness but a technology in which content, style, and form signal the presence and affectivity of others. For literary studies, vitality forms can foreground the signals of affectivity in a work's formal organization. Form shapes and animates its contents to signal a situation for affective experiences in all their manifold potential. This is not to dismiss the importance of content but to elevate it as the subject of particular ways of feeling and knowing. Stern insists that vitality forms are "fundamental and primary" (*Forms* 25)—in other words, inextricable from their contents—not to lower the importance of categorical affects but to emphasize their dynamism. Anger is never simply anger but anger with a specific form of timing, intensity, shape, and rhythm. To read for affective form is to shift analytic focus from the discursive—which carries with it the structuralist implication that abstract forms produce subjects—to the entwining of affective signals and conjuncturally embedded discourses, the patterning of elements for emotive and affective ends which binds discourses and dispositions, abstractions and ways of feelings.

The model for affective form, then, is not language but music. Smith uses music metaphorically, but Stern is quite literal when he insists that "our subjective experience has more in common with music than with a digital code" ("Introduction" 14).[35] Too strong a reliance on the content or discursivity of a situation overshadows the importance of the production of experience through its dynamic shaping through time, rhythm, shape, and force.[36] To illustrate this point, Stern turns to temporal arts such as music, dance, theater, and cinema.[37] The rhythm, shape, force, and timing of performances demonstrate that it is the style of form that affects in a film more than its discursive representation of emotion. Like Bergson, Deleuze, and others, Stern emphasizes the noncognitive solicitation of affect by insisting that for humans "all action and thought pass" through "imagined movement" (*Forms* 134). In Smith's situation, the spectator reflects himself into the position of the sufferer. By contrast, Stern's vitality affects signal experiences of motion and thought prior to identification as a kind of suspended motion, signals through which one may be moved without moving. It is experience embodied and suspended.[38]

What does this mean for literary studies? The dead-end of formalism remains a threat. For a written text, Stern's account of embodied experience can seem too simple, directly transmissible, and unthreatened by textual drift. After all, the mediation of the text allows for slippages in the apparent fullness of textual affectivity. How can a theory of affective form get past this problem? To begin, we should follow the lead of Garrett Stewart and his concept of *the phonotext*, what Stewart describes as the process in silent reading by which a text is subject to embodied uptake yet also experiences a "degree of independence from the scriptive aspect of writing" (*Reading* 28). For Stewart, the possibility of syllabic drift or of misreading at this level of interface reveals "the contestation of style at its inner horizon" (*Reading* 31), an interior rift as textual mediation produces affectivity yet slips and drifts in the unique event of a silent reading and its suspended bodily uptake. The result leads Stewart to track phonological compression and lexical drift and thus to elaborate the affectivity of reading itself, a process that in Dickens can be found in the slippages, drifts, and compressions of his novels.

As much as this opens space for many kinds of readers, however, it also suggests that the text is the sole source of drift and affectivity. Sociality and affectivity threaten to become mere textual effects. A fine position for a Derridean—*il n'y a pas de hors-texte*—but one that reduces everything to the discursive and the signifying. How can we address a text's discursive ambiguities and its nondiscursive ones—in short, how can we engage with the situation of a text and its readers as embedded in a world that includes the asignifying and nondiscursive? Part of the solution can be found in the work of Felix Guattari. Building on Stern's discussion of vitality affects, Guattari uncovers what he calls a "being before being" (*Chaosmosis* 125) in "an infant's early experiences ... [because they] do not dissociate the feeling of self from the feeling of the other" (*Chaosmosis* 6). The openness of this experience, one which is at once undivided in the attunement of infant and caregiver and soon to be divided in the experience of individuation, allows for the production of what Guattari terms *transversality*. For Guattari, this term describes a pragmatic process by which new forms or subjectivities may be produced by encouraging transversal lines of flight, an open process that connects and disconnects semiotic systems and asignifying systems such as the organic, biological, technological, and aesthetic.[39] Gary Genosko usefully describes Guattari's conception of transversality as "militant, social, undisciplined creativity" (81). It is this militant process of creativity, one that begins from the fraught indetermination of being that Guattari calls "the included middle" (*Three Ecologies* 36), which suggests the work of an asubjective affective form. The text offers a potentially shared affectivity and a pragmatic set of fractures and lines that radiate outward to connect or disconnect manifold systems in the production of a creative event.

Such claims might seem out of keeping given Guattari's reputation in literary studies as an advocate of minor literatures and countercultures. After all, transversality describes the process by which a writer such as Kafka reshaped German language and literature by producing new aesthetic machines, what Guattari and Deleuze describe elsewhere as interfaces between the human, the technological, and the natural that are irreducible to subject and object and connect and disconnect the discursive and the affective (that is, they stutter and...and...and and or...or...or...). Yet Guattari's understanding of art as a transversal articulation should be read alongside his insistence that "the work of art is a being of sensation and nothing else" (*What is Philosophy?* 164). Guattari's account of the original aesthetic machine, the refrain (*la ritournelle*), describes its use of rhythm and melody to turn a disorganized milieu into "a territorial assemblage" (*Thousand Plateaus* 312). From this perspective, art occurs whenever "the expressive is primary in relation to the possessive" (316)—in other words, whenever something exceeds its function as a marker of somebody or something's possession.[40] Expressive components signal affects when they cease to be the simple expression of ownership. Transversality, then, is the creative yoking of elements that provides opportunities to encounter and reconfigure those sensations anew. Taken together, Stewart and Guattari's ideas suggest texts engage in a transversal process of creative articulation by which elements are connected and disconnected and mediated and embodied with all their discursive ambiguities and shifts. Readers are not so much *caught up* in a represented feeling as allowed to enter into a transversal process that includes manifold ways of feeling and doing. Affective form attends to these articulations by analyzing the text's production of a situation and its situatedness.

Yet here too the dead-end of formalism threatens to return. To treat art as a transversal production of sensation suggests that the yoking of elements by a form simply enchains any reader. How to keep difference from disappearing in affective becoming? For theorists in affect studies, the crux has been to emphasize that an affective situation contains a plurality of experiences. In wrestling with Guattari's notion of undisciplined creativity, Brian Massumi reconceptualizes sympathy itself as situational, nonidentificatory, and not limited to the human. Massumi's theory of sympathy begins from an examination of how animal play-fighting "brings acts belonging to different arenas together *in* their difference" (*What Animals* 4). For Massumi, participants in play fighting are part of a shared situation, one which creates a "zone of indiscernibility" (25) that allows them to engage with fighting as play.

Drawing on Stern's work, Massumi explains this indetermination as the interaction of emotions and vitality affects: emotions assert similitude (*this playing is* like *fighting*) while vitality affects show difference (*this is playing, not fighting*). For Massumi, new forms and aesthetic creations emerge from the indetermination of emotion and affect in these spaces that maintain difference as difference. This *is-is not* aspect of the aesthetic is what Guattari called the included middle, a yoking of elements that retains their irreducibility. Recall that vitality forms qua style translate emotional content into other forms, sharing, intensifying, or dampening. By unpacking the affective specificities of this situation, Massumi highlights their differences as differences and delinks them from subject positions. Instead we discover a situation of emotions and vitality forms that constitute what Massumi calls a new form of sympathy. No longer a question of shared feelings, sympathy is for Massumi "*not identificatory*, and it in no way involves an undifferentiation" because it is "the dynamic form of the situation" (77). Rather, sympathy describes the feelings in a situation "of what, potentially, passes between [participants]" (77). *Potentially* matters a great deal here. By arguing that sympathy is "the affective consciousness of the situation's dynamism" (78), Massumi focuses his attention on the kinds of affectivity in a situation, its vitality affects and its categorical ones, rather than the subjective experience of an emotion. No longer the transmission of feeling from one participant to another, sympathy becomes a multiplicity of feelings within a situation and a prepersonal "affective consciousness [that] 'sympathizes' with ... the *dynamic form* of what is coming, affecting one and all, differently together, and as thematically oriented" (78).

If we are wondering "What about Dickens?", this reformulation of sympathy may help. Massumi suggests this sympathy reveals an affectivity in works that otherwise seem merely sentimental. At first glance, sentimentality in art re-territorializes animal sympathy as human emotion, an editing process that narrows and personalizes a situation. Yet sentimental texts may undergo a deterritorialization in their uptake that return them to sympathy's creative openness. Our earlier examples from Dickens illustrate the point: on the one hand, the sentimental coherence of emotion between David and Agnes; on the other hand, the more open yet less personalized affect of the situation of Rosa's performance. The openness of sympathy and the plurality of affect, however, do not inhabit a completely indeterminate and undeterminable perspective. Rosa's affect is in part eruptive and asignifying—it is a feeling that evades textual account—but it is also part of a discursive history—a transversal line or rift—in which women are abused by entitled men, class status and wealth protect their abusers, and the social and economic situation encourages destructive attachments. To engage with the openness of affect in a text is not to denude it of its singularities but to engage with their formation or reformation of a new situation, a new territory. The goal of an analysis that draws out the singularities of a situation is to discover the ways in which it may be recomposed in transverse ways through intensities and asignifications.

Affect studies describes this interanimation of singularities in a situation using another auditory metaphor, *resonance*—that is, intensities produced by the coupling of disparate elements in their disparity which then amplify an affect.[41] Wai Chee Dimock turns this notion of resonance into a powerful model for transhistorical criticism by foregrounding the ways in which elements may inform and transform textual reception. Dimock argues that because noise is necessary and meaningful to the creation of aural resonance, resonance provides "a helpful analogy for the phenomenon of semantic change" (1061). Cultural, semantic, and semiotic elements become the noise of textual reception that resonate to produce the paths of textual reception and analysis. Resonance has transhistorical import: new noise, new resonance. As Dimock explains, "resonance is a generative (and not merely interfering) process, one that remakes a text while unmaking, that pays tribute to time both as a medium of unrecoverable meaning and as a medium of newly possible meaning" (1062). Resonance thus offers one function to describe the creative yoking of disparate elements in difference, a conceptualization of a situation as constituted by difference in difference, historically situated and capable of change. In short, a function for reading the interplay of text, context, reader, writer, social, and historical situation, of embedded and disembedded histories and experiences.

Affective form describes this yoking of elements in their difference as signals able to produce manifold intensities and historical meanings. Its elements may draw on the representation of emotion but the signals it offers do not mean to capture or communicate one simple emotion as such. Rather, they are signals for affective situations, pluralities of feeling that the patterning of elements and the intensities that they produce. The patterning of elements in *Oliver Twist* produce situations in which vulnerability, dependence, and violence are inexorably linked and bound to their historical situation, most importantly to the New Poor Law and the end of the apprenticeship period following the abolition of slavery in the British West Indies. The elements of *The Old Curiosity Shop* include representations of love and anxiety that are patterned to produce intensities of feeling about place and belonging that cohere around discourses of human economic precarity in the 1840s. The elements of *David Copperfield* draw from the discourses of character in Victorian culture and are patterned to resonate with the social, economic, and political work of trust in professional work in the 1850s, a resonance that operates through feelings of surprise at trust's consistency or failure. And the patterning of elements in *Great Expectations* takes its representations of shame and contempt and draws them into a resonance with a cultural search for new forms of militant masculinity able to protect white

British culture from threats to its dominance at home and abroad, a style of feeling that focuses on the suspense of feeling itself.

Although resonance insists on the disparity of its elements, it too may still seem to produce its results by necessity. Elements may be yoked but a signal is present in a kind of state of indifference. Resonance may fail. Sara Ahmed's work offers perhaps the most important analysis of failures and divergences within situations, textual, historical, and contemporary as an underlying politics of emotion. Ahmed draws on Max Scheler's analysis of *feeling with*, which highlights categorical elaborations of the different felt relationships between subjects and objects. Scheler distinguishes five affective levels within sympathy, each more rarified than the next: identification, vicarious feeling, fellow feeling, benevolence, and love.[42] Ahmed tends to focus on Scheler's distinction between vicarious feeling, which coheres around shared objects, and fellow feeling, in which one feels for another without knowledge of the object.[43] For Ahmed, this distinction between object-relations reveals the ways in which inequalities, most especially gendered and racialized ones, imbue the differential transmissions of emotions and affects between subjects and objects.[44] Ahmed's work is especially important for revealing how pre-existing intentionality informs the ways one might feeling with another. As she writes in *The Cultural Politics of Emotion*, *"one feels with or for others only insofar as one feels 'about' their feelings in the first place"* (*Cultural Politics* 41). For Ahmed, this cuts both ways: "the sociality of emotion, for me, can also refer to the situations in which we feel quite differently; when we do not even share a feeling though something is shared (it might even be a disagreement)" (*Cultural Politics* 218). If the situations of Massumi or Guattari or Smith too readily smooth their differences, the situation for Ahmed is fundamentally structured by difference, a kind of shared object that individuals relate to with distinct ways of feeling and that are crisscrossed by decisions and doings. Situations are radically fissured, fundamentally marked by difference.

The importance of this radical difference that inhabits affective situations becomes clear in Ahmed's discussion of mood. Phenomenology and affect studies often treat mood as a shared affective experience of lower intensity than an affect or emotion. For Ahmed, mood reveals the labor that undergirds a situation and its affects and the ways in which mood may be used to discipline behaviors in social spaces. Ahmed returns to Stern's work on vitality affects to describe the work of emotional management that moods demand, what she terms "mood work" ("Not in the Mood" 19). Ahmed argues that mood work relies upon misattunement, the imperfect stylistic refraction of another's emotion and affect performed in order to reshape them. Ahmed emphasizes that this work is unevenly distributed and tends to fall the heaviest upon those historically excluded or marked by differences of gender, race, or sexual orientation. Moreover, when those outside a mood refuse to perform its work, the desire of those in that mood to remain within it leads them to turn upon those resisters and treat them as objects to be dealt with. Ahmed's account of mood, then, reveals the work of resonance. From Smith to Guattari to Massumi, the notion of the situation and of resonance gesture toward the ways that individuals may be differently implicated affectively yet resists foregrounding the conflict that informs these transversal productions because they insist that affect precedes subjectivity. Ahmed's account of mood work reinserts subjectivity and thus brings to the fore something hinted at by Smith's musical metaphor: the sufferer is expected to work to bring himself into harmony with the spectator. Smith's vision of social harmony, then, depends upon the affective work of the dominated sufferer. To refuse such work threatens that sufferer with further suffering.

Mood work thus shifts our understanding of affect in aesthetics. That one should or should not be caught up in a text's affects is fundamental to any encounter with a text or work of art—in essence, whether one is willing to bear the costs of engaging in a dynamic form of affective experience to reinforce an emotion one may or may not have—and it has been sidestepped only to the degree that one embraces Kantian disinterest. To read is to do a kind of mood work. Much as affect can precede subjectivity, it is nonetheless bound up with moment-to-moment experiences and histories. A text may offer us a line of becoming but we might well respond it, "I am not in the mood." Resonance has difficulty recognizing this resistance, so Smith's account of the encounter between sufferer and spectator is again useful. The spectator controls the emotion of the composition, its tonality, while the sufferer is in charge of its vitality affects, its rhythm. It is the sufferer's performance of a vitality affect that makes a spectator feel.

Rhythm thus marks the power and the limits of resonance. The importance of rhythm to the composition of feeling appears in Gilles Deleuze's discussion of Francis Bacon. Deleuze explains that art may turn to rhythm when it wishes to cause sensation without resonance. For Deleuze, all of Bacon's paintings engage with sensation but only at times aim to produce connections between figures in his paintings or between frames in his triptychs. Resonance may occur when figures in Bacon's paintings appear in a "struggle or confrontation … [that couple] diverse sensations in two bodies" (58), a process of coupling and intensification that recalls Massumi's discussion. At other times, however, Bacon uses figures that Deleuze claims simply inform one another. These produce what Deleuze calls "a common fact" (58)—what we might call a situation—and the indifference of these figures makes *"rhythm itself … the Figure"* (60). Deleuze describes three rhythms, what we might think of as three kinds of vitality affects: an active rhythm that varies in increasing ways and amplifies itself, a passive rhythm that operates in converse fashion, and an attendant rhythm that provides a point of measurement for active and passive rhythms. Multiple rhythms exist irreducibly within a common fact or situation. With significant resonance in a work, rhythm's differences may be "merged together with the melodic lines, the points and counterpoints, of a coupled figure" (61). Although focused on Bacon, Deleuze's discussion underscores the importance of rhythm in aesthetics overall. To capture the differences and divergence of a situation, one must attend to its rhythms, even when they seem merely part of a resonance. Much as attention to affect traces a musicality in its coupling of disparate parts, its interactions of rhythm, tone, and timber, of melody and form are haunted by atonalities and arrhythmias.

Here, then, we might describe narrative fiction not as producing a shared or sharable experience but rather signaling situations that are plural and asubjective, open and dynamic, a shaping and reshaping that posits a continued creative event that demands work and has the decided possibility of not being an event at all. The crux of these happenings is not cognitive but affective. Or more properly, how a situation allows a form and a reader to do something and how that doing is embedded in worlds and ways of being that encourage or resist this something doing. Affective form thinks through what a text does in terms of the patterns and elements that signal *feelings with*. It is thus engaged with the representation of emotions yet distinct from a study of emotions. An affective form is not a historical snapshot of an emotion but of the ways of doing and feeling embedded in a particular textual, historical, material, and political situation, ways that open lines of flight to other situations.[45] What matters is the coupling of differences and their attempts to signal intensities. One might say that to read for affective form is to sift texts for these signals by attending to their couplings and uncouplings at the level of the text and of the binding of these processes to historical, social, and political discourses. A text signals intensities, resonances, and rhythms through its yoking of form and content, the embedded- and disembedded-ness of its conjuncture, and its readers' relations to these elements. By examining a text's creation of situations for feeling with and their potential refusals and resistances, affective form engages with feeling without insisting that affect is an innately modernist or postmodern cultural concern. Instead, it hears those resistances as stutters in the consistency of a form that open to historical, material, and political analysis.

We return then to where we began: Why Dickens? The answer has much to do with Dickens's exclamation about *The Chimes*: "What a thing it is to have Power!" Dickens's work engages directly with affective intensity and is littered with signals that have particular resonances in his time and that have changed over the long history of his cultural uptake. Those signals are deeply informed by rhythm, an important aspect of Dickens's style that is at once well-recognized and under-theorized.

As Robert Douglas-Fairhurst contends in his study of Dickens's rhythms, "Dickens is at once irresistible as a source of examples [for critics interested in rhythm] and stubbornly resistant to being explained away by a single theory" (77). Dickens's rhythms—his narrative variations, his use of blank verse rhythms, and his use of rhetorical turns such as anaphora, antistrophe, litotes, and syllepsis—operate in multiple registers and encourage a variety of intellectual and affective postures in his prose. Malcolm Andrews explores Dickens's comic productions in rhythmic terms as comic timing, exploring the ways in which he orchestrates the syntax of individual sentences against interruptions, incongruities, and delays of information.[46] Yet Dickensian rhythms are not simply comic. As Douglas-Fairhurst notes, Dickens's "writing allowed the private rhythms of the self to find themselves within, and also assert themselves against, the larger rhythms of the social world" (89). If no one theory can capture Dickens's rhythms, we might well say that is because they are part of the vitality forms of particular works. One cannot understand rhythm in Dickens on its own precisely because rhythm is but one aspect of a larger composition, one that needs other elements to be sensible, either for the yoking of resonance or for the sudden indifference and strangeness of tonalities and rhythms against the patterning of other elements. The letter of Dickens's texts thus draws us inexorably into discussions of the resonances and rhythms that make up his affective situations, of the ways in which the patterned elements of his texts operate and of the resonances the noises of his culture, history, and economic situation create. It is also to suggest our readings are themselves new transversal creations. Here, we find that reading for affective form can matter not because we wish to share in a feeling but because sometimes we are very much not in the mood.

Notes

1 Similarly, Grossberg notes that questions of affect arose for him "not in the context of a theoretical debate—it was not simply a theoretical move—but rather as a tool in the service of a political-analytic problem [for my students and my teaching]" (Grossberg and Behrenshausen 1002).
2 As Sara Ahmed rightly notes, there has been an "evacuation of certain styles of thought (we might think of these as the 'touchy feely' styles of thought, including feminist and queer thought) from affect studies" (*Cultural Politics* 207).
3 See Alber and Zunshine.
4 On overdetermination, see Althusser, *For Marx* 87–128. For a useful critique of Althusserian totality, see Hall 97–126, esp. 100, 104, and 113.
5 Jameson discusses the ramifications of Althusser's theory of totality and expressive causality in *Political Unconscious* 13–20.
6 For my discussion of totalization in Caroline Levine's *Forms*, see the introduction.
7 See Foster, "Marx's Theory of Metabolic Rift" and *Marx's Ecology*. Jason W. Moore offers a different articulation of the idea, arguing that it is

———. *Lenin and Philosophy and Other Essays.* Translated by Ben Brewster. New York: Monthly Review Press, 2001.

Ammaniti, Massimo, and Pierfrancesco Ferrari, "Vitality Affects in Daniel Stern's Thinking—A Psychological and Neurobiological Perspective," *Infant Mental Health*, vol. 34, no. 5 (2013). DOI: 10.1002/imhj.21405

Andrews, Malcolm. *Dickensian Laughter: Essays on Dickens and Humor.* Oxford: Oxford University Press, 2013.

Armstrong, Nancy. *How Novels Think.* New York: Columbia University Press, 2006.

Bain, Alexander. *The Emotions and the Will.* John London: W. Parker and Son, 1859.

Bell, Michael. *Sentimentalism, Ethics, and the Culture of Feeling.* London: Palgrave, 2000.

Berlant, Lauren. *The Female Complaint.* Durham, NC: Duke University Press, 2008.

Brennan, Teresa. *The Transmission of Affect.* Ithaca, NY: Cornell University Press, 2004.

Boltanski, Luc. *Distant Suffering: Morality, Media, and Politics.* Cambridge: Cambridge University Press, 1999.

Burdett, Carolyn. "Is Empathy the End of Sentimentality?," *Journal of Victorian Culture*, vol. 16, no. 2 (2011), pp. 259–74.

Butler, Judith. *The Psychic Life of Power.* Stanford: Stanford University Press, 1997.

Chander, Manu Samriti. *Brown Romantics: Poetry and Nationalism in the Global Nineteenth Century.* Lewisburg: Bucknell University Press, 2017.

Chandler, James. *An Archeology of Sympathy: The Sentimental Mode in Literature and Cinema.* Chicago: University of Chicago Press, 2013.

———. *England in 1819.* Chicago: University of Chicago Press, 1998.

Damasio, Antonio. *The Feeling of What Happens: Body and Emotion in the Making of Consciousness.* New York: Harcourt, 1999.

Dames, Nicholas. *Amnesiac Selves.* Oxford: Oxford University Press, 2003.

Deleuze, Gilles. *Francis Bacon: The Logic of Sensation.* Translated by Daniel W. Smith. Minneapolis: University of Minnesota Press, 2004.

Deleuze, Gilles, and Felix Guattari, *A Thousand Plateaus.* Translated by Brian Massumi. Minneapolis: University of Minnesota Press, 1987.

Dickens, Charles. *David Copperfield.* Edited by Jeremy Tambling. New York: Penguin, 2004.

Dimock, Wai Chee. "A Theory of Resonance," *PMLA*, vol. 112, no. 5 (October 1997), pp. 1060–71.

Doane, Mary Ann. *The Desire to Desire: The Woman's Film of the 1940s.* Bloomington: Indiana University Press, 1987.

Dolar, Mladen. "Beyond Interpellation," *Qui Parle*, vol. 76, no. 2 (Spring/Summer 1993), pp. 75–96.

Douglas-Fairhurst, Robert. "Dickens's Rhythms." *Dickens's Style*, edited by Daniel Tyler. Cambridge: Cambridge University Press, 2013, pp. 73–92.

Eagleton, Terry. *The Ideology of the Aesthetic.* Oxford: Basil Blackwell, 1990.

Felski, Rita. *The Limits of Critique.* Chicago: University of Chicago Press, 2015.

Flatley, Jonathan. *Affective Mapping: Melancholia and the Politics of Modernity.* Cambridge, MA: Harvard University Press, 2009.

28 As Mladen Dolar notes, although Althusser draws from Lacanian psycho-analysis here, by making recognition "the necessary and sufficient condition of ideology" (Dolar 80), Althusser insists on a more totalizing notion of subjectivation than Lacan would allow.

29 See Smith, *Theory* 1.1.10:15.

30 Members of the anti-psychology movement in Britain such as R.D. Laing and David Cooper were pioneers in this work but their importance lies less in their discoveries than in the responses they generated. See Brennan 12–15; Guattari, *Chaosophy* 119–21. Tompkins's work on affect begins in the 1960s but focuses on individual affective experience more than transmission. See Alexander.

31 See Tomkins 75–80.

32 As Stern discusses, prior researchers engaged with vitality without insisting on its separation from the emotions (Stern, *Forms* 33–55). Damasio rechristens vitality affects "background feelings" and offers a list of "prominent" ones: "fatigue; energy; excitement; wellness; sickness; tension; relaxation; surging; dragging; stability; instability; balance; imbalance; harmony; discover" (286). Damasio closely links background feelings to moods, which he describes as "made up of modulated and sustained background feelings as well as modulated and sustained feelings of primary emotions" (ibid.).

33 See Stern, *Interpersonal* 138–61.

34 Grant argues that eighteenth-century music theory helps describe the problem of affect studies' relation to signification, a situation that he traces through contemporary uses of musical analogies in affect studies. Grant turns to the problem of attunement via eighteenth-century musical theory as a way of thinking but does not engage with Stern's work on attunement and vitality forms. Although Grant rightly suggests a turn to the aesthetic object as a signal, one that bridges intention and non-intention, his suggestion leaves us without an analytic framework because we have no specificities that would allow us to understand what vitality affects are or do.

35 See also Stern, *Forms* 51–54, 82–84.

36 In "Musicality," Trevarthen describes this process of rhythmic attunement between individuals as "sympathy—for body *form* and for body *movement*" (171) and adds in a footnote that Smith's discussion of sympathy includes references to mirrored postures and gestures.

37 See Stern, *Forms* 53.

38 Subsequent research in psychology on vitality forms embeds them within a "biobehavioral system that is regulated, at the brain level, through complex neurochemical systems and circuits that are involved in reward and in motivation" (Ammaniti and Ferrari 368). This turn to the neurochemical informs affect studies most well-known account of affect transmission, Teresa Brennan's. Brennan expands the parameters of this biobehavioral system to include more broadly social bases for shared feelings. For Brennan, the permeability of individual affective experience should lead one to consider affects as embedded in group dynamics and atmospheres, and she suggests that an individual's affective permeability may a result of olfactory apperceptions of hormones and pheromones. Brennan's focus on the olfactory overturns the impermeability of the individual subject for a sensory engagement with the situational. See Brennan 51–73.

39 See Guattari, *Chaosmosis* 24.

40 For Guattari, each is a "formal machine, transversal to every modality of Expression and Content" (*Chaosmosis* 23). Guattari draws on Hjelmslev's discussion of Expression/Content but insists that one should "[shatter] the

concept of substance in a pluralistic manner, and … promote the category of substance of Expression not only in semiology and semiotics, but in domains that are extra-linguistic, non-human, biological, technological, aesthetic, etc." (*Chaosmosis* 24).

41 See Massumi, *Parables* 25–26. This notion of feedback also appears in Silvan Tomkins account of affective resonance, though Tomkins emphasizes that this resonance produces heightened intersubjective relations.

42 See Scheler 96–102.

43 See Scheler 12–15. Importantly, Ahmed's use of Scheler denudes Scheler of his conservative politics and the ways in which his ethics mean to map a via media between Kantian and Utilitarian ethics. See Werner Stark, "Editor's Introduction," Scheler ix–xlii.

44 See Ahmed, *The Cultural Politics of Emotion, The Promise of Happiness, Queer Phenomenology, Willful Subjects.*

45 In this respect, affective form may suggest Jonathan Flatley's account of reading for mood. Flatley's Heideggerian notion of mood—that is, the difficult to translate *Stimmung*—offers "a critical practice that can attend to that situatedness, and that depends less directly on my own aesthetic experience" (151). Mood, for Flatley, is a way to consider how a text addresses a mood outside the text and the ways in which it "[attunes] to that mood in order to shift or change it" (150). My argument here, however, focuses on situations/conjunctures rather than moods for two reasons. The first is rooted in affect studies. As neurologist and cognitive theorist Antonio Damasio argues that Stern's vitality affects are tightly linked to moods but not reducible to them. Damasio argues that moods are "made up of modulated and sustained background feelings as well as modulated and sustained feelings of primary emotions" (286). The second is methodological. As Walter Benn Michaels objects, to focus on mood as such can elide the importance of intentional affective turns. Affective form, by contrast, begins with these questions of intentionality and then considers the ways in which a text's situations and historical situatedness may open other interpretative pathways.

46 See Andrews, *Dickensian Laughter* 50–76.

References

Ablow, Rachel. "Introduction." *The Feeling of Reading*, edited by Rachel Ablow. Ann Arbor: University of Michigan Press, 2010, pp. 1–10.

Ahmed, Sara. *The Cultural Politics of Emotion*. 2nd edition. London: Routledge, 2015.

———. "Not in the Mood." *New Formations: A Journal of Culture/Theory/Politics*, vol. 82 (2014), pp. 13–28.

———. *The Promise of Happiness*. Durham, NC: Duke University Press, 2010.

———. *Queer Phenomenology*. Durham, NC: Duke University Press, 2006.

———. *Willful Subjects*. Durham, NC: Duke University Press, 2014.

Alber, Jan. "Natural Narratology." *Routledge Encyclopedia of Narrative*, edited by David Herman, Manfred John, Marie-Laure Ryan. London: Routledge, 2005, pp. 394–95.

Alexander, Irving E. "Silvan Tomkins: A Biographical Sketch." *Shame and its Sisters*, edited by Silvan Tomkins. Durham, NC: Duke University Press, 1999, pp. 257–60.

Althusser, Louis. *For Marx*. Translated by Ben Brewster. London: Verso, 2006.

———. "Reading for Mood," *Representations*, vol. 140 (Fall 2017), pp. 137–58.

Foster, John Bellamy. *Marx's Ecology*. New York: Monthly Review Press, 2000.

———. "Marx's Theory of Metabolic Rift: Classical Foundations for Environmental Sociology," *American Journal of Sociology*, vol. 105, no. 2 (1999), pp. 366–405.

Frazer, Michael. L. *The Enlightenment of Sympathy: Justice and the Moral Sentiments in the Eighteenth Century and Today*. Oxford: Oxford University Press, 2010.

Gallagher, Catherine. *Nobody's Story: The Vanishing Acts of Women Writers in the Marketplace 1670–1820*. Berkeley: University of California Press, 1994.

Genosko, Gary. "The Life and Work of Felix Guattari: From Transversality to Ecosophy." *The Three Ecologies*, edited by Felix Guattari. New York: Bloomsbury Press, 2000, pp. 49–86.

Grant Roger Mathew. "Music Lessons on Affect and Its Object," *Representations*, vol. 144, no. 1 (2018), pp. 34–60.

Grossberg, Lawrence. *Cultural Studies in the Future Tense*. Durham, NC: Duke University Press, 2010.

Grossberg, Lawrence, and Bryan G. Behrenshausen. "Cultural Studies and Deleuze-Guattari, Part 2: From Affect to Conjunctures," *Cultural Studies*, vol. 30, no. 6 (2016), pp. 1001–28, DOI: 10.1080/09502386.2016.1173476

Guattari, Felix. *Chaosmosis: An Ethico-Aesthetic Paradigm*. Translated by Paul Bains and Julian Pefanis. Bloomington: Indiana University Press, 1995.

———. *Chaosophy: Texts and Interviews, 1972–77*. Edited by Sylvère Lottringer. Los Angeles: Semiotext(e), 2009.

Hall, Stuart. *Cultural Studies 1983: A Theoretical History*. Edited with an Introduction by Jennifer Daryl Slack and Lawrence Grossberg. Durham, NC: Duke University Press, 2016.

Hall, Stuart, and Doreen Massey. "Interpreting the Crisis," *Soundings*, vol. 44 (spring 2010), pp. 57–71.

Heidegger, Martin. *Being and Time: A Translation of Sein und Zeir*. Translated by Joan Stambaugh. Albany: SUNY Press, 1996.

Hobbes, Thomas. *Human Nature and De Copore Politico*. Edited by John Charles Addison Gaskin. Oxford: Oxford World's Classics, 1994.

Home is Where the Heart Is: Studies in Melodrama and the Woman's Film. Edited by Christine Gledhill, London: British Film Institute, 1987.

Hughes, John. *Affective Worlds: Writing and Feeling in Nineteenth-Century Literature*. Eastborne: Sussex Academic Press, 2011.

Hume, David. *A Treatise of Human Nature*. Edited by David Fate Norton and Mary J. Norton. Oxford: Oxford University Press, 2000.

Hutcheson, Francis. *Philosophical Writings*. Edited by Robin Downie. London: Everyman, 1995.

Jaffe, Audrey. *Scenes of Sympathy: Identity and Representation in Victorian Fiction*. Ithaca, NY: Cornell University Press, 2000.

James, William. *Principles of Psychology*, vol. 2. Mineola, NY: Dover, 1950.

Jameson, Fredric. *The Political Unconscious*. Ithaca, NY: Cornell University Press, 1981.

Jevons, William Stanley. *The Coal Question*. London: Macmillan, 1865.

Kaplan, Fred. *Dickens and Mesmerism: The Hidden Springs of Fiction.* Princeton: Princeton University Press, 1975.

———. *Sacred Tears: Sentimentality in Victorian Literature.* Princeton University Press, 1987.

Keen, Suzanne. *Empathy and the Novel.* Oxford: Oxford University Press, 2010.

Khalip, Jacques. "Virtual Conduct: Disinterested Agency in Hazlitt and Keats," *ELH*, vol. 73, no. 4 (Winter 2006), pp. 885–912.

Lobis, Seth. *The Virtue of Sympathy: Magic, Philosophy, and Literature in Seventeenth-Century England.* New Haven: Yale University Press, 2015.

Lukács, Georg. *History and Class-Consciousness.* Translated by Rodney Livingstone. Cambridge, MA: MIT Press, 1981.

Marshall, David. *The Figure of Theater: Shaftesbury, Defoe, Adam Smith, and George Eliot.* New York: Columbia University Press, 1986.

Massumi, Brian. *Ontopower: War, Power, and the State of Perception.* Durham, NC: Duke University Press, 2015.

———. *The Politics of Affect.* London: Polity, 2012

———. *What Animals Teach Us About Politics.* Durham, NC: Duke University Press, 2014.

Michaels, Walter Benn. "Grimstad on Experience, Flatley on Affect: A Response," *Nonsite*, 1 January 2018. Accessed 8 January 2018. http://nonsite. org/editorial/grimstad-on-experience-flatley-on-affect

Moore, Jason W. *Capitalism and the Web of Life.* London: Verso, 2015.

———. "Transcending the Metabolic Rift: A Theory of Crises in the Capitalist World-Ecology," *Journal of Peasant Studies*, vol. 38, no. 1 (2011), pp. 1–46.

Riffaterre, Michael. "Syllepsis," *Critical Inquiry*, vol. 6, no. 4 (Summer 1980), pp. 625–38.

Scheler, Max. *The Nature of Sympathy.* Translated by Peter Heath. New Brunswick, NJ: Transaction Publishers, 2008.

Sedgwick, Eve Kosofsky. *Touching Feeling.* Durham, NC: Duke University Press, 2003.

Silverman, Kaja. *The Acoustic Mirror: The Female Voice in Psychoanalysis and Cinema.* Bloomington: Indiana University Press, 1988.

Smith, Adam. *An Inquiry into the Nature and Causes of the Wealth of Nations.* Edited by Edwin Cannan. Chicago: University of Chicago Press, 1976.

———. *The Theory of Moral Sentiments.* Edited by Knut Haakonssen. Cambridge: Cambridge University Press, 2002.

Stern, Daniel. *Forms of Vitality: Exploring Dynamic Experience in Psychology, the Arts, Psychotherapy, and Development.* Oxford: Oxford University Press, 2010.

———. *Interpersonal World of the Infant: A View from Psychoanalysis and Developmental Psychology.* New York: Basic Books, 1985.

———. "Introduction." *The First Relationship: Infant and Mother*, edited by Daniel Stern. Cambridge, MA: Harvard University Press, 2002, pp. 1–15.

Stewart, Garrett. "Ethical Tempo of Narrative Syntax: Sylleptic Recognitions in *Our Mutual Friend*," *Partial Answers: Journal of Literature and History of Ideas*, vol. 8, no. 1 (January 2010), pp. 119–45.

———. "Lived Death: Dickens's Rogue Glyphs." *Dickens's Style*, edited by Daniel Tyler. Cambridge University Press, 2013, pp. 231–53.

————. *Reading Voices: Literature and the Phonotext.* Berkeley: University of California Press, 1990.

Terada, Rei. *Feeing in Theory: Emotion after the Death of the Subject.* Cambridge, MA: Harvard University Press, 2003.

Tomkins, Silvan. *Shame and its Sisters.* Edited by Eve Kosofsky Sedgwick and Adam Frank. Durham, NC: Duke University Press, 1999.

Trevarthen, Colwyn. "Musicality and the Intrinsic Motive Pulse: Evidence from Human Psychobiology and Infant Communication," *Musicae Scientia* (1999), pp. 155–215, DOI: 10.1177/10298649000030S109

Turner, Mark. *The Literary Mind: The Origins of Thought and Language.* Oxford: Oxford University Press, 1998.

Wark, McKenzie. *General Intellects: Twenty-Five Thinkers for the Twenty-First Century.* London: Verso, 2017.

————. *Molecular Red: Theory for the Anthropocene.* London: Verso, 2015.

Williams, Linda. *Playing the Race Card: Melodramas of Black and White from Uncle Tom to O.J. Simpson.* Princeton, NJ: Princeton University Press, 2001.

————. "When the Woman Looks." *Re-Vision: Essays in Feminist Film Criticism,* edited by Mary Ann Doane, Patricia Mellencamp, and Linda Williams. Los Angeles: American Film Institute, 1983, pp. 83–99.

Women in Film Noir. Edited by E. Ann Kaplan. London: British Film Institute, 1998.

Zunshine, Lisa. *Why We Read Fiction: Theory of Mind and the Novel.* Columbus: Ohio State University Press, 2006.

2 *Oliver Twist*
Dependence, Violence, and Slavery

We begin our discussion of Dickens with *Oliver Twist*, a novel that is at once more coherent and integrated than *The Pickwick Papers* yet lacks the unity often ascribed to Dickens's later works. Perhaps best known for its dramatic tonal disparities, the novel's uneasy movements from one emotional tonality to another makes it an exemplary text for affective form as an analysis of the ways of doing and feeling embedded in a particular textual, historical, material, and political situation. As I argue in Chapter 1, affective form does not mean to uncover a unified emotional tone but rather a set of affective conjunctions and disjunctions that one may follow like fractures through sheets of ice, waiting and watching for the moment one may open to another space. Affective forms do not unify texts so much as suggest the rifts by which a text's something doing becomes a doing something else, a rift that we follow through form, affect, and history. For most readers, the novel's shifts from bleak satire to slapstick comedy, from realist depictions of poverty and crime to theatrical climaxes of terror and violence counterpoised with sentiment-laden scenes of idyllic middle-class life, are inextricable from its satire and indictment of the New Poor Law. I argue that attention to the novel's tonal instabilities reveals a rift that opens the affective form of *Oliver Twist* to the history of the abolition of slavery. In this way, we see how the novel makes certain forms of life grievable, to use Judith Butler's term, while treating others as of no consequence. Without a doubt, the depiction of the poor in *Oliver Twist* means to expose how precarity, as Butler's explains, means "that each of us is constituted politically in part by virtue of the social vulnerability of our bodies," and that our social vulnerability means to be "attached to others, at risk of losing those attachments, [and] exposed to others, at risk of violence by virtue of that exposure" (*Precarious* 20).

One could take *Oliver Twist* as a straightforward attack on human precariousness if one overlooked the novel's tonal instability. Indeed, the novel's most discussed scenes recognize the disparities inflicted by the New Poor Law and argue that the poor and their children are lives worthy of recognition and grief. *Oliver Twist* effectively treats the New Poor Law as a mechanism of what Isabell Lorey terms "precarization," the ways in which a society distributes the fundamental vulnerability of social life in radically disparate ways. Yet precarization also denotes a mode of governance and subjection that means to thwart the discovery of shared interests among the precarious. As Lorey notes, "the precarious cannot be unified or represented, their interests are so disparate that classical forms of corporate organizing are not effective" (9). It is this disparity of interests and the difficulty of understanding their points of connection that inform the tonal instabilities of *Oliver Twist* in ways Dickens likely did not intend. As we will see, the affective form of *Oliver Twist* reveals a pattern of elements signaling sympathy for the vulnerable that link the novel not only to the New Poor Law but also to the abolition of slavery in the West Indies. Tonal instabilities whipsaw readers between satire and seriousness, grotesque comedy and terrifying violence that allow its figurations of vulnerability to resonate across situations. Yet the rhythms of these shifts in generic register reveal that this novel most well-known for its defense of the poor suggests a more fraught view of precarity and its distributions when questions of class confront those of race.

The tonal inconsistency of *Oliver Twist* is famously a subject of explicit narratorial concern. For scholars, this passage reveals Dickens's reliance on melodrama for his emotive and affective mechanisms. Sally Ledger contends that Dickens's theatrical effects create a "melodramatic affect" (4) bound to the narrative's social critique and linked to a continual oscillation between scenes of laughter and tears. As Ledger emphasizes, Dickens's readers understood his style as bound to his "propensity to shift the affective gears from pathos to laughter and back again" (7). Dickens comments on this at the beginning of Chapter 17, as the narrator defends his shifts in tone, genre, and feeling by drawing a comparison to melodrama: "it is the custom on the stage, in all good, murderous melodramas, to present the tragic and the comic scenes, in as regular alternation as the layers of red and white in a side of streaky, well-cured bacon" (17:129). Yet the novel's variations in emotion and style mean to reinforce its claims to verisimilitude. As the narrator explains,

> such changes appear absurd; but they are not so unnatural as they would seem at first sight. The transitions in real life from well-spread boards to death-beds, and from mourning-weeds to holiday garments, are not a whit less startling; only, there, we are busy actors, instead of passive lookers-on, which makes a vast difference. The actors in the mimic life of the theatre, are blind to violent transitions and abrupt impulses of passion or feeling, which, presented before the eyes of mere spectators, are at once condemned as outrageous and preposterous.
>
> As sudden shiftings of the scene, and rapid changes of time and place, are not only sanctioned in books by long usage, but are by

many considered as the great art of authorship: an author's skill in his craft being, by such critics, chiefly estimated with relation to the dilemmas in which he leaves his characters at the end of every chapter: this brief introduction to the present one may perhaps be deemed unnecessary. If so, let it be considered a delicate intimation on the part of the historian that he is going back to the town in which Oliver Twist was born; the reader taking it for granted that there are good and substantial reasons for making the journey, or he would not be invited to proceed upon such an expedition. (17:129–30)

Although melodrama's apparently "absurd" contrasts permeate everyday life, we overlook them, the narrator insists, because "we are busy actors, instead of passive lookers-on." Our position as spectators is the problem. As "mere spectators," we are inclined to condemn "violent transitions and abrupt impulses of passion or feeling," a situation that recalls the spectator of moral sense philosophy and sentimentality. The narrator suggests instead a certain readerly activity and experience to overcome spectatorship's passivity, a kind of dynamic affective engagement. Yet such activity, the narrator realizes, may be at cross purposes with the judgments of literary critics. Their chief aesthetic criterion is the patterning of sequences, a process that forces readers to take on the position of passive spectator. (*Wait, the scene is over? Where are we now?*) The text's streaky bacon is made up of these conflicting affective and moral demands, a streakiness that pulls us between affect and sentimental spectatorship.

The contents of these scenes and their streakiness connect the novel's affective strategies to its conjuncture. Elaine Hadley argues that *Oliver Twist* exemplifies what she terms "the melodramatic mode" (3), a rhetorical response to the emergence of nineteenth-century market society and its forms of governmentality which deploys pathos alongside patriarchal norms to offer "a reactionary rejoinder to social change" (3). For Hadley, the novel's melodramatic streakiness means "to break down the barriers between the readers and the characters in the novel, symbolically forestalling, as opponents of [the New Poor Law] had done, the critical distance and emotional forbearance of spectatorship" (118). Yet, as Hadley rightly notes, the novel's use of melodramatic form also conjures the spectatorial distance that the narrator's reflection on streakiness critiques and thus threatens to fold the novel's project back into the mechanisms of market society. Importantly, Hadley's account says little about the novel's comedic and satirical turns and focuses instead on the novel's sensational criminal scenes and melodramatic familial ones. This is perhaps justifiable since the novel's initial readers and adapters found its serious and realistic scenes the most affecting.[1] Reviewers focused on its grim representations of poverty and its rejection of sentimentality rather than its satirical sequences. For T.H. Lister, "the merit [of *Oliver Twist*] lies chiefly in the details" and he encourages Dickens not "[to convert] a certain Mr Monks, who figures in the latter chapters, into a mere melo-dramatic villain of romance" (95). A piece in *The Monthly Review* focuses on the "grave and serious passages" of the novel's conclusion (30) and includes lengthy extracts from Fagin's revelation of Nancy's betrayal, Nancy's murder, Sikes's flight, and Fagin's final night. In *The Quarterly Review*, Richard Ford similarly emphasizes that Dickens "tells a tale of real crushing misery in plain, and therefore most effective, language; he never *then* indulges in false sentimentality, or mawkish, far-fetched verbiage" (90). Stage adaptations were similarly grim. Charles Almar's adaptation, the first following the end of the novel's serial run, performed Sikes's murder of Nancy in the dark. Later adaptations played up its gruesomeness. In the 1840s, performances of the story at the Victoria performed the murder on stage to allow the audience to hiss at Sikes; the Licenser of plays banned *Oliver Twist* from the stage for a period as a result.[2]

Yet it would be a mistake to elide the comedic fat from the serious lean in an analysis of the novel's affective form. Indeed, the comic components were noted in its initial reception. Although the grim seriousness of the tale affected its staging, stage adaptations nonetheless also retained some of the novel's comic sequences, though often it seems as a result of the desire to stage a realization of George Cruikshank's illustration of Mr. Bumble and Mrs. Corney (*OT* 23:183).[3] Almar truncates the novel's opening scenes to begin with a realization of this comic scene, and Charles Zachary Barnett retains the two comic characters as well.[4] The novel's illustrations by Cruikshank also serve as crucial indicators of the text's streakiness. Consider a scene such as Sikes menacing Nancy as he recovers from his illness. Nancy faints and the scene shifts suddenly into comedy. Cruikshank illustrates Fagin and the Artful Dodger holding Nancy upright while Bates "[gives] her a whiff of fresh air with the bellows" (*OT* 39:308). The image of the group in a kind of droll scrum suits Bates's subsequent comic encomium on Sikes's provisions but the tone shifts again as Fagin and Sikes turn to their schemes. This alternation of the comic and threatening produces a representational mode that informs both Dickens's work and those of writers he admired such as Smollett and Swift, the grotesque. As Philip Thomson explains, the grotesque is in effect an unresolved conflict between the comic and terrifying—a description that suggests the tonal ambivalence of *Oliver Twist*—and the reactions that it generates are similar in kind to those generated by confrontations with apparently abnormal physical forms.[5] In terms of genre, we might describe *Oliver Twist* as an experiment in grotesque melodramatic realism. The purpose of this grotesqueness is at times, as James Kinkaid argues, to encourage laughter while producing "an uneasy emotional response at being forced into the same isolation the novel portrays" (*Dickens* 54). Laughter is a crucial part of the novel's affective form, and attention to the ways the text mixes the comic, the serious, and the terrifying reveals a particular rhythm for the feelings of precarity. To understand the text's affective form, then, we must discover in the text's grim seriousness a historical streakiness to match that of its tone. For this reason, we turn our attention to the New Poor Law and the abolition of slavery.

Free Labor, Slavery, Apprenticeship

Critics of *Oliver Twist* have long recognized the New Poor Law's importance to the novel, but to grasp the novel's affective form, the New Poor Law needs to be understood through and in tension with the abolition of slavery. This is in part because the newly reformed Parliament took up the question of abolition and Poor Law reform simultaneously (Drescher, *Mighty Experiment* 130) and because the post-abolition apprenticeship system that preceded actual freedom for the enslaved did not end until 1838, the year *Oliver Twist* appeared. Yet to read the novel against the history of slavery as an institution does not mean to "speak the unspeakable," to use Paul Sharrad's phrase. One of the few critics to sift *Oliver Twist* for the effects of slavery, Sharrad traces slavery's absent presence through the novel's brief references to the West Indies and rightly notes that the text has little explicit engagement with the problems of Empire and evinces no interest in the direct representation of slavery. I would suggest instead that the feelings and concepts that informed arguments about the New Poor Law and the abolition of slavery evoke the problems of slavery in *Oliver Twist*. One can locate these feelings first in the novel's satirization of the New Poor Law as the urge to protect the vulnerable, feelings that extol a benevolent paternalism and the benefits of a stable social hierarchy. As we will see, the central figure for these feelings is Oliver as a vulnerable child who is forcibly apprenticed, an idea that evokes the post-abolition apprenticeship system and brings to the foreground the period's understanding of labor as either free or coerced.

The question of free labor—labor not indentured to a master or bound to the land—drove the New Poor Law. As Karl Polanyi documents, the law's purpose was to create a national free labor market.[6] The Speenhamland system of out-of-door relief which preceded the New Poor Law was an economic defense of longstanding social hierarchies, inscribing laborers in a position of dependence to local landowners by offering working men monetary support to supplement their wages. The elimination of Speenhamland's out-of-door relief meant to force workers to become free laborers who moved about in search of work. Free labor posed a problem, however, in terms of social control. Workers forced off the land were effectively disembedded from traditional social hierarchies. In Polanyi's account, the central innovation of the New Poor Law was to pair direct controls over the impoverished with market discipline. There was the workhouse which forcibly separated husbands and wives and replaced social relief with humiliation and social violence. The threat of the workhouse meant to ensure workers were held under a new kind of dominance, the impersonal discipline of the market place. Yet the architects of the New Poor Law understood market discipline to be driven by a simply physiological urge. Without out of door relief, advocates of the law argued, hunger would drive people into wage labor.

This feeling—psychology would call it a drive—pervades Dickens's representation of the workhouse and workhouse labor. When Oliver rebels at the undertaker Sowerberry's, the Beadle Mr. Bumble tells Mrs. Sowerberry: "It's not Madness, ma'am .... It's Meat" and counsels her to "leave him in the cellar for a day or so, till he's a little starved down" (*OT* 7:50–51). Out-of-door relief becomes an opportunity to reinforce hunger. Bumble describes to Mrs. Corney an instance in which he provided out-of-door relief to a poor family by giving them inedible food. He explains that this kind of "out-of-door relief, properly managed— properly managed, ma'am,—is the porochial safeguard" (23:179). The purpose is plain enough: inedible food out of the workhouse or unlivable conditions in it will dissuade the poor from seeking aid and to seek work instead. Hunger was at the heart of free labor. It would force those who could work to take whatever work was available and those who could not to die. Hunger, as Mr. Bumble's joke indicates, was to be the source of control over free labor.

This conception of free labor operated in tandem with the abolitionist framing of slavery. Slavery, in historian David Brion Davis's words, was "totally dependent upon physical torture" (*Age of Revolution* 466). To be free as a worker simply meant not to be subject to violet coercion. Nowhere is the reduction of free labor to the absence of violence clearer than in the closing of *The History of Mary Prince*.[7] Prince's closing comparison of West Indian slaves to British workers captures this notion of free labor. "No slaves here [in England]," Prince writes:

> no whips—no stocks—no punishment, except for wicked people. They hire servants in England; and if they don't like them, they send them away; they can't lick them. Let them work ever so hard in England, they are far better off than slaves. If they get a bad master, they give warning and go hire to another. They have their liberty. That's just what *we* want. (38)

The reduction of the free worker to the worker free of whips and stocks was by design. As Davis notes, "much of the early British antislavery writing reveals an almost obsessive concern with idealizing hierarchical order" (*Age of Revolution* 377). By treating free labor as merely free of violence, social hierarchy, inequality, and other distributions of

one motivator, but planters were uncertain whether former slaves would be willing to return to the plantation work for wages (Drescher 132).

The solution was the post-abolition system of apprenticeship. When the Slavery Abolition Act went into effect on August 1, 1834, the institution of slavery in the British Empire was replaced by what was to be a six-year period of imposed service for all the formerly enslaved. This new system of apprenticeship introduced institutions and mechanisms for social control modelled on those of the New Poor Law. If these were short-lived, this was, as Christopher Taylor notes, "an effect of the imperial state's attempt to refashion plantation Jamaica into an ideal-typical society culled from liberal political economic thought" (87). Part of the difficulty can be seen in the very term *apprentice*. The choice of language by Parliament rhetorically framed the formerly enslaved, as Thomas C. Holt explains, "as children needing to be reeducated as wage laborers and resocialized as citizens" (56). The language of apprenticeship not only infantilized the formerly enslaved, it also indicated that they remained open to physical coercion. Apprentices in Britain were legally subordinate to their masters and so too were the new apprentices of the West Indies. The difference between apprenticeship and slavery appeared in the introduction of a new bureaucracy of special magistrates, plantation police, and public workhouses.[10] Masters were stripped of their legal powers of coercion and special magistrates were instead tasked with "the role of former masters in enforcing work discipline" (Holt 58). Former slaves were legally obligated to work three-fourths of each week for their former masters in exchange for living allowances equivalent to those they had received during slavery; their subsequent free time was to be used to work for wages or for their own forms of free enterprise, in effect to train them as wage laborers.[11] In practice, apprentices often paid these masters a weekly hire rate and found work they preferred; this arrangement, however, legally demanded the agreement of the former master. In *The West Indies in 1837*, abolitionists Joseph Sturge and Thomas Harvey recount the case of one woman who could not get her former master to take a weekly hire arrangement and thus appealed for justice to the local magistrate. In response, the magistrate told her flatly: "You are the property of your master, and he can do what he likes with you" (Sturge and Harvey 140). By documenting the abuses of the apprenticeship system, Sturge and Harvey made clear how little apprenticeship was discernible from slavery.[12] Plantation owners and overseers often demanded extreme work hours to maintain sugar production and those who resisted confronted slavery's old tools, the whip and the treadmill. The mill quickly supplanted the whip as apprenticeship's symbolic tool of violence and women were its chief victims.[13] As Holt details, "the treadmill became emblematic of the abuses of the Jamaican prison system, which in turn symbolized that colony's general failure to make the transition from a slave to a free society" (107). It was the rampant abuse of the apprenticeship system that led to its sudden collapse. When the Colonial Office hired Captain J.W. Pringle to investigate the apprentice system in 1838, the Jamaican legislature unilaterally abolished it in an attempt to block his report (Holt 105).[14] Apprenticeship ended throughout the Empire shortly thereafter.

If hunger was one thread connecting the New Poor Law and the end of slavery, another was the political economic costs of poor relief and abolition. Working class resentment largely cohered around the willingness of Parliament to use tax money to pay the £20 million cost of abolition while insisting no money could be had for poor relief (see Drescher 160). As Virdee Satnam records, the decision to pay slaveowners while slashing poor relief seeded antipathies in the working class that would organize racial divisions for over a century.[15] In 1823, William Cobbett complained of William Wilberforce:

> it comes to this, that [abolitionists] want the inhabitants of this country and of Scotland and Ireland, to do something that shall make the West India Blacks *as well off* as the working part of the Whites in these countries. (515)[16]

Cobbett underlines an opposition between West Indian and British workers that would become more common later in the century: "the Black slaves had so many friends" in Parliament" and "the poor White slaves ... [appear] to have no friends at all in the House" (515). "Poor white slaves" became a commonplace of later Chartist and working-class rhetoric. The parallelism explains why, as Patricia Hollis notes, "from 1823 until the Garrisonian 1840s ... the abolitionist cause attracted little working-class support, much working-class indifference, and considerable working-class hostility" (295). The root of the problem was the apparent indifference of abolitionists to the poverty of white British people. Hollis documents that populist and working-class leaders such as Cobbett, Richard Oastler, and Bronterre O'Brien publicly argued abolitionists were "hypocrites, indifferent to poverty and suffering at home" (296). Like Cobbett, Oastler and O'Brien also used the language of "white slaves," and O'Brien argued that abolition would "proletarianize" the formerly enslaved (qtd. in Hollis 301).

Beginning in the late 1830s, this tension starts to appear in public meetings. Drescher notes that during "the final stages of the anti-apprenticeship campaign [in 1838] working class radicals interrupted a Birmingham mass meeting" (161). Two years later, Chartists would disrupt an antislavery meeting by declaring a la Cobbett "that English laborers were 'slaves working for idle Gentlemen'" (Drescher 161). Such arguments would come into greater relief in the 1840s as West Indian labor costs increased while British wages stagnated (Drescher 218). The nature of this antipathy is telling. Oastler and O'Brien both supported abolition but gave speeches that underscored the plight of white workers against those of the formerly enslaved. They often highlighted the state of children forced into the factory system. In their eyes, these children were worse off than those enslaved in the West Indies because they were unable to consent to work and (they believed) received worse treatment (cf. Hollis 298). Such arguments are in effect extensions of the division of free and coerced labor. By limiting slavery to labor violently coerced labor, poor law reformers and abolitionist discourse meant to limit what could be called slavery. Hunger was not violent coercion, they would argue. Yet by highlighting the poor children forced into work, Oastler, and O'Brien identified a class of worker unable to consent and subject to violent coercion in the workplace. What are British children in the factory system, they asked, if not slaves?

Dickens's Innocent and Savage Children

Here we return to Dickens and *Oliver Twist*. Children are the pivot linking the New Poor Law and apprenticeship, apprentices as children, children as slaves. Dickens's depiction of children in *Oliver Twist* captures this division in a way that shows us something about his view of children overall. Kinkaid rightly notes that Dickens produces two kinds of children in his work. On the one hand, an innocent child like Oliver who adults may "mould and watch and manipulate" ("Construction" 37) and, on the other hand, a suppressed savage child. This savage child also has two sides, Kinkaid writes, appearing either as a "noble savage" a la Rousseau or as one of "natural depravity" ("Construction" 33).[17] When these categories are attached to the New Poor Law and apprenticeship, we find a perverse allegory in *Oliver Twist*. Oliver suggests the innocent exploited children of Oastely and O'Brien, and Charley Bates and the Artful Dodger become the novel's savage children and criminal apprentices. The Dodger is introduced as "a snub-nosed, flat-browed, common-faced boy... but he had about him all the airs and manners of a man" (8:57). As the naturally depraved child, the unrepentant Dodger is transported to the colonies for his city-based savagery and his question to Oliver during their first meeting evokes the typical punishment of post-slavery apprenticeship: "Was you never on the mill?" (*OT* 8:58). By contrast, Charley Bates is the novel's noble savage. Although he too is one of Fagin's child apprentices, earning his keep by picking pockets and possibly prostituting himself as suggested by the narrator's persistent convention of calling him Master Bates, Bates shows moral traits late in the novel.[18] When Sikes arrives at the thieves' hideout on Jacob's Island, Bates attacks him and announces his presence to the angry mob outside. This change of heart saves Bates from the fate of the novel's other criminal child savages. The narrator informs readers that Bates "turned his back on the scenes of the past" and "from being a farmer's drudge, and a carrier's lad, he is now the merriest young grazier in all Northampton-shire" (53:439). One might object that Bates does not redeem himself so much as become a poacher. Indeed, the line may be a comic allusion to "The Northamptonshire Poacher," a folk song that begins "When I was bound apprentice in famous Northamptonshire, / I served my master truly for seven long year, / Then I took up game-poaching, on this you now must hear" (Kennedy 568).[19] Whether Bates is a poacher or a grazier, he escapes his bad apprenticeship in the city to become in the country what he once was only in satire, his own master.

Hence it is curious that Bates is also the only character who mentions West Indian slavery. Bates delivers an encomium upon the food he and Fagin have brought for Sikes and Nancy, including "a pound and a half of moist sugar that the niggers didn't work at all at, afore they got it up to sitch a pitch of goodness,—oh no!" (39:311). Bates evokes enslaved labor to dismiss it. The absence of racialized labor connotes the sugar's purity, as though extended contact with "the n------" will cause it to lose its "goodness." The racist language and metaphors in this speech are striking in their historical context. As historian Seymour Drescher records, racial epithets and arguments were strikingly absent from the Parliamentary debates over abolition, and only became common as the British experiment in abolition came to seem an economic failure.[20] The word is also uncommon in Dickens. It does not appear in *Sketches by Boz* or *The Pickwick Papers*. Dickens uses a French variant once in his letters of the 1830s: writing to a friend arrested for climbing a lamppost, he refers to the police as "a rascally set of *Negurs*" (*Letters* 1, 14).[21] In *Nicholas Nickleby*, the cruel schoolmaster Squeers avoids the epithet when he says "a slave driver in the West Indies is allowed a man under him to see that his blacks don't run away or get up a rebellion" (9:108). In Dickens's discussion of slavery in *American Notes*, the word appears only once via a newspaper quotation. Bates's use of the word, then, is unusual and I think meaningful. It is a class marker, one that may intimate the racial resentments simmering in some quarters of the working classes during the late 1830s. That Bates uses the word suggests that the noble savage in *Oliver Twist* is a redeemable *white* savage.

Dickens's view of slavery and race thus begins to come into focus earlier than critics have thought. Grace Moore argues that Dickens's notions of race harden in the early 1850s as he moves toward the virulent racism that would mark his reaction to the Indian Uprising of 1857 (on which see my discussion in Chapter 5).[22] At the root of this turn, Moore explains, is Dickens's ability to separate his support for abolition from his support for those who were enslaved (cf. 240). This distinction marks *Bleak House*, where Dickens depicts abolitionists as more concerned for distant others than for those on their very doorstep, what he memorably terms "telescopic philanthropy."[23] Mrs. Jellyby's first appearance in a fireless room implies that abolitionists have let the domestic hearth go cold for "the welfare of their species all over the country" (4:48). The properly domestic and locally sympathetic Esther offers a damning judgment of the Jellybys of the world that echoes Cobbett's thirty years before:

> It struck me that if Mrs. Jellyby had discharged her own natural duties and obligations before she swept the horizon with a telescope in search of others, she would have taken the best precautions against becoming absurd, but I need scarcely observe that I kept this to myself. (38:563)

Strangely, although Mrs. Jellyby is a satire of abolitionists and her scheme is effectively the same as the plan to resettle the formerly enslaved in Sierra Leone, her dialogue focuses not on slaves but "the natives" (*BH* 44, 48, 50, 51, 52). The word *slave* appears only four times in the novel, twice from Skimpole, first in his discussion of his debts (*BH* 15:233), then in reducing "the case of the slaves on American plantations" to one for his aesthetic enjoyment (*BH* 18:273). The apparent mockery of Skimpole's reduction of slavery to an aesthetic concern does not stop the text from using the word as a metaphor when Richard's lawyer compares his work on Jarndyce and Jarndyce as "like a galley slave" (*BH* 23:343), or when Mrs. Jellyby's daughter Caddy tells Esther after learning that one of Mrs. Jellyby's male philanthropists has asked to marry her: "I won't be a slave all my life, and I won't submit to be proposed to by Mr. Quale" (*BH* 14: 201). In effect, the word becomes a metaphor to capture exploitation and overwork while those who had been or could be enslaved become people outside or beyond what Dickens's understood as the space of civilization. This rhetorical distinction gives us a better sense of what Moore means by Dickens's separation of support for abolition and support for the enslaved. *Slave* comes to denote labor made unfree by violence and coercion and *native* enslaved peoples.

This division seems to inform the organization of children in *Oliver Twist* and Dickens's 1842 discussion of slavery in *American Notes*. Intriguingly, in *American Notes*, slavery is for Dickens the source of painful feelings. Of a dinner in Baltimore, he writes "though I was, with respect to [slavery], an innocent man, its presence filled me with a sense of shame and self-reproach" (*AN* 1.8:127).[24] When he reaches Virginia, he refuses to travel beyond Richmond because of his distaste for what he calls "the pain of living in the constant contemplation of slavery" (1.8:140), and he blames slavery for creating such "an air of ruin and decay" (2.1:151) that he was "grateful … that I was not doomed to live where slavery was, and had never had my senses blunted to its wrongs and horrors in a slave-rocked cradle" (2.1:154). The book's final chapter, devoted to slavery, is as Meredith L. McGill rightly notes "a radical change in tone and mode" (126). Although a substantial portion of the chapter consists of newspaper advertisements for runaways plagiarized from Theodore Weld's 1839 abolitionist pamphlet, *Slavery As It Is: Testimony of a Thousand Witnesses*, it also includes Dickens's description of slavery as a relation of power separable from race.[25] In a crucial passage, Dickens attacks those who own slaves but "admit the frightful nature of the Institution in the abstract" (*AN* 2:9:250):

> The ground most commonly taken by these better men among the advocates of slavery, is this: 'It is a bad system; and for myself I would willingly get rid of it, if I could; most willingly. But it is not so bad, as you in England take it to be. You are deceived by the representations of the emancipationists. The greater part of my slaves are much attached to me. You will say that I do not allow them to be severely treated; but I will put it to you whether you believe that it can be a general practice to treat them inhumanly, when it would impair their value, and would be obviously against the interests of their masters.'
>
> Is it the interest of any man to steal, to game, to waste his health and mental faculties by drunkenness, to lie, forswear himself, indulge hatred, seek desperate revenge, or do murder? No. All these are roads to ruin. And why, then, do men tread them? Because such inclinations are among the vicious qualities of mankind. Blot out, ye friends of slavery, from the catalogue of human passions, brutal lust, cruelty, and the abuse of irresponsible power (of all earthly temptations the most difficult to be resisted), and when ye have done so, and not before, we will inquire whether it be the interest of a master to lash and maim the slaves, over whose lives and limbs he has an absolute control! (2.9:251–52)

The source of slavery's painful feelings for Dickens becomes much clearer. For an author whose fame begins with the story of a servant particularly attached to his master, it is important that Dickens foregrounds the slave owner's paternalist assumption that "my slaves are much attached to me." The situation, Dickens insists, fundamentally differs from that of Sam Weller and Mr. Pickwick. For Dickens, the horror of slavery is not the attachment of master and servant but of dependents subject to "brutal lust, cruelty, and the abuse of irresponsible power (of all earthly temptations the most difficult to be resisted)." It is a horror of the mistreatment of dependents. Race, as we will see, is another thing altogether.

The Abuse of Irresponsible Power: Oliver as Apprentice

The affective form of *Oliver Twist* means to signal the many different ways one might respond to the horror of the abuse of irresponsible power. Its grim seriousness, its terror, and its satire map the corners of revulsion that the text signals. This form relies on the repeated use of a particular affective situation to signal intensities of feeling: a vulnerable dependent threatened with violence by a grotesque master or guardian. Certainly, such signals could be seen in action when theaters dramatized Sikes's murder of Nancy. Recall the audiences hissing Sikes during the murder. The intensity of the scene led Dickens's friends to insist it was too histrionic to be included in his public readings of the 1860s.[26] Nancy's murder, however, is merely the climactic episode in a pattern of situations in which a guardian threatens a vulnerable person. For much of the novel, Oliver is the privileged locus of vulnerability, a status that explains his limited characterization. As one of Dickens's innocent children, Oliver is, as Kinkaid argues, receptive to the molding of adults. Such molding takes place through Oliver's unique kind of receptivity. Oliver is a character who "instead of possessing too little feeling, possessed rather too much" (4:29), which the novel indicates makes him particularly affected by circumstances and able to affect those around him. Yet Oliver's receptivity to feeling is matched by his receptivity to a generalized notion of morality, something the text captures in Oliver's ability to pray, a skill that Dickens pointedly withholds from the street urchin Jo in *Bleak House*. Taken together, Oliver is a figure meant to signal the confluence of affective receptivity and moral conscience.

These qualities are crucial to the text's presentation of Oliver as a vulnerable dependent. Without them, attention drifts from feeling and from moral receptivity. It is also important that the novel's illustrations by Cruikshank highlight situations that show Oliver as vulnerable. Two stand out as scenes that Martin Meisel describes as "embodying a 'situation' memorably typifying Oliver's plight" and that thus ensure "the resolution in both cases is less memorable and less significant than the situation, which, as an image, is made lasting" (55). The first is Oliver's request to "the master" (2:12) for more gruel, a request that reveals another wrinkle in the New Poor Law's focus on hunger to produce free labor. Oliver was "desperate with hunger" (2:12), the narrator explains, which makes him not a docile worker but a "reckless" one (2:12), and thus "the master aimed a blow at Oliver's head" (2:12). The illustration underscores the physical inequality of this confrontation. The diminutive and vanishingly thin Oliver stands in silhouette before the master who not only towers over Oliver but is also turned in a three-quarters profile toward the frame to emphasize his solidity and power.

If the language of mastery here suggests slavery, Oliver's near-apprenticeship to the chimneysweep Gamfield, the second scene illustrated by Cruikshank, elaborates this situation of vulnerability and makes a stronger discursive connection to the post-abolition situation in the West Indies. Oliver's situation with the master is satirical yet distressing, and Gamfield is a more immediately comical figure. He is introduced with a comedic syllepsis as he tries to work out his finances "in a species of arithmetical desperation, ... alternately cudgeling his brains and his donkey" (3:16). Gamfield's brutal relationship with his donkey is part of the larger satire of apprenticeship and its violence. It also reveals one way in which the text distinguishes its comedic scenes of violence from its terrifying ones: the use or omission of the word *violence*. Gamfield's brutality is violent without being "violent." The sequence is instead grotesquely comic:

> Mr. Gamfield growled a fierce imprecation on the donkey generally, but more particularly on his eyes; and, running after him, bestowed a blow on his head, which would inevitably have beaten in any skull but a donkey's. Then, catching hold of the bridle, he gave his jaw a sharp wrench, by way of gentle reminder that he was not his own master; and by these means turned him round. He then gave him another blow on the head, just to stun him till he came back again. Having completed these arrangements, he walked up to the gate, to read the bill. (3:16–17)

The narrator's genteel rephrasings of Gamfield's cursings and his insistence that the donkey is uniquely impervious to violence makes this scene of animal cruelty grotesquely humorous. The use of litotes makes this abuse a series of gifts ("bestowed" "gave") while the language of master and servant highlights the physical vulnerability of not being one's own master. Central to the sequence's satire is that Gamfield is manifestly unsuited to be the kind of good master Dickens imagines with the master servant relationship in *Pickwick*. Yet one of the workhouse board members, "having witnessed the little dispute between Mr. Gamfield and the donkey... saw at once that Mr. Gamfield was exactly the sort of master Oliver Twist wanted" (3:17). Gamfield limns the contours the novel's focus on human precarity by offering readers a glimpse of a more expansive precarity of life created by the novel's grotesque villains.

The negotiation of Oliver's apprenticeship with the workhouse board highlights Gamfield's grotesqueness and violent character for its comedy while conjuring the malignant apprenticeship of the West Indies. Like masters in Britain and former West Indian slave owners, Gamfield is to be paid for taking Oliver as his apprentice, but as in the abolition debate this cost is the subject of political argument and economic calculation. The board offered a premium of £5 to anyone willing to take Oliver but after weighing Gamfield's work and his reputation for beating apprentices to death, they haggle and settle on £3 15s. One board member argues that Oliver would "be cheap with nothing at all, as a premium"— true enough; it is payment to own someone else's labor—and adds "he wants the stick, now and then: it'll do him good; and his board needn't come very expensive, for he hasn't been overfed since he was born. Ha!

ha! ha!" (3:19). Like much of the laughter in the novel's satirical scenes, the gentleman's laugh is double voiced: Gamfield and the rest of the board share his merriment over cheap, coerced, and nearly starved labor while the narrator signals readers to laugh at the moral ugliness of these calculators of human labor and misery. This simultaneous laughter of and at the grotesque is a conjuring of multiple feelings—of horror, of satirical laughter—which reveals the political economic consensus that coercion and starvation are the proper mechanisms for disciplining the workforce.[27]

Oliver's appearance, however, alters the scene's tone. The narrator focuses on Oliver's tears ("he began to cry very piteously" [3:19], "tears rolled down the poor child's face" [3:20]), and his description of Oliver being "released from bondage" (3:19) underlines the scene's suggestion of slavery (Bumble has just fetched Oliver from confinement). Nevertheless, unlike the inescapable mass apprenticeships enacted by the Slavery Abolition Act, Oliver escapes his apprenticeship after the magistrate's "gaze encountered [his] pale and terrified face" (3:21). Oliver pleads to the magistrate "that they would order him back to that dark room—that they would starve him—beat him—kill him if they pleased—rather than send him away with that dreadful man" (3:22). His "pale" and palpable terror seems to move the magistrate more than the specifics of his plea. If Oliver asking for more is a scene staged and illustrated to signal an affective situation for readers, the scene of Oliver, Gamfield, and the magistrate is a diegetic staging of moral spectatorship. The magistrate makes a moral judgment based on the visual appearances of "a pale and terrified" child and a man whose "villainous countenance was a regular stamped receipt for cruelty" (3:21). The situation of vulnerable dependent, terrifying man, and moral spectator is the novel's central patterning of elements for its affective form, one that signals feelings of vulnerability and dependence and that the narrative tries to reinscribe as sentimentality: a "pale and terrified" dependent pleading to be saved from a terrifying man represented as physically villainous or abnormal.

It is the comic grotesqueness of the villain that first stands out in this situation. While Gamfield disappears from the novel after this episode, Oliver encounters other versions of Gamfield in the many grotesque men who demand his labor and threaten his life, from the Sowerberries and Noah Claypole to Fagin and Sikes. The text presents the undertaker Sowerberry, to whom Oliver is legally apprenticed, as a figure as grotesque as Gamfield, a man who looks like Death himself, "a tall, gaunt, large-jointed man, attired in a suit of thread-bare black" yet "was in general given to professional jocosity" (4:26). This grotesqueness is most apparent in one of the scenes Victorian readers lauded its realism, the parochial funeral. The scene's apparent realism lies in its use of detail and its underscoring of hunger's role in this new world of social discipline: the dead woman's husband cries to Sowerberry, "I say she was starved to death" (5:39), and Bumble offers the nearly starved remaining family the minimum of relief, "a half-quartern loaf and a piece of cheese" (5:40). Sowerberry's commercial eagerness and lack of feeling on either side of this pathetic scene creates a series of rhythmic shifts that heighten its effects, from his greeting of Bumble's appearance "with a lively countenance" as he asks, "order for a coffin, eh?" (5:36), to his informing Oliver that the day's work—collecting the body from a nearly starved family and stuffing it into an overfull mass grave—is "nothing when you *are* used to it, my boy" (5:41).

Oliver's experience at Sowerberry's reinforces what the scene of Oliver before the magistrate suggests: that Oliver should not be an apprentice at all. Oliver's apprenticeship to Sowerberry attacks the very qualities that mark Oliver as a character: his receptivity to feeling and morality. Oliver's feelings undergo a continued assault, beginning with his sleeping quarters among the coffins and continuing through his experience of parochial funerals and mourning. Perhaps worse still, the text implies, Sowerberry commodifies Oliver's prayers. The text's horror of apprenticeship marks the appearance of that always pregnant object in Dickens, the blacking-bottle, which here conveys medicine to the woman Oliver helps bury. As Bumble recounts, the parochial surgeon sent it by his "prentice" (5:36). To be an apprentice in this world is to be forced into acts which expel fellow feeling and to embrace a world of hunger and work.

That Oliver resists this emotional reduction in the face of continued domination and abuse is never adequately explained. For much of the novel's early pages, he simply endures. The narrator recounts,

> that Oliver Twist was moved to resignation by the example of these good people, I cannot, although I am his biographer, undertake to affirm with any degree of confidence; but I can most distinctly say, that for many months he continued meekly to submit to the domination and ill-treatment of Noah Claypole. (6:42)

Only when Claypole attacks Oliver's feelings for his mother using "a jeering tone of affected pity" (6:44) do readers see his resistance. We should recall here the distinction between affect and emotion. What matters to Oliver is not Claypole's emotion as much as his way of doing this emotion, his tone and the affectedness of his pity. The violence done to Oliver's feelings by Claypole's affect draws Oliver into his own violent display. Oliver's rejection of Claypole's affectation and his abuse is perhaps the only sequence in which Oliver exhibits the melodramatic violence which the narrator encourages readers to wish upon Oliver's grotesque abusers. Oliver here has "the violence of his rage" and "an energy he had never known before" (6:44)—or since, really, given his actions throughout the rest of the novel. Oliver's rejection of domination at

Sowerberry's ends his formal apprenticeship and sends him to London. Although it is de rigueur to see the narrative's shift to the city and its Newgate plot as a retreat from its satire of the New Poor Law, this shift does not alter its affective form. Its situation remains almost unchanged but now minoritized by the attachment of apprenticeship to Fagin.

Fagin, Anti-Semitism, and Race

In Fagin, the grotesqueness of Oliver's former masters becomes racialized through the use of anti-Semitic imagery, from Fagin's stage Jew description as "villainous-looking and repulsive face... obscured by a quantity of matted hair" (8:63) to the satanic overtones of his standing shrouded in smoke, toasting fork in hand, preparing non-kosher food.[28] For Dickens, Fagin's Jewishness was part of the tale's seriousness. When he defended the representation of Fagin in 1863—he had leased Tavistock House to a Jewish solicitor and his wife, Eliza Davis, raised the issue—he argued

> Fagin in *Oliver Twist* is a Jew, because it unfortunately was true of the time to which that story refers, that that class of criminal almost invariably was a Jew. But surely no sensible man or woman of your persuasion can fail to observe – firstly, that all the rest of the wicked dramatis personae are Christians; and secondly, that he is called "The Jew", not because of his religion, but because of his race. If I were to write a lie, I should do a very indecent and unjustifiable thing but I make mention of Fagin as the Jew, because he is one of the Jewish people, and because it conveys that kind of idea of him, which I should give my readers of a Chinaman by calling him a Chinese. (*Letters* 10, 269–70)[29]

For Dickens, Fagin's Jewishness describes "his race." Although Dickens's use of the word occurs after his explicitly racist work of the 1850s, his use of *race* to describe an ethnic group in anthropological or biological terms may help us to understand his thought process in the 1830s as his usage in this letter dates to the sixteenth century.[30] Dickens saw Fagin's Jewishness as a form of radical difference. This difference was not so much religious or cultural—though it certainly was that as well—as it was physical. The text's racialization of Jewishess relies on the insistence of the Jew as physically grotesque and, like Gamfield, "villainous-looking." This racialization is most apparent in its emphasis of the Jew as marked by physical differences, most especially that of the nose, a recurrent trope of anti-Semitic representation. When Fagin first meets Claypole, the two try to intimate their understanding of one another by tapping their noses, beginning with Fagin tapping his. Nevertheless, the narrator explains, Claypole cannot imitate Fagin's gesture, "his own nose being not large enough for the purpose" (42:342). Similarly, Barney, the novel's other Jewish character, possesses only one trait: his "words: whether they came from the heart or not: made their way through the nose" (15:113).

For most critics, Fagin's depiction as a grotesque racialized figure is of less interest than his structural isolation. In his influential reading, Murray Baumgarten emphasizes that Fagin's Jewishness isolates him— Baumgarten dismisses the novel's other Jewish character, Barney—from British and Jewish culture and custom. For Baumgarten, Fagin's isolation and role as the novel's scapegoat draws out an implicit parallel with Oliver that the novel rejects by placing them in murderous opposition. From this perspective, the text's anti-Semitism can seem an unfortunate result of conflicting structural and cultural discourses. By contrast, for Susan Meyer, the novel's anti-Semitism is inseparable from its discussion of "the English treatment of the poor" (240). For Meyer, Dickens's discussion of the treatment of the poor focuses on its unchristian qualities, and she argues that Fagin's acceptance of Oliver signifies "[Christians] have become worse than the Jew" (244). Meyer's argument finds some support in Dickens's defense to Mrs. Davis—"all the rest of the wicked dramatis personae are Christians"—but avoids his racialization of Jewishness.

When placed alongside the novel's use of apprenticeship, this racialization reveals the novel's anti-Semitism to signal an inversion of racial domination, one like that the institutions of West Indian apprenticeship and the New Poor Law meant to quell. Although the rebellious apprentice has its own storied place in British history, and its most famous rebellious apprentice, Jack Sheppard, would receive his own long-running serialization in *Bentley's Miscellany* as *Oliver Twist* finished its serial run, Fagin captures this threat of a world turned upside down. Throughout, Fagin is menaced by the possibility of rebellious apprentices. Sikes tells him:

> I wonder they don't murder you ... If I'd been your 'prentice, I'd have done it long ago; and—no, I couldn't have sold you arterwards, though; for you're fit for nothing but keeping as a curiosity of ugliness in a glass bottle, and I suppose they don't blow glass bottles large enough. (13:95)

Fagin's race makes him an unnatural master for Sikes, and his description of Fagin "as a curiosity of ugliness" links his imagined rebellion to the imperial hobby of collecting physical specimens "in a glass bottle." To overthrow his Jewish master, Sikes implies, would be to reassert a particularly white British supremacy.

The novel's racist fear of "the Jew" does not focus on the threat of corruption by physical contact like that in Bates's account of his West

Indian sugar. Instead, it is a fear of moral corruption due to dependence on the Jew. Fagin is obsessed with bringing people into and under his power. The chief threat he poses to Oliver is his plan to implicate Oliver in the robbery of the Maylies', making Oliver, as Fagin tells Sikes, "ours for his life" (19:153). Fagin's corruption, like that of Sowerberry's, operates through feeling. He asserts, "Once let him feel that he is one of us; once fill his mind with the idea that he has been a thief; and he's ours!" (19:153). Oliver's receptivity to feeling thus threatens to become the basis of his corruption. Fagin, like a New Poor Law administrator, means to use feeling to make Oliver a self-directed worker, a free laborer in the criminal marketplace. To achieve this end, though, Fagin turns not to the mechanisms of the New Poor Law, hunger and humiliation, but to those of West Indian apprenticeship, violent coercion. For Fagin, coercion is prior to feeling. He explains to Monks: "I had nothing to frighten him with; which we must always have in the beginning, or we labor in vain" (26:205). Fagin thus forces Oliver to participate in a robbery and Oliver acts only under the constant threat of death from Sikes should he disobey.

Yet coercion fails, a result the text ascribes to a capacity for resistance that at first glance seems to reside chiefly in Oliver. If Oliver feels more than anyone, the text implies, he illustrates an inborn capacity to feel for others that the world has otherwise neglected. Oliver's innate moral sense thus implies a moral sense available to all if even a weak and frightened Oliver can become so "firmly resolved that, whether he died in the attempt or not, he would make one effort to dart upstairs from the hall, and alarm the family" (22:174). It is this moral sense that informs the narrator's call to readers to extend their capacity to feel to those caught in poverty and crime:

> Oh! if when we oppress and grind our fellow-creatures, we bestowed but one thought on the dark evidences of human error, which, like dense and heavy clouds, are rising, slowly it is true, but not less surely, to Heaven, to pour their after-vengeance on our heads; if we heard but one instant, in imagination, the deep testimony of dead men's voices, which no power can stifle, and no pride shut out; where would be the injury and injustice, the suffering, misery, cruelty, and wrong, that each day's life brings with it! (*OT* 30:233)

This densely intertextual passage weaves together sentimental language with language from the Bible and Evangelical opposition to slavery. The notion of a crime against humanity bearing down on Britain recalls William Wilberforce's 1823 pamphlet against slavery, which calls it "a national crime" (3) and includes repeated pleas for his "fellow-creatures."[31] Slavery as a marker of the nation's corruption and fall pervades abolitionist literature in tract and literary form. Anna Letitia Barbauld's implored Wilberforce almost forty years prior, in 1791, "But seek no more to break a nation's fall, / For ye have saved yourselves—and that is all" (1.116–17).[32] Yet Dickens's narrator uses this language of national corruption to defend Cobbett's white slaves and demand that readers bestow their thoughts on the oppression and coercion of "our fellow-creatures." That the narrator's demands are a result of Oliver's suffering at the hands of the grotesquely racialized Fagin indicates the extent of the text's displacements of the enslaved as people. In his coercive power and racialized figuration, Fagin offers a figure able to hold together the problems of slavery as both master *and* slave.

By contrast, Oliver seems free of all racial determinations. Released from the threat of apprenticeship, crime, work, and race, he enters a prelapsiarian state of white British middle classness at the Maylies, a place where work is simply the pleasurable experience of freely given effort. Thus, he exclaims to Rose Maylie:

Oh! dear lady, if I could but work for you; if I could only give you pleasure by watering your flowers, or watching your birds, or running up and down, the whole day long, to make you happy; what would I give to do it! (32:248)

For Oliver and the text, there is no greater pleasure than the fantasy of (white, British, and male) work free of hunger and coercion.[33]

Violent Violence and the Vulnerable

Once Oliver is removed to middle class safety, Fagin comes to exert his powers of coercion and domination on Nancy. As a young woman, Nancy provides the novel with a figure that reinflects its affective situation of dependence, vulnerability, and the abuse of irresponsible power through gender. From her introduction, Nancy is subject to near constant coercion by men, from her first trip to the police station to find Oliver to her collection of Oliver in the street and her conveying him to Sikes. Unlike Oliver, this coercion seems to have been effective. Hints from Fagin imply that Nancy continues to be subject to his command, making Nancy a kind of apprentice, one Fagin has lent to Sikes and can reclaim at will. Yet Nancy is more degraded in this experience than Oliver as an apprentice. Fagin means to incite her anger by comparing her to Sikes's dog: "If you want revenge on those that treat you like a dog—like a dog! Worse than his dog, for he humours him sometimes—come to me" (44:362). Although his incitement fails, this suggestion of Nancy's animalization frames Sikes as master of the domestic space and a double for Gamfield. Indeed, the chimneysweep's treatment of his donkey—that "blow on his head, which would inevitably have beaten in any skull but a donkey's"—foreshadows Nancy's death.

Nancy reveals the articulation of the text's patterning of elements to a particular affective form. She shares with Oliver, Mr. Bumble, and Mrs. Corney the uneasy distinction of being one of the text's semantic loci for narrative violence. The words *violence* and *violent* tend to cluster around her and Oliver and denote physical force (e.g., "violent termination" [2:15] and "violent consequences" [5:35]), intensity (e.g., Oliver kicking the door of the Sowerberrys' coal cellar "with a violence that rendered every other sound inaudible" [7:51]), or comic hyperbole (e.g., with Mr. Bumble and Mrs. Corney).[34] Throughout, the narrative associates *violence* with Nancy as an intensity of action or excess of passion. When Bulls Eye tries to attack Oliver, she "[struggles] violently with" (16:125) Sikes to protect him and "[stamps] her foot violently (16:126) in protest of their treatment; when Fagin tells her of his plan to make Oliver part of Sikes's robbery, she offers a "temporary display of violence" (26:203), which amounts to "a compound of feelings" (26:203); when she tracks Fagin and Monks, she moves with "extreme haste and violence" (39:315) before she takes to the streets with a "violent run" (39:317) that would "keep pace with the violent current of her own thoughts" (39:317); and fights off a "violent outbreak" (44:360) when Sikes prevents her from meeting with Rose a second time.

As the narrative progresses, the text's violent intensities come to intersect with violent physical force, as in this doubled usage: "The violent agitation of the girl, and the apprehension of some discovery which would subject her to ill-usage and violence, seemed to determine the gentleman to leave her, as she requested" (46:376). Violence's contrasting usages offer counterpoints of emotional intensity and physical threat, the one building on the other in a reciprocal pressure. This semantic violence then attaches to Fagin the grotesque racialized figure of master and slave as he manipulates Sikes into Nancy's murder. The narrator describes the two as

> they sat over against each other, face to face, [Fagin] looked fixedly at him, with his lips quivering so violently, and his face so altered by the emotions which had mastered him, that the housebreaker involuntarily drew back his chair, and surveyed him with a look of real affright. (47:378)

After Fagin reveals Nancy's betrayal, Fagin's violence becomes Sikes as he attacks a door, "expending fruitless oaths and violence" (47:381). Fagin then asks Sikes "You won't be—too—violent, Bill?" (47:382). The semantic violence clustered around Nancy thus takes on plotted form as Fagin's subsequent clarification increases the word's polyvocality: "not too violent for safety" (47:382).

The novel's figurations of apprenticeship, which serve as situations to signal affective and sentimental possibilities, here receive a strong affective form, violence, a way of doing and what is done, a confluence of intensity and physical force. Dickens revised this line for his public reading in a way that reinforces its ambiguity: "not too—<u>violent</u>—for—for—<u>safety</u>" (242).[35] If the em-dashes indicate the reading's rhythm, underlining specifies its hierarchy of emphases: violence is what is to be done but the emphases underscore safety, making what is violent also a way of doing violence. Fagin means for Sikes not to be too violent in his violence. The redundancy of Fagin's implication of a violent violence intimates something like what Daniel Stern terms a "vitality form," a fusion of a way of doing with what is done (see Chapter 1). To call violence part of the novel's affective form is not to treat it as what Sianne Ngai calls a text's emotional tone, an overarching emotion that organizes the feeling of a text. Rather, it is a way of doing embedded in what is done, a polyvocality that helps articulate the shifting tonalities of the text's streaky bacon. If the narrative of *Oliver Twist* is a loose assortment of situations remembered more for their effects than their plotted outcome, violent violence describes its rhythm of intensities as it shifts violently in and between scenes. The problem of streaky bacon—the tension between what is felt and what is seen in the orchestration of scene shifts and spectatorship—is a problem of intensities, suddenness, and physical force, of a violent violence.

This violent affective form reaches its apex in Nancy's murder, though the only semantically "violent" act of the scene is when Sikes "struggled violently, to release his arms" from her grasp (46:383). The scene is itself radically streaky. Unlike the narrator's remediation of Gamfield's beating of his donkey for comedic effect, the narration of the activity of violence in Nancy's murder is sparse. Once Sikes struggles free of Nancy's grip, the scene is under-narrated to produce image and implication: Sikes "beat [his pistol] twice with all the force he could summon, upon the upturned face that almost touched his own" (47:383). The description of Sikes's command of "force" and the figural proximity of their faces signal a bodily experience rather than a sight to be judged. The chapter moves frantically between a narration that suggests a witnessing moral agent and one that signals an affective experience of violence through Sikes's body and consciousness:

[Nancy] staggered and fell: nearly blinded with the blood that rained down from a deep gash in her forehead; but raising herself, with difficulty, on her knees, drew from her bosom a white handkerchief—Rose Maylie's own—and holding it up, in her folded hands, as high towards Heaven as her feeble strength would allow, breathed one prayer for mercy to her Maker.

It was a ghastly figure to look upon. The murderer staggering backward to the wall, and shutting out the sight with his hand, seized a heavy club and struck her down. (47:383)

The first part of the passage constructs a melodramatic tableau with one undulating, highly stylized sentence as Nancy kneels in prayer, Rose's white handkerchief in hand. The narrator deploys three instances of consonance that nearly lift the sentence into blank verse (*blinded...blood, high... Heaven, mercy...Maker*). With its brief conjuring of "a ghastly figure to look upon," however, the scene pivots. Ghastly for whom? For readers but also for the murderer, who shuts out the sight with his hand. The narrator fades as moral spectator. Instead, the passage approaches Sikes's consciousness in its sounds, enacting his revulsion of Nancy as an unnarrated hiss captured in the echoing sibilant *s* of *ghastly, staggering, shutting, seized*, and *struck*. The murder is thus caught in this narrated shift between the seen and the felt.

The effect of this confrontation between the moral seen and the morally problematic felt are inextricable from the novel's persistent affective situation of a vulnerable dependent, a grotesque guardian, and a witnessing moral agent. The result is a kind of discursive autoinsemination and affective mise-en-abyme, a semantic urge toward repetition and felt excess. This is what it means to be an affective form, to conjoin textual content, affective signals, and conjunctural discourses in a particular pattern of affects. The scene of Nancy's murder is thus followed by another sequence of emotional intensity, Sikes's flight from the law, again figured as a confrontation between the vulnerable and the grotesque. Sikes, however, has become vulnerable as "that morning's ghastly figure [follows] at his heels" (48:388), a situation that signals for readers Sikes's "agony of fear" (48:389) while insisting on a continued moral judgment of Sikes for the murder. The novel's late intensities turn again and again on the resituating of this affective situation: Sikes and Bates on Jacob's Island, witnessed by the furious crowd; Sikes and the furious crowd, witnessed by the reader; Fagin in prison, the death sentence a grotesque master, and witnessed first by his jailers, readers, and Oliver. Time and again, the affective situation occurs first as visual and tightly bound to the staging of a spectatorial sequence in moral sense philosophy and then as a signal for feeling. Consider the scene of Fagin awaiting execution, illustrated by Cruikshank and described visually from without before the narrator hones in on Fagin's "helpless desperate state... with gasping mouth and burning skin, [he] hurried to and fro, in such a paroxysm of fear and wrath" (52:430). Yet such descriptions are perhaps not meant to make Fagin a more moral character or convey morality to the reader. Kinkaid argues that Fagin offers a "vigorous and persuasive life-force in the novel" (*Dickens* 72). For Kinkaid, readers may feel sympathy for Fagin as a result of the novel's laughter which has exposed readers' stodgy middle-class assumption. Laughter certainly matters to Fagin's depiction but his final scene signals its affects through *force* more than laughter. Fagin's grotesqueness ensures that any signals for sympathy confront a real and formal limit: Fagin goes to his death but that death is not a scene for Oliver or the reader to witness or to feel. Instead, the text offers Oliver falling into a swoon after their final dialogue, a result of Fagin's state and his refusal to join Oliver in a final prayer (see *OT* 52:435). As the leader of a band of savage apprentices, Fagin dies an unrepentant savage too.

Signals of felt intensities in *Oliver Twist* thus hinge on the novel's staging of situations which dramatize the abuse of irresponsible power, an abuse that Dickens would later use to explain the evils of slavery and to avoid engaging with enslaved peoples who appeared to him so physically different from himself. The resulting discursive indetermination of this focus on the vulnerable and their abuse thus allows figures for British poverty and precarity to suggest the precarity of those formerly enslaved by the British empire. Figures of apprenticeship run throughout *Oliver Twist* not to comment on apprenticeship as such but on the vulnerability of those who are dependent and abused by those who oversee their labor. The violent violence of the text's affective form is the dynamic force of these discursive blurrings, producing both scenes that signal intensities and that produce the text's broader tonal instability. This is not to suggest violence should be understood as a metonym for affect, that affect and violence are simply asignifying and nondiscursive. The violent violence of *Oliver Twist* is embedded in its narrative discourse and its representations of violence. Its presentation of signals for violent feelings are predicated on a complex history of social, economic, and political domination in Britain and in the West Indies. In its tonal inconsistencies and signals of affective possibility, *Oliver Twist* shows an affective form to be a patterning of an array of affects, intensities, genres, and conjunctural forces. Its elements operate together to suggest a way of feeling the precarity produced by the British state in the late 1830s, and in the conjuring of this set of feelings, the novel intimates divisions between workers that the production of precarity encourages. The novel's attack on the New Poor Law comes to evoke the indifference of the working classes to abolition as a result of their own impoverishment. In its treatment of apprenticeship, the novel enfolds the problem of post-slavery Empire into itself as a theme and as a radical exterior, an outside that seems to escape the text's thematic interests. *Oliver Twist* thus insinuates telescopic philanthropy *avant la lettre*: the white working poor are present and worthy of concern, the black working poor are distant and not. The novel's racialization of Fagin offers a raced figure able to bear the blame for Britain's poor white child slaves. Yet the racism that hovers over the text may not keep the novel's affective scenes from resonating in unexpected ways, signaling felt experiences with otherness that the novel's sentimentality and politics otherwise elide. The very instability of the novel's form, its violent violence, can allow its affecting typifying scenes to come loose from its narrative and become something else again. How else, one might ask, could one go from the grim seriousness of *Oliver Twist* and Fagin's execution to the musical comedy of Lionel Bart's *Oliver!* (1960) and Fagin's happy exit with the Artful Dodger into the sunset?[36]

Notes

1 My discussion here draws on Nicholas Dames's insight that the propensity of Victorian reviewers to include enormous chunks of a novel's text indicates scenes they believed were most significant to the feeling of a text. T.H. Lister includes extensive quotes from scenes of Oliver's birth and his mother's death, of Bumble and Sowerberry's first conversation, of Oliver and Sowerberry collecting the body of a woman starved to death by the parish and her subsequent funeral, of Oliver's first encounter with Fagin, including learning how to pick a pocket, and of Sikes and Fagin planning the break-in to Mrs Maylie's home. *The Monthly Review* includes lengthy extracts from Fagin's revelation of Nancy's betrayal, Nancy's murder, Sikes's flight, and Fagin's final night. Richard Ford's review of the novel in *The Quarterly Review* eschews lengthy excerpts. See Dames, "On Not Close Reading."
2 See Hollingshead 188–90.
3 Key illustrations for realization include "Oliver escapes being bound apprentice to a sweep" (*OT* 23), "Mr Bumble and Mrs Corney taking tea" (*OT* 183), "The last chance" (413), and "Fagin in the condemned Cell" (431).
4 Meisel rightly notes that Almar draws on Cruikshank's illustrations for the first half of the novel than the second, though this may also be a result of the play opening ten days after the novel finished publication. See Meisel 252–57.
5 See Thomson 21–27.
6 Ellen Meiksins Wood demonstrates that agrarian capitalism and the creation of market precedes the structural reorganizations that are crucial for Polanyi's argument in *The Great Transformation*. Polanyi's account of the Speenhamland system, however, remains a useful exposition of the ways in which the political attempted to carve out resistant spaces to the extension of commoditization and the expansion of market discipline to more forms of labor.
7 Prince's narrative should be understood as both a personal narrative and a rhetorically shaped appeal for abolition. See Salih's introduction to the Penguin edition of *The History of Mary Prince*, especially xiii.
8 See Drescher, *Mighty Experiment* 19–33.
9 See E.P. Thompson, *Whigs and Hunters*, and *Customs in Common* 185–258.
10 As Holt notes of Jamaica, the role of the special magistrate in this arrangement often depended on where the magistrate had been recruited. Magistrates from the West Indies used their power to reinstate slavery, while those from Britain tended to view their role as authorities in the construction of a post-slave society. See Holt 58.
11 See Holt 48–49.
12 See also Davis *Age of Revolution* 270.
13 The treadmill, first imported to the West Indies from Britain soon after its invention in 1818. Although the treadmill held symbolic import, it should be noted that men and women on the treadmill were often whipped while walking it. See Holt 105–12, and Higman 243.
14 Different regimes of social control would appear in the decade that followed, most importantly the use of rent to control access to land, but 1838

marks the end of the legal regime of apprenticeship. Apprenticeship's abrupt end in Jamaica produced months of argument between its legislature, the Colonial Office, and Parliament, and resulted in tensions between local and imperial control that would simmer for decades until the events at Morant Bay in 1864 led to systemic changes in colonial governance. On the role of rent as social control, see Davis, *Problem of Slavery in the Age of Emancipation* 281.

15 See Virdee 1–73.

16 The year 1823 marks a shift in tactics for abolitionists, including new interest in migration and the gradual abolition of slavery, as well as the replacement of Wilberforce by Thomas Fowell Buxton as the new abolitionist leader in Parliament. See Davis, *The Problem of Slavery in the Age of Emancipation* 263–64.

17 This discussion of the savage recalls a 1853 piece in *Household Words* by Dickens titled "The Noble Savage." Dickens attacks a showing of native South Africans at St. George's Gallery in Hyde Park Corner for threatening to reanimate an "affectionate yearning toward that noble savage" ("The Noble Savage" 337). Dickens's discussion means to undermine Rousseau's notion of the uncorrupted primitive as instead an instance of "dire uniformity" (338). Dickens insists the savage is not innocent of modern society's corruptions but rather mired in a dull cultural homogeneity, and thus even "the ceremonies with which [the savage] faintly diversifies his life are, of course, of a kindred nature" (338). My thanks to James Buzzard for bringing this piece to my attention.

18 See Wolff.

19 "The Northampton Poacher" is one of many variants of the popular song "The Lincolnshire Poacher," the opening line of which varies between "When I was bound apprentice..." and "I was born a labourer...". For the "apprentice" variant, see Bell 216–17. For the "labourer" variant, see Roud and Bishop 342. I am indebted to Timothy F. Stunt for bringing this allusion to my attention.

20 See Drescher 128. Thomas Carlyle's 1849 "The Occasional Discourse on the Negro Question" struck his initial upper middle class audience as vulgar for its racist picture of Quashee and its urging of a return to slavery, but readers had embraced Carlyle's position and language when he republished it in 1853 as "The Occasional Discourse on the Nigger Question." By the 1850s, the racial epithet could then be found in publications as diverse as *The Times* and *The Northern Star.*

21 To H.W. Kolle, January 1833. Dickens adds a note to explain this strange usage that says "Blacks, not Browns," meaning, apparently, the slang coppers for the police.

22 Moore notes that the piece satirizes the views attributed to Dickens by abolitionist Lord Denman as a result of Mrs. Jellyby. See Moore 239.

23 On the emergence of racism in the 1850s, see Drescher 217–22, and Virdee 32–37.

24 Arthur A. Adrian argues that Dickens's understand of slavery was much along the lines of Carlyle, reflecting on Dickens's description of slavery as a result of "paltry republicanism which recoils from honest service to honest man" (320).

25 For McGill, Dickens's plagiarism undermines one of the central arguments that Dickens made on this trip, in favor of international copyright. See McGill 127.

26 See Hollingshead 190.

27 Nor is this the only instance of troubling moral calculations in which one man sells another, or in which such a sale generates grotesque laughter. Consider this scene with Fagin and the landlord of the Three Cripples:

> 'I say,' said the other, looking over the rails, and speaking in a hoarse whisper; 'what a time this would be for a sell! I've got Phil Barker here: so drunk, that a boy might take him!'
>
> 'Ah! But it's not Phil Barker's time,' said the Jew, looking up.
>
> 'Phil has something more to do, before we can afford to part with him; so go back to the company, my dear, and tell them to lead merry lives— *while they last*. Ha! ha! ha!'
>
> The landlord reciprocated the old man's laugh; and returned to his guests. The Jew was no sooner alone, than his countenance resumed its former expression of anxiety and thought. (26:200).

These two make tidy sums providing information to the police and turning over acquaintances to the law, a routine practice in the years before the formation of the more professionalized Metropolitan police force. Here, though, the language emphasizes the sale of a man, with his merchants considering whether his market value matches his current value to them, and seems to generate the same kind of shared laughter at the exploitation of the man's vulnerability. Yet here the laughter is forced, induced to indicate a shared economic interest.

28 A push for Jewish emancipation also occurred in the early 1830s. See Feldman 36–47, Nord, and Stone.
29 For discussion of the repeated uses of "the Jew" as an epithet, see Grossman.
30 See "race, n.6," 1b, 1c, and 1d.
31 See Wilberforce 19, 33, 36, 45, 51. In one early passage, Wilberforce offers a similar set of rhetorical devices:

> A nation which besides the invaluable benefit of an unequalled degree of true civil liberty has been favoured with an unprecedented measure of religious light with its long train of attendant blessings has been for two centuries detaining in a state of slavery beyond example rigorous and in some particulars worse than Pagan darkness and depravity hundreds of thousands of their fellow creatures originally torn from their native land by fraud and violence. Generation after generation have thus been pining away and in this same condition of ignorance and degradation they still for the most part remain. (19)

32 Anna Laetitia Barbauld, "Epistle to William Wilberforce, Esq. on the Rejection of the Bill for Abolishing the Slave Trade" (1791), l.116–17.
33 In a Freudian slip, the text does suggest at one point that the only truly free work may writing, buying, and selling of books. See OT 14:103.
34 See "violence, n." *OED Online*, Oxford University Press, January 2018, www.oed.com/view/Entry/223638. Accessed 9 March 2018.
35 I have emended Collins's italics with the manuscript underlinings.
36 On Bart's stage adaptation and its reinvention of the novel's Jewishness, see Weltman.

References

Adrian, Arthur A. "Dickens on American Slavery: A Carlylean Slant," *PMLA*, vol. 4, no. 67 (1952), pp. 315–29.

Almar, George. *Oliver Twist A Serio Comic Burletta in Four Acts*. New York: Samuel French, 1864.

Barbauld, Anna Laetitia. "Epistle to William Wilberforce, Esq. on the Rejection of the Bill for Abolishing the Slave Trade (1791)." *The Works of Anna Laetitia Barbauld*, edited by Lucy Aikin. Cambridge: Cambridge University Press, 2014, pp. 173–79.

Barnett, Charles Zachary. *Oliver Twist; or, The Parish Boy's Progress: A Drama in Three Acts Adapted from the Novel by Mr Charles Dickens.* 10 Middle Row, Holborn: J Duncan & Co., 1838.

Baumgarten, Murray. "Seeing Double: Jews in the Fiction of F. Scott Fitzgerald, Charles Dickens, Anthony Trollope, and George Eliot." *Between Race and Culture: Representations of "the Jew" in English and American Literature*, edited by Bryan Cheyette. Stanford: Stanford University Press, 1996, pp. 44–61.

Bell, Robert. *Ancient Poems, Ballads, and Songs of the Peasantry of England.* London: John W. Parker and Son, 1857.

"Bentley's Miscellany for November." *The Examiner, the Ballot*, 1555 (19 November 1837), pp. 740–41.

Butler, Judith. *Precarious Life: The Powers of Mourning and Violence.* London: Verso, 2004.

Cobbett, William. "To William Wilberforce. On the State of the Cotton Factory Labourers, and on the Speech of Andrew Ryding, Who Cut Horrocks with a Cleaver," *Cobbett's Weekly Register*, vol. 47, no. 9 (30 August 1823), pp. 514–58.

Dames, Nicholas. "On Not Close Reading: The Prolonged Excerpt as Victorian Critical Protocol." *The Feeling of Reading*, edited by Rachel Ablow. Ann Arbor: University of Michigan Press, 2010, pp. 11–26.

Dickens, Charles. *American Notes for General Circulation.* Edited by Patricia Ingham. New York: Penguin, 2004.

———. *Bleak House.* Edited by Stephen Gill. Oxford: Oxford World's Classics, 1996.

———. *The Letters of Charles Dickens: The Pilgrim Edition, Volume 1: 1820–1839.* Edited by Madeline House and Graham Storey. Oxford: Oxford University Press, 1965.

———. *The Letters of Charles Dickens: The Pilgrim Edition, Volume 10: 1862–1864.* Edited by Graham Storey and Margaret Brown. Oxford: Oxford University Press, 1998.

———. *Oliver Twist.* Edited by Kathleen Tillotson. Oxford World's Classics, 2008.

Davis, David Brion. *The Problem of Slavery in the Age of Emancipation.* New York: Alfred A. Knopf, 2014.

———. *The Problem of Slavery in the Age of Revolution, 1770–1823.* Oxford: Oxford University Press, 1999.

Drescher, Seymour. *The Mighty Experiment.* Oxford: Oxford University Press, 2004.

Engerman, Stanley L. "The Land and Labour Problem at the Time of the Legal Emancipation of British West Indian Slaves." *West Indies Accounts: Essays on the History of the British Caribbean and the Atlantic Economy in Honour of Richard Sheridan*, edited by Roderick A. McDonald. Kingston: University of the West Indies, 1996, pp. 297–318.

Feldman, David. *Englishmen and Jews.* New Haven: Yale University Press, 1994.

Ford, Richard. "Art. IV – Oliver Twist; or, the Parish Boy's Progress," *The Quarterly Review* vol. 64, no. 127 (June 1839), pp. 83–102.

Grossman, Jonathan. "The Absent Jew in Dickens: Narrators in *Oliver Twist, Our Mutual Friend,* and *A Christmas Carol,*" *Dickens Studies Annual,* vol. 24 (1996), pp. 37–58.

Hadley, Elaine. *Melodramatic Tactics: Theatricalized Dissent in the English Market Place, 1800–1885.* Stanford: Stanford University Press, 1995.

Higman, Barry William. *Slave Populations of the British Caribbean, 1807–1834.* Kingston: University of West Indies Press, 2013.

Hollingshead, John. *My Lifetime,* vol. 1. London: Sampson Low, Marston & Co., 1895.

Holt, Thomas C. *The Problem of Freedom.* Baltimore, MD: Johns Hopkins University Press, 1992.

Kennedy, Peter, editor. *Folksongs of Britain and Ireland.* London: Oak Publications, 1975.

Kinkaid, James. "Dickens and the Construction of the Child." *Dickens and the Children of Empire,* edited by Wendy S. Jacobson. London: Palgrave, 2000, pp. 29–42.

———. *Dickens and the Rhetoric of Laughter.* Oxford: Oxford University Press, 1971.

Ledger, Sally. "'Don't Be So Melodramatic!': Dickens and the Affective Mode," *19: Interdisciplinary Studies in the Long Nineteenth Century,* vol. 4 (2007). http://19.bbk.ac.uk/index.php/19/article/viewFile/456/316

Lister, Thomas Henry. "Dickens's Tales," *The Edinburgh Review,* vol. 68, no. 1 (October 1838), pp. 75–96.

Lorey, Isabell. *States of Insecurity: Government of the Precarious.* Translated by Aileen Dereig. London: Verso, 2015.

McGill, Meredith L. *American Literature and the Culture of Reprinting, 1834–1853.* Philadelphia: University of Pennsylvania Press, 2003.

Meisel, Martin. *Realizations: Narrative, Pictorial, and Theatrical Arts in Nineteenth-Century England.* Princeton, NJ: Princeton University Press, 1983.

Meyer, Susan. "Anti-Semitism and Social Critique in *Oliver Twist,*" *Victorian Literature and Culture,* vol. 33, no. 1 (2005), pp. 239–52.

Moore, Grace. "Reappraising Dickens's 'Noble Savage,'" *The Dickensian,* vol. 98, no. 458 (2002), pp. 236–43.

Nord, Deborah Epstein. "Dickens's Jewish Question: Pariah Capital and the Way Out," *Victorian Literature and Culture,* vol. 39, no. 1(2011), pp. 27–45.

"Oliver Twist, or the Parish Boy's Progress," *The Monthly Review,* vol. 1, no. 1 (January 1839), pp. 29–41.

Prince, Mary. *The History of Mary Prince.* Edited by Sara Salih. New York: Penguin, 2004.

"race, n.6." *OED Online.* Oxford University Press, January 2018, www.oed.com/view/Entry/157031. Accessed 19 March 2018.

Roud, Steve, and Julia Bishop. *The New Penguin Book of English Folk Songs.* London: Penguin, 2014.

Satnam Virdee, *Race, Class, and the Racialized Outsider.* New York: Palgrave, 2014.

Sharrad, Paul. "Speaking the Unspeakable: London, Cambridge and the Caribbean." *De-Scribing Empire: Post-colonialism and Textuality*, edited by Alan Lawson and Chris Tiffin. London: Routledge, 1994, pp. 201–17.

Smith, Adam. *An Inquiry into the Nature and Causes of the Wealth of Nations*. Edited by Edwin Cannan. Chicago: University of Chicago Press, 1976.

Stone, Harry. "Dickens and the Jews," *Victorian Studies*, vol. 2, no. 3 (1959), pp. 223–53.

Taylor, Christopher. *Empire of Neglect: The West Indies in the Wake of British Liberalism*. Durham, NC: Duke University Press, 2018.

Thompson, Edward Palmer. *Customs in Common*. New York: The New Press, 1993.

———. *Whigs and Hunters: The Origins of the Black Act*. London: Pantheon Books, 1975.

Thomson, Philip. *The Grotesque*. London: Metheun & Co., 1972.

"violence, n." *OED Online*. Oxford University Press, January 2018, www.oed.com/view/Entry/223638. Accessed 9 March 2018.

Weltman, Sharon Aronofsky. "'Can a Fellow Be a Villain All His Life': *Oliver!*, Fagin, and Performing Jewishness," *Nineteenth-Century Contexts*, vol. 33, no. 4 (2011), pp. 371–88.

Wilberforce, William. *An Appeal to the Religion, Justice and Humanity of the Inhabitants of the British Empire in Behalf of the Negro Slaves in the West Indies*. London: J. Hatchard and Son, 1823.

Wolff, Larry. "'The Boys Are Pickpockets, and the Girl Is a Prostitute': Gender and Juvenile Criminality in Early Victorian England from 'Oliver Twist to London Labour'," *New Literary History*, vol. 27, no. 2 (Spring 1996), pp. 227–49.

Wood, Ellen Meiksins. *The Origin of Capitalism: A Longer View*. London: Verso, 2017.

3 The Old Curiosity Shop
Love, Anxiety, and Inheritance

Affective form reveals the streaky tonalities of *Oliver Twist* and its depiction of domination and vulnerability to be intimately bound to the violence of its conjuncture. What might it uncover of the often derided sentimentality of *The Old Curiosity Shop* (1840–41)?[1] Were our analysis to focus on emotion, we would begin with Dickens's grief for his sister-in-law, Mary Hogarth. Affect, however, directs our attention not to emotion but to the something doing in the way a text signals emotion and produces a dynamic pattern of feeling which articulates it to its conjuncture. From this perspective, we look not for intimations of an emotion that we would expect to find—the affective fallacy *par excellence*—but for productive figurations or situations that yoke disparate elements in the text, something akin to the affective situation in *Oliver Twist* of the vulnerable child, grotesque villain, and judging spectator. The threat posed by Quilp to little Nell suggests a similar threat of the grotesque but the novel's plot hinges upon the persistent separation of these two figures rather than repeated stagings of their confrontation. Much as the novel's prose draws on the language of sentimentality, its affective situation is not one of sufferer, villain, and spectator as in *Oliver Twist* but a more diffuse derealization of sentimental spectatorship in Nell's passage through a villainous social world. Nell and her grandfather move from place to place to escape Quilp, and the novel follows the two in their flight, Quilp in his search for them, and Kit, Nell's friend and former servant, in his attempt to protect the two from Quilp. The novel consists of tableaus of transit and passage, of movement from one place to another that are meant to move readers in sentimental fashion by making them spectators of Nell's suffering in an indifferent world yet also conjures something more. The precarity of her existence, like Oliver's, is a result of the political economic organization of British society, one that has unevenly distributed the precariousness of existence. The novel's affective situation, then, is one of precarious transit, of punctual scenes drawn from an otherwise indivisible experience of movement, a situation that may recall Zeno's paradox of the arrow, always in motion and always at rest.[2]

This affective situation of transit works in tandem with the novel's use of inheritance as an initiating plot device. In other novels, Dickens uses this device as a mechanism for plotted suspense. In *Martin Chuzzlewit* and *Our Mutual Friend*, inheritance effectively operates as a suspense mechanism for their marriage plots. Once inheritance's deferral ends, these plots can be brought to a close: Martin Chuzzlewit marries Mary and returns to his grandfather's good graces and John Harmon marries Bella Wilfer and receives his inheritance regifted by the kindly Mr. and Mrs. Boffin. In *Bleak House*, Dickens further draws out the thematic meaning of this narrative device. The narrative deferral of inheritance comes to infect life itself as the promise of inheritance deprives characters like Richard Carstone, Miss Flite, and Mr. Gridley of their ability to act or think of the future. Only John Jarndyce's renunciation of inheritance opens a path to escape a life spent waiting. If inheritance in *Bleak House* emphasizes the openness and irresolution that makes it a functional plotting device, in *The Old Curiosity Shop*, it suggests a more radical focus on the irresolution of suspense. In this text, inheritance is impossible to achieve and empty from the start. Nell's grandfather imagines a fortune to leave his granddaughter, but he has nothing for Nell to inherit. At least Jarndyce v. Jarndyce began with a fortune.

As a conjunction of the impossible and the empty, inheritance offers the novel a figure for the precarity of its affective situation, a precarity created by staggering economic inequality. The introduction of the inheritance plot in the novel's opening pages reveals the scope of this inequality. Nell's grandfather explains to the visiting Master Humphrey his plans for an extravagant and entirely imaginary bequest:

> I would leave [Nell]—not with resources which could be easily spent or squandered away, but with what would place her beyond the reach of want for ever. You mark me, sir? She shall have no pittance, but a fortune. (3:34)

Nell's grandfather understands that to leave Nell without a fortune would be to abandon her to the kinds of scenes which will make up the bulk of the novel, a life not just of work but of sexual exploitation, abuse, starvation, and death. It is not enough to leave her with some resources in this world. She must be put beyond the reach of want forever. For most readers, her grandfather's dream is mere delusion, but the novel's attention to the precarity of existence and to monetary incomes reveals it to be integral to the novel's affective form. Real numbers can be put to the grandfather's dream. By bringing together representations of wealth in nineteenth-century literature and the economic history of wealth, economist Thomas Piketty demonstrates that from the nineteenth century through the twenty-first century, extreme wealth can be calculated as somewhere between 50 and 100 times the national average income, a level of wealth supported by the figures in the novels of Jane Austen and Honoré de Balzac.[3] In the 1840s, Britain's average income was about £35 a year and one character in *The Old Curiosity Shop* receives this as a yearly wage: the schoolmaster who takes charge of Nell and her grandfather and gives them a place to live next to the Gothic churchyard where Nell will eventually be buried. The average income is a princely sum to this character. The schoolmaster is "delighted" at his new situation and exclaims upon seeing his new home: "Five-and-thirty pounds a year in this beautiful place!" (46:352). To place Nell beyond the read of want, her yearly income would be an astronomical £1,750–£3,500. Such an income would be expected to come from investments at an annual rate of return of three percent, the standard rate of return for British Consols. To earn that yearly, Nell would need a monstrous fortune, a sum between £58,000 and £117,000. The grandfather's fantasy of escape from precarity, the emotional basis for his gambling and mental decline, is the pursuit of an impossible sum. Yet his drive to give Nell an inheritance will manage to place her beyond the reach of want forever—in her grave, propelled there by the desires that attach to this imagined inheritance. Inheritance and the desires it solicits are not simply urges to be overcome or ignored in this novel but a fantasy of the impossible means necessary to escape precarity. To grasp the novel's affective form will require an analysis of the novel's use of inheritance as a kind of passage, whether the passage of money, objects, or emotions between characters and the novel's readers. The resulting form reveals a complex interweaving of the political and economic with the affective and the sentimental.

Inheritance and Land Reform as Discourses of Inequality

The novel's evocations and failures of inheritance help unveil the intertwining of political economic discourses and the affective in Britain during the 1840s. Its impasses and failures in the novel suggest the ways in which the increasingly limited sphere of "proper" political economy understood inheritance as a political concern rather than an economic one. Economists thus offered only modest critiques of inheritance law as thwarting market exchange. By contrast, popularizing and populist forms of political economy—most especially those offered by the Chartists—treated inheritance as fundamental to the economics of inequality by allowing an already well-off aristocracy to further accumulate wealth. By the 1860s, this populist argument against inheritance had lost its currency, in part due to the diminishing sway of Chartism and the success of the Anti-Corn Law League, whose arguments against the Corn Laws were premised on a critique of aristocratic privilege. Even Karl Marx's thought bears evidence of this shift. In 1843, Marx subjected primogeniture to withering analysis in *Critique of Hegel's Doctrine of the State*.[4] By 1869, however, Marx declared to the Fourth

Annual Congress of the International Working Men's Association—an audience that included many former Chartists—that "the right of inheritance is only of social import insofar as it leaves to the heir the power which the deceased wielded *during his lifetime*" (Marx, "Report"). Where the Chartists had once placed the critique of inheritance at the center of their demands for land reform, Marx now insisted that "the abolition of the right of inheritance can never be the starting point of such a social transformation" (ibid.).

To grasp this shift, one must turn to the analysis of inheritance that began in the years immediately prior to the French revolution. In France and England, discussions of inheritance focus on "real property"—that is, titles, estates, and land—more than portable property such as financial assets or other commodities. Two strains of thought dominated these discussions. Supporters of existing inheritance laws stressed the importance of paternal authority in the disposition of real property. Without paternal control of family resources, they argued, social order would crumble. By contrast, supporters of limitations to testamentary freedom believed that the division of large estates would spur economic activity by increasing the number of interested landowners. Adam Smith briefly argues against primogeniture for these reasons in *The Wealth of Nations* by appealing to familial fairness, noting that "nothing [could] be more contrary to the real interest of a numerous family, than a right which, in order to enrich one, beggars all the rest of the children too" (1:409). One might see this line of argument used by Quilp—rarely the sign of a good argument—when he tells Nell's brother, Fred: "I always will say... that when a rich relation having two young people—sisters or brothers, or brother and sister—dependent on him, attaches himself exclusively to one, and casts off the other, he does wrong" (182). Jeremy Bentham suggests a more concrete approach in *Supply Without Buthen* (1795) by encouraging the state to decrease the concentration of real estate by receiving and dividing the estates of the childless wealthy. In France, supporters of limits to inheritance stressed not only their economic benefits but also their affective ones. Changes to inheritance law, they argued, would encourage greater comity within families by eliminating the tyranny of primogeniture and paternal authority and thus would promote greater comity in society itself. As sociologist Jens Beckert notes in his comparative history of inheritance law, the Marquis de Mirabeau was a key proponent of this argument. In a letter, Mirabeau underscored that these alterations to inheritance law were necessary because "the feelings and habits that are crucial to public happiness arise at the domestic hearth" (qtd. in Beckert 31).

Questions of inheritance, then, were understood to be questions of political and economic power. In England, Edmund Burke premises his conservative analysis of government and political power in *Reflections on the Revolution in France* upon existing inheritance law as an unchanging state of nature. He inveighs, "By a constitutional policy working after the pattern of Nature, we receive, we hold, we transmit our government and our privileges, in the same manner in which we enjoy and transmit our property and our lives" (33). No surprise, then, that those who wished to alter the social order argued that the natural order and inheritance laws must be changed. The Jacobins were especially attuned to inheritance as an important social mechanism for the transmission of wealth and power. In 1794, they eliminated testamentary freedom, though their short-lived control of the state meant this change in law was not permanent (see Beckert 35–36). In the years that followed the revolution, French law introduced limited restrictions to testamentary freedom. The Code Civil enforced the equal division and sale of large estates among children and imposed new restrictions on the division of inheritances with an eye toward equality; however, it also included an expansion of the testamentary rights of smaller estate holders. As Beckert notes, this expansion of inheritance law to include those with fewer resources had a political purpose: it "was supposed to restore paternal authority within the family" (37). Later conservative attacks on the Code Civil's limitations to inheritance would also invoke this call for increased paternal authority.[5]

In the 1830s, however, France saw the appearance of a contrasting argument about inheritance, this time from the Saint-Simonians. Rather than questions of real property and primogeniture, the Saint-Simonians highlighted a moral demand to work. In 1830, they demanded, in their words,

> the abolition of all privileges of birth, without exception, and consequently the destruction of inheritance, the greatest of these privileges, the one which to-day embraces them all, and whose effect is to leave to chance the distribution of social privileges among the small number of those who wish to lay claim to them, and to condemn the most numerous class to depravity, ignorance and poverty. (qtd. in Blanqui 501)

The problem of primogeniture and entails was no longer a question of domestic happiness but a moral demand that all who live in a society work. For the Saint-Simonians, inheritance must be eliminated because "it sanctions for some the impious privilege of idleness, that is to say, of living on the labor of others" (ibid.). Inherited wealth thus authorizes the existence of a parasitic class and distributes work according to "the chance of birth" (ibid.).

It will take almost twenty years for this argument to appear in political economy, the result of a crucial shift in political economic thought which occurred almost simultaneous with the French revolution. For pre-revolutionary Physiocrats like François Quesnay, the lynchpin of economic productivity was the land, and who owned land mattered for how it would be worked.[6] Adam Smith threatened the primacy of land in political economic analysis by insisting that productive labor was not reducible to agriculture but instead consisted of any labor that "adds to the value of the subject upon which it is bestowed" (*Wealth* 1:351).[7] At the turn of the nineteenth century, T.R. Malthus reasserted the Physiocratic position in new form: because population increases faster than the means of subsistence, the productivity of land matters more than the productivity of labor. Inheritance as primogeniture remained an economic problem for Malthus because it limited access to land and its produce.[8] David Ricardo, however, put an end to this argument and to the economic importance of inheritance with his analysis of rent and food prices. By focusing on the labor that makes land productive, Ricardo placed the question of land ownership outside economic analysis except insofar as they inhibit how land is used. Land will be cultivated and pay rent based on its fertility, according to Ricardo, because capital seeks to maximize its returns. If prices rise, this is due to increased labor costs, not increased land costs. As he explains, "the reason why...raw produce rises in comparative value is because more labor is employed in the production of the last portion obtained, and not because a rent is paid to a landlord" (38). The fertility of the land, the interests of capital, and the amount of labor needed to work the land—these are economic questions. Who owns the land is not.

As a result, in the 1830s and 1840s, inheritance is a topic of scattered import for political economy. Parliament releases four reports on real property from 1829–33, but political economists had little to say about inheritance until 1848 when John Stuart Mill attacked inheritance in his first edition of *Principles of Political Economy* and John Ramsay McCulloch published a defense of inheritance as inextricable from private property as such.[9] Intriguingly, Mill came to the question of inheritance not through political economy but his familiarity with the Saint-Simonians. In his *Autobiography*, Mill writes that he first encountered the Saint-Simonian school as "they were just beginning to question the principle of hereditary property" and that he "was by no means prepared to go with them even this length" (5:98). By the time of he began writing *Principles of Political Economy*, however, Mill admits that he had become "far more heretical" than he "had been in the days of [his] most extreme Benthamism" (7:137). This heresy includes a shift in Mill's view of inheritance law. His initial argument reads much like Bentham. Primogeniture and entails should be eliminated, Mill thought, as a way to "[mitigate] the inequalities consequent on these institutions" (7:137). Nevertheless, as Mill developed his position, he came to take a position all but indistinguishable from the Saint-Simonians. This shift may have also been a result of the influence of Thomas Carlyle. Inheritance should be limited by law, Mill comes to believe, as a result of the

Biblical injunction "that they who do not work shall not eat" (7:138),[10] a suggestion Carlyle makes in *Past and Present* (1842), writing scornfully:

> Aristocracy has become Phantasm-Aristocracy, no longer able to *do* its work, not in the least conscious that it has any work longer to do. Unable, totally careless to *do* its work; careful only to clamour for the *wages* of doing its work,—nay for higher, and *palpably* undue wages, and Corn-Laws and *increase* of rents; the old rate of wages not being adequate now! (3.1:142–43)

Mill's discussion of inheritance can be understood as part of this shift in the discourse about inheritance from land to work. Note that Mill locates his ideas about inheritance outside the realm of economics proper even though he offers them in a book ostensibly about political economy. Inheritance is an issue of distribution and public morals, not production, and he writes that the state should not limit the right of testamentary freedom but rather the maximum that one might inherit (232). More broadly, Mill argues "it may be affirmed that in a majority of instances the good not only of society but of the individuals would be better consulted by bequeathing to them a moderate, than a large provision" (229). Elaborating this idea through familial feeling, Mill asserts that all children should be provided for in terms no less generous than those society feels due illegitimate children: "To such a child it is generally felt that there is due from the parent, the amount of provision for his welfare which will enable him to make his life on the whole a desirable one" (230). Mill admits, however, that class expectations will likely urge parents to bequeath more than this due:

> When the children of rich parents have lived, as it is natural they should do, in habits corresponding to the scale of expenditure in which the parents indulge, it is generally the duty of the parents to make a greater provision for them than would suffice for children otherwise brought up. (230)

A longstanding critic of unreflecting habit, Mill means to highlight a potentially corrosive class privilege and to encourage limits to inheritance that would foster industriousness;[11] however, he stops short of arguing against wealthier parents providing portions that would allow their children to remain comfortable members of the class in which they were raised. Much as Mill bolsters the demand to work as a limit to inheritance, he does not launch a full assault on class privilege.

By contrast, Chartist demands for land reform in the 1840s directly attacked inheritance, a result of their focus on economic inequality. An 1840 editorial in the *Northern Star* described such inequality as a problem of "the acquisition and accumulation, in individual hands, of large heaps of wealth and property by the oppression and starvation of the people" (qtd. in Chase 66). Chartists viewed inheritance as one of the key mechanisms that transmitted "heaps of wealth and property" across generations. Initially, Chartists followed a Utilitarian line of argument that legal protections for inheritances should be eliminated in order to release land for small holders to work. Their proposed solution, however, was not a radical redistribution of land but rather expanded legal "access to, rather than ownership of, the land" (Chase 70). Although the Chartist Land Company launched in 1845, historian Malcolm Chase notes that the "commitment to agrarian reform...had been central to Chartism almost from its inception" (65). In 1839, the Chartist National Convention issued a declaration in favor of "taking into public ownership any land that had once been 'appropriated to public and general use'" (64). In his 1841 pamphlet *Remedy for National Poverty and National Ruin*, Feargus O'Connor promoted reclaiming wastes for small landholders to work by hand.

The Chartist land plan, then, is the most immediately historically adjacent discussion of inheritance to Dickens's novel and treats it as a question of work and access to land.[12] Thus while the desire for an impossible inheritance drives the novel's plot, its narrative is marked by questions of work and inequality raised by inheritance and access to the land, ideas that we can see were well established in populist discourse during the novel's initial serialization from April 1840 to February 1841. By the early 1840s, the Saint-Simonian demand to work had become part of the Chartist analysis of the problems of property ownership and intergenerational wealth transfer. Mill's discussion appears later but usefully illustrates the kind of solutions that suggested themselves to middle class reformers like Dickens. In this way, arguments about inheritance reveal the coherence of the novel's seemingly divergent narrative trajectories of Nell, Kit, and Dick Swiveller. Taken as a pair, Nell and Swiveller map the limits of respectable escapes from work, either through death or an acceptably modified inheritance, and the good-natured Kit provides the proper relation to work and wealth in its most limited form.

The novel's failed inheritance plot thus leads Nell through a decline from a seemingly well-off middle-class position—"looked upon as affluent" (48:363) in her relative's words—to a life of poverty marked by work and leading inexorably to death. The failure of the grandfather's attempts to marshal a fortune for her to inherit first loads him with cares and then mortgages his belongings to Quilp. The failure of his plan to create an inheritance inaugurates Nell's turn to work. She pleads with her grandfather to flee the shop and his cares, telling him "we may beg, or work in the open roads or fields, to earn a scanty living, rather than live as we do now" (9:79–80). For punitively economical middle-class characters like Miss Monflathers, Nell can seem to be not industrious enough. She asks Nell rhetorically, "Don't you know that the harder you are at work, the happier you are?" (31:240). Yet the text goes to some lengths to show Nell as unremittingly industrious. She tries her hand at a variety of work-like tasks, from mending puppet clothes and making nosegays to leading tours through Jarley's waxworks and opening and closing a church. Nell's industriousness, however, does nothing to promote the happiness that Miss Monflathers attributes to work. Instead, the novel links work throughout to a world of mummified life, what Theodor Adorno aptly describes as "the object world of the bourgeois sphere" (177). For Adorno, the world of the novel is the world of the commodity. Since Nell can neither grasp nor escape the mummified life of the commodity, she is finally sacrificed to it.

Adorno's focus on the novel's commodity world usefully directs our attention to a crucial feature of the novel's treatment of work: it turns the worker into an object. Although it is a near truism to liken Nell's commodity world to Marx's talking table, perhaps most especially given the novel's use of puppets and waxworks, what many overlook is that the world of Marx's talking table is the world of circulation not production. Indeed, Adorno faults the novel for this reason. Yet in its focus on circulation, the novel's commodity-centric world is a fantasy of escape raised by the problems of inheritance—that is, it is a fantasy bound up with an analysis of inequality focused on the ways in which capitalism distributes wealth. Adorno's analysis inaugurates a line of criticism that draws connections between novel's focus on objectification and death. Claire Wood suggests these foci for the novel reveal Dickens's ambivalence toward the Victorian commercial culture of death and burial (see Wood 59). By contrast, John Bowen argues that the novel's use of objectification subordinates questions of commerce to those of mourning and figures "the simultaneous necessity and impossibility of mourning" (143). Inheritance by contrast provides a historical discourse that links death and objectification, and economic inequality and the novel's persistence use of punctual scenes of transit for its affective situation. Inheritance produces inequality, creating an object world of wealth predicated on death and demanding from the poor nothing but endless toil, and death is omnipresent because inheritance demands a death. As we will see, Nell's death inverts this demand and allows the wealth that would have passed between generations in a family to move instead into the wider world.

If Nell and her death figures the refusal of inheritance, then Dick Swiveller captures its moderation. For Swiveller, work is at odds with his conception of himself as a gentleman of expectations. Inherited wealth, Swiveller insists, should free gentlemen from the object world of work so that they can act and spend as they like. He thus focuses his attention on an aunt who promised him a substantial inheritance and Nell, whose inheritance he hopes to gain by marriage. When both his inheritance campaigns falter, Swiveller is persuaded by Quilp to accept a clerkship with

Sampson Brass, a position that could be mistaken for work except that it does not pay, makes few demands on his time, and requires and provides no professional skills. With work too a dead letter, Swiveller quickly approaches his financial nadir. After an extended illness, he finds himself trapped in his room because all his clothes have been pawned for food. An unexpected but limited bequest from his aunt rescues him from pecuniary ruin, but Mr. Witherdeen informs him,

> If you had been another sort of nephew, you would have come into possession (so says the will, and I see no reason to doubt it) of five-and-twenty thousand pounds. As it is, you have fallen into an annuity of one hundred and fifty pounds a year. (*OCS* 66:504)

Swiveller's lost inheritance—possible but not obtained—is nearly half the size of Nell's imagined fortune. Yet Swiveller's greatly reduced inheritance reflects his new moral standing. It allows him to maintain his class status yet does not encourage him to return to his spendthrift ways. It also, however, keeps him from seeking productive work, a space that remains in the novel the world of the alienated commodity. Instead, Swiveller's inheritance allows him to develop and deepen his familial and social feelings. He pays for the education of the young Marchioness before marrying her, which the text makes a joke about Swiveller's failed inheritance schemes. The narrator notes that he had "frequent occasion to remark at divers subsequent periods [to say of his wife] that there had been a young lady saving up for him after all" (73:552).

Sentimentality as Distributionist Critique

Swiveller's turn from inheritance to feeling indicates inheritance's role in the novel as a test of the power and limits of sentimentality. As critics have long noted, sentimentality imbues *The Old Curiosity Shop*. Biographers correlate this sentimentality with Mary Hogarth's death, drawing on Dickens's reflections in personal letters during the novel's composition.[13] Scholars are more equivocal about the function of sentimentality in Dickens's work. Fred Kaplan argues for the direction application of eighteenth-century moral sense philosophy to Dickens's work but notes that Dickens's otherwise pervasive reliance on "the moral sentiments" (*Sacred Tears* 62) does not keep him from creating villains such as Quilp who are seemingly devoid of those sentiments. As a result, Dickens seems to blame the social corruption of the sentiments for villainous behavior even as characters like Quilp, Kaplan writes, "challenge the assumption that moral sentiment is an innate human quality" (63). Although she does not discuss Dickens, Miriam Bailin importantly contests Kaplan's direct applicability of eighteenth-century philosophy to the Victorian period and argues that "Victorian pathos... is the emotional accommodation sentimentality offers to the experience of social mobility, in particular the competitiveness that underlies it" (1016). In Bailin's account, the affective problems solicited by a character like Quilp suggests a problematic rivalry at the heart of the sentimental, the result of "a struggle to suppress or transvaluate supervening obstacles to sympathetic identification (anger, hatred, and resentment, for instance) whose traces can still be felt in the outpouring of emotion that is meant to signal their absence" (1020). For other critics, these faultlines in the novel's sentimentality should be understood in terms of the political or generic. For Sue Zemka, the novel's "hysteria of sentimentality" offers a successful "mass response" to the potentially threatening "Jacobin carnivalesque" of the novel's grotesque figures (296); and Brad Fruhauff sees the novel's sentimentality and Gothicism as generic mechanisms that explore the threats to and promises of ethical action for the novel. Attention to the role of inheritance in the novel reveals the text's sentimentality to be bound to historicizable issues of inequality and social mobility. Although this interpretation suggests Bailin's account of the sentimental, the novel's engagement with social mobility operates without a clearly articulated rivalry between diegetic characters. If there is a rivalry at hand in the text, it is one that connects its affective situation of transit to its thematics of the transmission of objects, bodies, and emotions. The sentimentality of *The Old Curiosity Shop* thus urges us to imagine the passage of objects, bodies, and emotions as the contagious transmission of a positive moral sense between characters, yet these passages also suggest that the materiality of what is passed may undermine such feelings.

This tension appears most clearly with the characters that capture the novel's sentimental urges. For Nell and Kit, the moral sentiments almost invariably work, drawing other characters to them through a near spontaneous infection that the narrator makes explicit as "something contagious in Kit's laugh" (22:173). The resolution of the narrative—Kit's upward mobility and the spiritual regeneration created by Nell's death—may thus be understood in Kaplan's sense as the culmination of a textual re-education of the moral sentiments. The difficulty, of course, is that if sentimentality simply transmits from one character to another, the narrative would never occur. Quilp would be moved by Nell and Sampson would be moved by Kit. They are not. It is perhaps fairer to say that the novel's version of sentimentality imagines a general moral sense available to all and an anxiety that that this moral sense can fail. The two most noted emotions in the novel capture these urges. On the one hand, "love" signals the ways in which successful affective incitements may cohere social relationships. On the other hand, "anxiety" signals the troubling possibilities that they may fail. These twin emotions form the pincers by which Quilp means to catch Nell's grandfather by marrying Nell to Swiveller. The narrator describes this as Quilp "seeking to entrap the sole object of his love and anxiety into a connexion of which he knew he had a dread and hatred" (23:181). "Love and anxiety" here indicates anxiety's role in the novel. While love marks sentimental care, anxiety inflects it with instability. Throughout the text, anxiety inflects another emotion as a kind of modulation. The narrator speaks of 'sorrows and anxieties' (6:58), 'anxiety and distress' (9:76), 'depression and anxiety' (9:76), 'anxiety and surprise' (10:85), and 'anxiety and sorrow' (11:98). For a novel so widely known as sentimental, it is surprising that anxiety is its omnipresent emotion. Yet as phrases like 'care and anxiety' (16:133) and 'anxious and uneasy' (154) suggest, anxiety is less an emotion than a heightening of and potential threshold with another emotion. Anxiety, then, is not so much an emotion in the novel as a way of doing an emotion—in other words, an affect—and it reveals the fundamental precarity that organizes the novel's signaling of emotion and its attempts to instill love.

Anxiety is thus our byword for the novel's affective form, a pervasive style of feeling the precariousness of love in a world of extreme economic inequality. Indeed, it marks the very origin of the Old Curiosity Shop itself. When Nell's great uncle recounts how her grandfather came to open his shop, he explains that after falling into poverty, "the tastes he had cultivated were now to yield him an anxious and precarious subsistence" (69:526). The titular shop supports "an anxious and precarious" life and the novel that bears its name explores the qualities of that life. At the center of this life is the uneasy relationship between interior feeling and economic survival. Interior feelings—the grandfather's tastes—guide actions—his selection of objects—yet cannot guarantee economic subsistence. *The Old Curiosity Shop* is patterned by this anxiety generated by the disconnection of interior sensibility and external material subsistence. Either may fail. Both may fail. Precariousness and anxiety are the crux of the text, and its evocations of feeling mean to bring what is interior in line with what is exterior, to make feeling and economic distribution coeval.

Other critics have noted the importance of precariousness to the novel's sentimentality. Valerie Purton argues of the novel that "it is the knowledge of the precariousness of human identity against which the insistent rhetoric of sentimentalism militates" (108). Hilary Schor approaches a similar argument with her claim that Nell, in her age, flight, and death, represents the commodification of the female body and resistance to this commodification. Schor rightly links this problematic to the issue of inheritance and writes, "the role of the good, quiet, daughter…may well be to represent a patrimony she cannot, yet, possess for herself" (45). Schor's focus, however, falls on Nell's "pornographic" objectification (34) rather than the passages of objects and affects. What I want to emphasize as the novel's affective form is its suggestion that objects and emotions have no necessary mechanisms for passing from one to the other, that it wishes to bring them line yet intuits a potentially fundamental dissension. In this sense, the novel suggests Sara Ahmed's argument in *The Cultural Politics of Emotion* that the passage of objects may reveal dissension in affective experiences rather than simple emotional infections.[14] The novel's persistent turn to commodification certainly means to suggest a world in which the passing of objects between or away from characters signals fellow feeling. The passage of objects can thus reveal feelings that are otherwise obscure, a point that Master Humphrey emphasizes in the novel's opening pages:

> We are so much in the habit of allowing impression to be made upon us by external objects, which should be produced by reflection alone, but which, without such visible aids, often escapes us; that I am not sure I should have been so thoroughly possessed by this one subject, but for the heaps of fantastic things I had seen huddled together in the curiosity shop warehouse. (*OCS* 1:20)

That is, objects may impress upon us thoughts and feelings easily missed. In this case, "fantastic" objects associated with Nell impress Master Humphrey with her vulnerability. Yet the passage of these objects persistently threatens to mark dissensions of feeling and demands for possession. Hence Master Humphrey indicates that we should—though we often do not—recognize these feelings "by reflection alone"—that is, without objects.

Such an idea forms the basis for the novel's attempt to reclaim fellow feeling by reframing objects themselves as the threat to feeling. The text thus strips objects from Nell in a clarifying sentimental process, encouraging readers to discover without the "visible aids" of objects' sentimental connections. This objectless or dematerialized aspect of proper moral reflection in the novel resonates with its discussion of inheritance and feeling. Anxiety that the sentiments may fail—that emotions may not transfer—strips away possessions and their attendant vulnerability to misrecognition or capture. If the alienation of the object-world indicates a problem of economic distribution, of inequalities and failed transfers, then the novel suggests a new emphasis on dematerialized social connections. An extended passage near its mid-point describes differences in emotional attachments based on class and underscores this shift from material objects to be passed from hand to hand to immaterial ones. Inheritance here serves as the basis for an affective contrast between the landed elite and the landless lower classes:

> And let us linger in this place for an instant to remark that if ever household affections and loves are graceful things, they are graceful in the poor. The ties that bind the wealthy and the proud to home may be forged on earth, but those which link the poor man to his humble hearth are of the truer metal and bear the stamp of

Heaven. The man of high descent may love the halls and lands of his inheritance as part of himself, as trophies of his birth and power; his associations with them are associations of pride and wealth and triumph; the poor man's attachment to the tenements he holds, which strangers have held before, and may to-morrow occupy again, has a worthier root, struck deep into a purer soil. His household gods are of flesh and blood, with no alloy of silver, gold, or precious stone; he has no property but in the affections of his own heart; and when they endear bare floors and walls, despite of rags and toil and scanty fare, that man has his love of home from God, and his rude hut becomes a solemn place. (38:289)

For Andrew McCann, this section of the novel reveals "poverty is detached from any meaningful material context; it becomes the ennobling absence that frames more permanent, immaterial identifications" (191). I would add that it is where the text separates feelings of sociality from material circumstances, extricating poverty from the mechanism that produces material inequality. The passage continues by exhorting British political leaders "to improve the wretched dwellings in bye-ways where only Poverty may walk" in order to foster "that love of home from which all domestic virtues spring" (OCS 38:289). The narrator explains that this should be done because

> in love of home, the love of country has its rise, and who are truer patriots or the best in time of need—those who venerate the land, owning its woods, and stream, and earth, and all that they produce? Or those who love their country, boasting not a foot of ground in all its wide domain? (ibid.)

Immaterial familial feeling outweighs inheritance. It, not inheritance, should be the basis for a social order linking heaven and earth.

If Kit and Nell are the novel's avatars of this immaterial familial feeling of domesticity, who represents "the man of high descent" with his "associations of pride and wealth and triumph"? Here the depiction of Quilp as a grasping, tyrannical man becomes more meaningful. Mrs. Quilp's mother describes him as "the greatest tyrant that ever lived" (4:39) and the narrator associates Quilp with language from Shakespeare's best-known tyrant, Richard III, in a way that suggests he is an unaware aristocratic villain. When he devises his plot against Kit, Quilp uses language that suggests Richard's announcement of his villainy: Richard decries Edward "[crossing] me from the golden time I look for!" (3 Henry VI 3.3.129) while Quilp describes Kit blocking "a golden [opportunity] to us all" (51:388). Elsewhere, the narrator uses Shakespearean language to mark Quilp's unsuspecting similarity to a death-driven Richard: "Having no intuitive perception of the cloud which lowered upon his house, the dwarf was in his ordinary state of cheerfulness" (67:504). The result presents Quilp in language and intertextual reference as the very lowest form of a "man of high descent," a man of great wealth but also of perverse sexuality and grotesque physical appearance, a "demon" (48:367). His representation further emphasizes that Quilp has the feelings of a man of high descent. Pride motivates his plot against Fred and Dick due to sexual jealousy, wealth drives his plot to defraud Nell's grandfather and then her great-uncle, and triumph motivates his plot against Kit due to Kit's honesty.

Against these aristocratic feelings, the narrator argues for immaterial familial feelings of domesticity. The narrative, however, shows these too to be under threat. The novel's description of Chartists signals an unease about the domestic affections in the social world. The period leading up to the novel's publication was marked by recurrent Chartist uprisings, the most well-known being the Newport Rising in late 1839, and the novel dramatizes what appears to be one of these risings in a section first published in October 1840.[15] The narrator describes

> But night-time in this dreadful spot!—night, when the smoke was changed to fire; when every chimney spirited up its flame; and places, that had been dark vaults all day, now shone red-hot, with figures moving to and fro within their blazing jaws, and calling to one another with hoarse cries—night, when the noise of every strange machine was aggravated by the darkness; when the people near them looked wilder and more savage; when bands of unemployed labourers paraded the roads, or clustered by torch-light round their leaders, who told them, in stern language, of their wrongs, and urged them on to frightful cries and threats; when maddened men, armed with sword and firebrand, spurning the tears and prayers of women who would restrain them, rushed forth on errands of terror and destruction, to work no ruin half so surely as their own—night, when carts came rumbling by, filled with rude coffins (for contagious disease and death had been busy with the living crops); when orphans cried, and distracted women shrieked and followed in their wake—night, when some called for bread, and some for drink to drown their cares, and some with tears, and some with staggering feet, and some with bloodshot eyes, went brooding home—night, which, unlike the night that Heaven sends on earth, brought with it no peace, nor quiet, nor signs of blessed sleep—who shall tell the terrors of the night to the young wandering child! (45:341)

The text frames this Gothic scene of workers become "savage" as the source of terror for a "young wandering child" yet the subsequent paragraph reveals that Nell sleeps during the tumult after she "put up a prayer for the poor old man" (45:341). Like Oliver, Nell's purity is marked by her consistent recollection of prayer but her role here also reinforces the role of women in the novel as the caretakers of the domestic virtues and fellow feeling that the novel locates as the basis of the moral sense. The desolation of this scene coheres around the image of "maddened men, armed with sword and firebrand, spurning the tears and prayers of women who would restrain them." This depiction of women as the pleading avatars of thwarted domestic virtues against masculine Chartist savagery seems to have little basis in fact. As Dorothy Thompson notes, "women in the Chartist movement...were important, particularly between 1838 and 1843" (150). Nevertheless, the gendering indicates the true source of terror for the novel: the destruction of the moral sentiments as feelings of feminine domesticity and restraint. Nell thus provides this tableau of destroyed familial feelings with a clarifying figure, one that embodies the persistence of these feelings as frail and vulnerable.

For the novel, the key to diffusing the horror perpetrated by the failures of domestic feelings is for the world and the workingman to embrace that he has "no property but in the affections of his own heart" (38:289). At first, this appeal seems an ideological one suited to a world of the emerging proletariat and of Lockean private property. Yet for *The Old Curiosity Shop*, the proper form of dematerialization is one that demands affections—along with an attendant weak nationalism—operate with no objects passing between its subjects. To find properly felt social relations, the novel suggests that one should evaporate the objects that may block these feelings. Kit's quarter-holiday captures this experience of dematerialization as an explicit dematerializing of the objects that pass between characters. Throughout, Kit exemplifies the poor man and his portable domestic affections, whether working for Nell and her grandfather, at home with his mother, or with the Garlands. His family outing to the theater and an oyster house is the novel's most extended sequence of those affections expressed in actions and attitudes, providing Kit and his family with pleasure and cheer while linking them to a wider world. These are experiences of consumption, the turning of objects into personal feelings. (The service work they consume is of little interest in this tale.) From theater going to restaurant eating, the only material accumulation of these experiences is the "grotto" of oyster shells that Kit's brother Jacob builds on the table (39:301). This emphasis on the dematerialization of objects by a happy consumption runs through the novel, from Nell's dinner with the Punch men and the beer that Swiveller sends to Kit in prison to the restorative gifts of food from the single gentleman to an ailing Swiveller after he helps clear Kit's name and the celebratory feast that the Garlands throw Kit upon his release. Consumption is the basis of conviviality, the disappearance of objects to be replaced by the happy glow of satiety and fellow feeling. If affections of the heart in

Dickens never quite coincide with a case of heartburn, this is because the text's celebratory scenes of consumption are spaces for positive affective connection to bloom in the passing away of material objects.

Home without Home: Nell and the Domestic Non-Place

This immaterial or dematerializing demand on objects passing between characters marks characters as well. Much like Kit, Nell is a figure for the domestic virtues but one who also passes away. Nell's death is inextricable from her power to create feelings of domestic virtue in homes that are not homes. Her constant flight and the homelessness of the workingman's home suggest a spiritualization of what Marc Augé terms *non-places*, spaces dedicated to impersonal movement. Augé locates the non-place in twentieth- and twenty-first-century spaces of transit such as airports, train stations, and highways. Nell, too, is in transit, and the feelings that surround her allegorical experience often intimate what Augé calls the "melancholy pleasure" of the isolated traveler (70). Nell constructs the domestic affections in these non-places of transit by producing punctual events in spaces of increasingly de-realized community. In this way, Nell suggests another facet of the non-place: its use in late twentieth- and twenty-first-century societies of control to create seemingly undisciplined spaces that in fact rely on checkpoints to identify and control movements of people, money, information, and such. Nell produces moments that are not checkpoints for state power but rather punctual events of care and hospitality, checkpoints at which the domestic affections may be expressed without becoming bound to place. The movement here, then, is one of continual passages of anxiety—uncertainty, non-placeness—punctuated by events of love. Long before the rise of the technologies necessary for societies of control, the affective form of the novel gestures toward the ways in which affective checkpoints may compensate for the loss of striated social spaces and stitch individuals into unfamiliar smooth spaces instead. Hilary Schor is thus right that Nell is effectively an object within the text but Nell's objectification is inextricable from the text's delocalized notion of home. Nell becomes the object that creates domestic virtue at crucial intervals, making her a figure for the poor man's "love of home." The novel's inheritance plots and their attendant misrecognitions are thus tightly bound to this affective appeal. Nell's non-existent inheritance produces love against the anxiety of the self-interest and double-dealing that surround her. Her subsequent spiritualization of domestic virtues through death are part of a broader construction of an imagined national virtue divorced from multi-generational landownership.

The novel's relentless focus on death turns on this desire to imagine a national sense of belonging in which people are embedded in the land yet incapable of owning it, a kind of spiritual intimation of the later ideas of

Henry George. No episode makes this clearer than Nell's arrival at her final residence next to a decaying Gothic church. The narrator describes her turn to domestic virtue on their arrival, explaining that the decision "to make these dwellings as habitable and full of comfort as they could was now their pleasant care" (52:392) Yet the age of the church portends Nell's tenure there will be short and suggests that love of home comes with the knowledge that one owns no property, a feeling that the novel articulates to the familial feelings of the domestic virtues yet keeps distinct. The church's "aged walls" reveal "the solemn presence, within, of that decay which falls on senseless things the most enduring in their nature...of Death" and "filled [Nell] with deep and thoughtful feelings but with none of terror or alarm" (52:393). The insistence that these feelings speak of death and yet resist its terrors marks this passage as at once recalling and resisting the work of Graveyard poets like Robert Blair, works in which the horror of the grave was a key rhetorical strategy to evoke the sublimity of death. Yet in *The Old Curiosity Shop*, death causes no terror because life itself has become a home without property. This idea achieves its apotheosis in Nell's discussion of the untended gardens left on the graves in the churchyard. The sexton says that for some "it's melancholy to see these things all withering or dead" but he insists "tis a good sign for the happiness of the living" (54:407). Nell replies that "perhaps the mourners learn to look to the blue sky by day, and to the stars by night; and to think the dead are there, and not in graves" (ibid.). Nonetheless, she begins to tend the disused plots. The grave offers the central paradigm of one's relation to land as something held in trust, to be tended without ownership with the promise that one will pass into it, unavoidably, without pride or triumph, outside questions of descent or inheritance. Death itself, then, becomes an opportunity to reflect on life as a passage, the punctual events of domestic virtues and their necessary dematerialization.

As the crucial object mediating and cohering group feeling, Nell in her death reveals how shared affects are possible only by eliminating the objectification that figures their containment. Critics such as Claire Wood and Mary Elizabeth Hotz note that Nell's dematerialization in death coheres community, a view supported by the lesson the narrator offers on Nell's passing: "When Death strikes down the innocent and young, for every fragile form from which he lets the panting spirit free, a hundred virtues rise, in shapes of mercy, charity, and love, to walk the world and bless it" (72:544).[16] Nell's gender, youth, and death mark the novel's refusal of inheritance, one that embeds national and domestic virtues in a land that cannot be owned. Such objectified attachments must be buried, as it were, and virtue freed "to walk the world" like the emerging industrial working classes. This refusal of inheritance brings the novel to a close after the brother of Nell's grandfather, who has sought out Nell and her grandfather to restore their wealth, realizes the failure of his hopes. He appeals to his brother to return with him, describing how together they would be

> going home with no hope realized, that had its growth in manhood—carrying back nothing that we brought away, but our old yearnings to each other—saving no fragment from the wreck of life, but that which first endeared it. (71:538)

It seems nothing can be saved but familial attachment. Yet with the death of Nell's grandfather, the final object limiting the passage of familial feeling—the family—disappears. At this point, the surviving brother becomes an avatar of the virtues and "went forth into the world, a lover of his kind" (73:554). Nell's inheritance, never received, becomes instead charitable gifts bestowed, the narrator tells readers, on "those who had been kind to them [Nell and her grandfather]" (ibid.). This dematerialization of objects infects the land itself. When an aged Kit returns to the neighborhood of the old curiosity shop, he finds it gone and cannot recall where it had once stood. The novel closes with an exclamation underscoring this passage of objects and of time: "Such are the changes which a few years bring about, and so do things pass away, like a tale that is told!" (73:556). The Biblical language conjures a final and total dematerialization, words lost in the telling. What passes, passes away—people, feelings, buildings, and the stories told about them. The novel's focus on death, so clearly laden with other affective strains than those of wealth and inequality, reveals its affective form to be one of the passage of objects into emotions and of emotions into a coherent feeling of national belonging. Such feelings of belonging stand counterpoised to the feelings of landed wealth solicited by the language of inheritance, a language which the people of the 1840s used to grapple with Britain's pervasive and destructive economic inequality.

The Anxiety of Inheritance

The novel's closing appeal may leave readers with a sense that nothing can be inherited beyond the affective freight of compensatory "virtues" and "gentler nature." Such an answer may be resistant in its historical moment—it refuses to endorse land and inheritance as the basis of political power—but it also is to one side of the political and economic problems posed by inherited wealth. Whether this response is a sleight of hand substituting feeling for economic value or a construction of a specifically literary humanist value in contrast to the economic is difficult to say. The novel's sentimentality evokes both possibilities without endorsing either. Certainly, the novel's affective critique of inherited wealth is of a piece with other distinctions that evoke problems of inequality, perhaps most clear in its two concluding narrative strands of

Kit's persecution and Nell's death. There too, affect turns questions of inequality away from conflict by making poverty an existential problem and locates potential class antagonisms in personal grievance.

Dickens's view of inheritance in *The Old Curiosity Shop* reflects the political tensions raised by inheritance in the 1840s, though Dickens himself lacks a clear political alignment during this period. As biographers note, Dickens's experiences in America the following year revealed to him that he was not as much of a political radical as he thought and led him to reflect on the negative effects of the lack of a strong social hierarchy in America.[17] His political views in *The Old Curiosity Shop* suggest this equivocal view before Dickens realized it himself, a mixture of ideas that seem to draw as much from William Cobbett as from Richard Cobden while evincing a broad if unfocused sympathy for the poor.[18] When read against the political economic discussion of inheritance during this period, *The Old Curiosity Shop* becomes a text that limns the economic and affective fault lines of the moral sentiments. Dickens intervenes in the political economy of emotions with a critique of inheritance and landed wealth that at times seem more attuned to middle-class arguments against aristocratic privileges like those of the Anti-Corn Law League. ACLL leaders such as Cobden and John Bright took on landed wealth not through attempted reforms of inheritance but by advocating the benefits of free trade for workers and their employers, including the claim that stronger trading ties would end international conflict.[19] The novel's use of dematerialization, then, may carry one further valence: a freedom of movement that brings material and moral benefits to all.

The novel's use of love and anxiety, though, can unsettle the implication that Nell's death is the emotional equivalent of an end of protectionist tariffs. The "hundred virtues" seem the beneficial results of freer trade in sentiment, but the novel's pervasive anxiety disturbs this economic homology. Throughout, *The Old Curiosity Shop* suggests that anxiety is a result of mistaking what is outside for what is inside, and that interior feeling and economic survival must be brought into accord. This is the anxious and precarious existence of the Old Curiosity Shop itself, one predicated on a man's interior sense of taste yet without material guarantees that those tastes can support life. In a sense, then, the novel intuits an analysis of anxiety that appears almost a hundred years later. Anxiety, Gilbert Simondon argues, has been fundamentally misunderstood. Philosophers like Martin Heidegger treat anxiety as showing us our finitude and producing our sense of self. For Simondon anxiety remains central to the construction of individuality but it is not a result of the confrontation with death. Rather, anxiety is the result of a confrontation with the fullness of what precedes and produces selves, a mistaking of the formative potentials that precede individuality for what should make up that individuality.[20] This confrontation, Brian Massumi explains, can feel like "an unliveable tension" (160), a drive toward death as the subject confronts a fundamentally impossible demand to find what is most inside herself in what is outside her. One might understand the drive to death in *The Old Curiosity Shop* as a result of this attempt to overcome anxiety. The novel imagines an internalization and dematerialization of capitalism's preeminent bearer of potential, wealth. The difficulty of this fantasy produces the need for death, a move that allows the external object that produces anxiety to disappear and yield instead feelings of wholeness and satisfaction, a skein of emotions that Dickens understood best as the moral sentiments. For a discussion of the text's affective form, it is not the elimination of anxiety for the moral sentiments that matters so much as the nervous rhythm of anxiety that organizes the text's plotting and signaling of emotions, a rhythm that captures an inner desire to belong even as the means and mechanisms of belonging in the world seem to produce nothing but exclusion.

Notes

1 For readings of sentimentality in the novel, see Frauhoff, Bailin, Brown, Hotz 67–79, Kaplan, *Sacred* 39–70, Purton 102–09, Schor 19–46, Wood 58–105, and Zemka. For readings of the novel as an allegory of capitalism, see Adorno 171–77 and Bowen 132–56. Gareth Cordery offers one of the few historicizations of the novel's economics, and reads Quilp as a demonic embodiment of Cain and Hopkins's gentlemanly capitalism.
2 See Aristotle, *Physics* VI:9, 239b5.
3 See Piketty 410–14.
4 See Marx, *Early Writings* 57–198, esp. 164–87.
5 See Beckert 39–46 on Frederic Le Play's 1864 attack on testamentary freedom and subsequent political arguments.
6 See Meek 128–37.
7 See Smith 1:351–71.
8 See Malthus 139.
9 Mill returns to this issue with the Land Tenure Reform Association toward the end of his life. Arguments of the late 1860s and early 1870s, as part of the great moderation of the mid-century, are politically and economically distinct from those of the tumultuous forties. See Mill, *Programme.*
10 Mill here rephrases 2 *Thessalonians* 3:10, a passage that Carlyle subsequently uses to justify the re-instatement of slavery in his 1849 essay "Occasional Discourse on the Negro Question" and led to a break in friendship between Mill and Carlyle.
11 See Collini 121–69, esp. 154–55.
12 By 1850 the Chartists had abandoned these positions as they came to believe that modifications of inheritance laws would neither break up the concentration of land capital nor make it accessible to working people. See Chase 66.
13 See Ackroyd 226–27 and 318–19; and Kaplan, *Dickens* 120–21.
14 See Ahmed 1–16.
15 On Chartist risings in the late 1830s, see Thompson, *Dignity* 82–102. On the Newport rising, see Thompson, *Chartists* 79–86.
16 See Wood 57–58 and Hotz 91.
17 See Kaplan, *Dickens* 140–42.

18 On Dickens's relation to the radical press, see Ledger, esp. 106–41; for the influence of Cobdenite radicalism, see Shelden.
19 See Read 41–68, esp. 66–67.
20 Simondon's major works have yet to be translated in English. I draw here on discussions of Simondon's ideas in Massumi 159–65 and Scott 85–87.

References

Ackroyd, Peter. *Dickens*. New York: Harper Collins, 1990.
Adorno, Theodor W. *Notes to Literature*. Volume 2. Edited by Rolf Tiedemann. Translated by Sherry Weber Nicholsen. New York: Columbia University Press, 1992.
Ahmed, Sara. *The Cultural Politics of Emotion*. New York: Routledge, 2015.
Augé, Marc. *Non-places: An Introduction to Supermodernity*. London: Verso, 2008.
Bailin, Miriam. "'Dismal Pleasure': Victorian Sentimentality and the Pathos of the Parvenu," *ELH*, vol. 66, no. 4 (1999), pp. 1015–32.
Beckert, Jens. *Inherited Wealth*. Translated by Thomas Dunlap. Princeton, NJ: Princeton University Press, 2008.
Bell, Michael. *Sentimentalism, Ethics and the Culture of Feeling*. Houndsmills: Palgrave, 2000.
Bentham, Jeremy. *Supply without Burthen or Escheat vice Taxation*. London: J. Debrett, 1795.
Bergson, Henri. *Key Writings*. Edited by Keith Ansell Pearson and John Mullarkey. London: Bloomsbury Press, 2014.
Blanqui, Adolphe-Jérôme. *History of Political Economy in Europe*. Translated by Emily J. Leonard. New York: GP Putnam's Sons, 1880.
Bowen, John. *Other Dickens: Pickwick to Chuzzlewit*. Oxford: Oxford University Press, 2000.
Brown, Nicola. "Introduction: Crying Over Little Nell," *19: Interdisciplinary Studies in the Long Nineteenth Century*, vol. 4 (2007). Accessed 22 June 2017. www.19.bbk.ac.uk/articles/abstract/10.16995/ntn.453/
Carlyle, Thomas. *Past and Present*, edited by Richard Altick. New York: New York University Press, 2000.
Chase, Malcolm. "Chartism and the Land: 'The Mighty People's Question.'" *The Land Question in Britain, 1750–1950*, edited by Matthew Cragoe and Paul Readman. New York: Palgrave Macmillan, 2010, pp. 57–73.
Collini, Stefan. *Public Moralists: Political Thought and Intellectual Life in Britain 1850–1930*. Oxford: Clarendon Press, 1991.
Cordery, Gareth. "Quilp, Commerce, and Domesticity: Crossing Boundaries in *The Old Curiosity Shop*," *Dickens Quarterly*, vol. 26, no. 4 (2009), pp. 09–33.
Deleuze, Gilles. "Postscript on the Societies of Control," *October*, vol. 59 (1992), pp. 3–7.
Dickens, Charles. *The Old Curiosity Shop*. Edited by Norman Page. New York: Penguin, 2000.
Fruhauff, Brad. "The Devil You Know: Sentimentalism and Gothic Threat in *The Pickwick Papers* and *The Old Curiosity Shop*," *Victorians: A Journal of Culture and Literature*, vol. 122 (2012), pp. 77–89.

Hotz, Mary Elizabeth. *Literary Remains: Representations of Death and Burial in Victorian England*. Albany: SUNY Press, 2009.

Kaplan, Fred. *Dickens: A Biography*. Baltimore, MD: Johns Hopkins University Press, 1988.

————. *Sacred Tears: Sentimentality in Victorian Fiction*. Princeton, NJ: Princeton University Press, 1987.

Ledger, Sally. *Dickens and the Popular Radical Imagination*. Cambridge: Cambridge University Press, 2010.

Malthus, Thomas Robert. *An Essay on the Principle of Population*. Edited by Geoffrey Gilbert. Oxford: Oxford University Press, 1993.

Marx, Karl. *Early Writings*. Translated by Rodney Livingstone and Gregor Benton. New York: Penguin, 1992.

————. "Report of the Fourth Annual Congress of the International Working Men's Association, Held at Basle, in Switzerland, 1869." Accessed 21 June 2017. www.marxists.org/history/international/iwma/documents/1869/inheritance-report.htm.

Massumi, Brian. *The Politics of Affect*. Malden, MA: Polity, 2015.

McCann, Andrew. "Ruins, Refuse, and the Politics of Allegory in *The Old Curiosity Shop*," *Nineteenth-Century Literature*, vol. 66, no. 2 (2011), pp. 170–94.

McCulloch, John Ramsay. *Treatise on Succession to Property Vacant By Death*. London: Longman, Brown, Green, and Longmans, 1848.

Meek, Ronald. *The Economics of Physiocracy: Essays and Translations*. Cambridge, MA: Harvard University Press, 1963.

Mill, John Stuart. *Autobiography*. Edited by Jack Stillinger. Boston: Houghton Mifflin, 1969.

————. *Principles of Political Economy*. Amherst: Prometheus, 2004.

————. *Programme of the Land Tenure Reform Association with an Explanatory Statement by John Stuart Mill*. London: Longmans, Green, Reader, and Dyer, 1871.

O'Connor, Feargus. *Remedy for National Poverty and National Ruin*. Leeds: J. Hobson, 1841.

Piketty, Thomas. *Capital in the Twenty-First Century*. Cambridge, MA: Harvard University Press, 2014.

Purton, Valerie. *Dickens and the Sentimental Tradition: Fielding, Richardson, Sterne, Goldsmith, Sheridan, Lamb*. London: Anthem Press, 2012.

Read, Donald. *Cobden and Bright: A Victorian Political Partnership*. London: Edward Arnold, 1967.

Ricardo, David. *The Works of David Ricardo*. Edited by John Ramsay McCulloch. London: John Murray, 1888.

Scott, David. *Gilbert Simondon's Psychic and Collective Individuation*. Edinburgh: Edinburgh University Press, 2014.

Schor, Hilary. *Dickens and the Daughter of the House*. Cambridge: Cambridge University Press, 1999.

Shelden, Michael. "Dickens, 'The Chimes,' and the Anti-Corn Law League," *Victorian Studies*, vol. 25, no. 3 (1982), pp. 329–53.

Smith, Adam. *Wealth of Nations*. Edited by Edwin Cannan. Chicago: University of Chicago Press, 1976.

Thompson, Dorothy. *The Chartists: Popular Politics in the Industrial Revolution.* New York: Pantheon Books, 1984.

————. *The Dignity of Chartism.* Edited by Stephen Roberts. London: Verso, 2015.

Wood, Claire. *Dickens and the Business of Death.* Cambridge: Cambridge University Press, 2015.

Zemka, Sue. "From the Punchmen to Pugin's Gothics: The Broad Road to a Sentimental Death in *The Old Curiosity Shop,*" *Nineteenth-Century Literature,* vol. 48, no. 3 (1993), pp. 291–309.

4 *David Copperfield*
Trust, Surprise, and the Call Loan System

Although scholarship has long focused on the economic and emotive aspects of Dickens's work, my focus on the affects of precarity has tried to bring to the surface the ambivalences captured by the plurality of discourses and dispositions about economic precarity and moral judgment that imbue his texts. For *Oliver Twist*, violence, domination, and racialized threat gear narratorial and readerly sympathies multiply motivated by the agitation surrounding the abolition of slavery and Poor Law reform. *The Old Curiosity Shop* presents its sentimental scenes with a pervasive anxiety, inflecting its signals of emotion with the precarity of a world marked by economic inequality. In these early novels, precarity and affect operate together to produce reinforcing patterns or styles of feeling without necessarily cohering the presentation of emotion and style into a thematically coherent narrative. These novels instead present typifying scenes of emotion that suggest the almost unbearable non-cathartic stasis of Sianne Ngai's "ugly feelings," affects that "foreground a failure of emotional release" (9). Recall Oliver held before the magistrate while the villainous chimneysweep Gamfield looks on or Nell asleep in the midst of a Chartist rising. Yet in their loose plotting, these narratives do eventually make the emotions they signal the subject of catharsis: the dominator can be defeated, the threat or tension purged. Oliver thus escapes Fagin's grasp and Sikes and Fagin are captured and brought to justice. Death saves Nell from the materiality of the world, Kit escapes Quilp's nefarious scheme, and Quilp dies a violent death much like Sikes as he attempts to escape justice.

In narrative terms, this schema of unbearable tension and catharsis is the result of two conflicting desires, one to heighten the affects of a particular scene and another to construct a narrative through-line that resolves its heightened affects. This conflict suggests a distinction that Byung-Chul Han notes between feelings as temporal and narratable and affects as atemporal and resistant to narration.[1] This distinction offers an important insight for our discussion as we move from Dickens's early work to his so-called mature or late work. In his early work, Dickens draws on melodrama and sentimentality to bridge this temporal discontinuity between narrative feeling and scenic affect yet the typifying scenes of these novels often seem to exist autonomously from their plotting. This discontinuity allows Dickens's early novels to draw out the affective and historical ambivalences of their conjunctures in punctual episodes and with suggestive but discordant narratives. Hence Sally Ledger's argument that Dickens's alternating of scenes of laughter and tears creates a "melodramatic affect," which suggests this ambivalence of narrative form is a rhythm that signals alternating emotions without molding them into a single coherent feeling. Such alternations of emotive signaling remain in Dickens's later novels, but these texts more tightly integrate theme, rhetoric, and plot to bring feeling and affect into a new kind of copresence. Dickens's shift toward this kind of integrated narrative begins with *Dombey and Son* (1848), but *David Copperfield* (1850) best illustrates how he works with the ambivalences of this new relation between felt narrative and affective scene.

A deeply freighted semi-autobiographical text, *Copperfield* is Dickens's publicly proclaimed "favourite child" (1867 preface to the novel). Part of its power is no doubt due to the scenes of suffering that reflected Dickens's biographical experience, most especially his embarrassment, humiliation, and shame for his father's imprisonment for debt and his work at Warren's Blacking Factory. As Rosemarie Bodenheimer writes, "whether he hid it or idealized it, Dickens's childhood would always feel like a Shadow that clings and will not be forgotten" (61). In *Copperfield*, Dickens grapples most directly with his childhood in scenes that, as Harold Bloom notes, contain an intensity of pathos "out of all proportion to the fictive experience" (8). If *Copperfield* is, as Bloom claims, "the first therapeutic novel" (6), it is so because Dickens found a form that allowed its affectively dense scenes to become narratively meaningful: the fictional autobiography. David, then, is rightly at the center of critical accounts of the novel. As character-narrator, David is the narrative's simultaneous subject and object and scholars treat him as a kind of Hobbesian Leviathan. He lords over the novel's multitude of characters, creating a unified text by folding other characters into his narrative of self. For Audrey Jaffe, David as a character-narrator takes great pains to assume the position of a Lacanian Subject Supposed to Know and thus to make everyone else a narrative object. David's narration positions himself against his past while putting up the pretense that his observations and objectification of others are purely incidental. D.A. Miller similarly views David as a *hypocrite lecteur* whose narrative command allows the novel to evoke strong affects and to divorce them from narrative content. As the novel's narratorial subject, David creates and protects his unique and free interiority by emptying his character of specificity. For Miller, David's command of other characters' experiences allows him to keep secret his own subjectivity and thus to present and obscure Dickens's own.[2] The result of this narratorial sleight of hand reveals David to be the model liberal subject, one defined by his willingness to find freedom in submission to social discipline. When critics turn their attention to questions of feeling and emotion in the novel, David appears similarly hypocritical. In Joseph Litvak's reading of resentment in the novel, David's need to distinguish himself from his servants allows him to empty himself hypocritically of responsibility.[3] In all these accounts, David is the novel's feeling subject and a stand-in for Dickens the man. Thus David is a subject bent on obscuring the nature and origin of his feelings. Even when his feelings are taken as central to the novel's project, they are about something else. Rachel Ablow argues the novel exemplifies a vision of sympathy that "[encourages] love in its readers rather than identification" (24). The novel's incitements to love thus stage conflicts between David's idealization of the people he loves and their reality. When Steerforth transgresses his idealization by David, David treats him as dead long before he dies in the novel's climactic shipwreck. For Ablow, Agnes thus takes the status of ideal-real object and narrative endpoint. Drawing on Garrett Stewart's argument in *Dear Reader* that Dickens creates the literary as a supplemental space to the domestic, Ablow views David's closing encomium of Agnes as an incite-ment of love for the novel form itself.

Affective form suggests that David's centrality and Agnes's privileged position in the novel's conclusion are part of the text's attempt to solve a formal literary problem and a conjunctural one. Together, they mean to resolve a tension between narrative feeling and affectively dense scene and to offer a solution to the nearly unlivable economic precarity of the Victorian era. Such a reading admits the importance of the autobi-ographical without reducing the novel to it. As Dickens's biographers note, his early experience of poverty marks nearly all of his fictional texts and likely gave him the lived experience necessary to produce the affective textures of economic precarity in our readings thus far: the violence of domination and the anxiety of an indifferent world of mon-strous inequality. *David Copperfield* marks a shift insofar as it turns the problem of precarity into the basis for a positive project, one that grounds affective scene and temporal narrative in a shared problematic. In this way, the novel's engagement with affect and with history come to produce what we now recognize as an organizing thematic. One may glimpse this project in the novel's structure as a fictive autobiography, a form that appears to give the tale its narrative coherence. Its thematic co-herence, however, is not simply a result of biographical unity. Biography provides temporal connections between events. Thematic coherence re-lies instead on atemporal connections between elements, what I describe in Chapter 1 as a yoking of elements in affective resonance. The elements that share features here are not elements that suggest the construction of self via autobiography but rather trust's role in escaping precarious material circumstances. Yet shared features are not enough to put ele-ments into resonance. As we will see, these elements are also discursively overdetermined and put into operation in affectively dense scenes in which trust is broken or restored. Once yoked to a temporally connected series of events, the conjunction of elements with shared features, of discursive overdetermination, and of affectively dense scenes produces a narrative thematic.

Agnes's importance as the narrative endpoint provides a semantic foothold for analyzing this thematic, the notion of trust. Agnes is the novel's proper conclusion because its narrative ends once David realizes the truth behind Agnes's rhetorical question: "If you cannot confidently trust me, whom will you trust?" (25:374). David's closing panegyric to Agnes frames her as the apotheosis of domestic and familial trust, the contrasting "good angel" in the house to Steerforth's untrustworthy homewrecking "bad angel" (25:374). Agnes thus brings forward trust as a key narrative element in the novel's first pages. From the first, trust is a multi-generational problem that yokes personal relationships and economic practicality. In the opening chapter, David's aunt, Betsey Trotwood, introduces the issue of trust as she interrogates his pregnant mother about the name of her house:

> 'Why Rookery?' said Miss Betsey. 'Cookery would have been more to the purpose, if you had had any practical ideas of life, either of you.'
>
> 'The name was Mr. Copperfield's choice,' returned my mother. 'When he bought the house, he liked to think that there were rooks about it.'
>
> The evening wind made such a disturbance just now, among some tall old elm-trees at the bottom of the garden, that neither my mother nor Miss Betsey could forbear glancing that way. As the elms bent to one another, like giants who were whispering secrets, and after a few seconds of such repose, fell into a violent flurry, tossing their wild arms about, as if their late confidences were really too wicked for their peace of mind, some weatherbeaten ragged old rooks'-nests, burdening their higher branches, swung like wrecks upon a stormy sea.
>
> 'Where are the birds?' asked Miss Betsey.
>
> 'The—?' My mother had been thinking of something else. 'The rooks—what has become of them?' asked Miss Betsey.
>
> 'There have not been any since we have lived here,' said my mother. 'We thought—Mr. Copperfield thought—it was quite a large rookery; but the nests were very old ones, and the birds have deserted them a long while.'
>
> 'David Copperfield all over!' cried Miss Betsey. 'David Copperfield from head to foot! Calls a house a rookery when there's not a rook near it, and takes the birds on trust, because he sees the nests!' (1:17–18)

The problem of trust first appears, then, as a threat. The willingness to trust threatens one's ability to navigate life's material demands. David's tale is about this particular Scylla and Charybdis. The as yet-unborn David may not be his father but his readiness to take what he sees on trust certainly makes him "David Copperfield from head to foot." Yet this is not to say the novel offers a pedagogy of trust. It does not teach David or its readers how to develop properly trustworthy relationships to better navigate economic precarity. Trust and practicality remain throughout in disharmony and only the featureless goodness of Agnes, in David's closing encomium, allows her "[to touch] the chords of my memory so softly and harmoniously, that not one jarred within me" (60:844).

The problem of trust thus appears in the novel as deeply personal and yet impersonal, almost abstract. Aunt Betsey muses on her belief that David will be born a girl and named after his aunt: as a guardian, her "care" must be to protect her niece "from reposing any foolish confidences where they are not deserved" (1:19). Her imagined role of trust is a veiled description of her past. Trust, then, is inextricable from a tension between the particular and abstract, what is and what should be: the David Copperfield who was and the David Copperfield who is yet to be, the Betsey Copperfield who was and the Betsey Copperfield who will never be. The novel dramatizes this tension through repetitions, most importantly of a love triangle of witting and unwitting rivals: Doctor Strong, Annie Strong, and Jack Maldon; Emily, Steerforth, and Ham; David, Dora, and Agnes; and David, Uriah Heep, and Agnes. These triangles and their attendant failures of trust threaten one's ability to survive and be recognized as a person, as the tales of Emily, the fallen woman Martha, and Steerforth indicate. This abstract problem of trust comes to suggest that properly reposed trust can be a socially reparative act, one that brings the particular back from abstract death through a particular affective valence. Mr. Pegotty brings Martha back from the brink of literal and social death by trusting her unreservedly, an act that Martha notes "in a low voice of astonishment" (47:691–2). Agnes similarly returns David to the social world and himself after the deaths of Dora, Ham, and Steerforth by "[telling] me, in her own fervent manner, what her trust in me was" (58:822).

The astonishment and fervency of these episodes indicates the centrality of intensity and surprise to the novel and its representations of trust. Surprise is the crux of the novel's affective form. It informs its model for the entwining of trust and social relationships, David's determinative experience of neglect and poverty. His betrayal by Mr. Murdstone reveals romantic rivalries (between Murdstone and David's father, and Murdstone and David himself) and the failures of trust they produce. Murdstone's betrayal is effectively a failure of the trust David's mother placed in him as her son's legal guardian and its effects on David are described as surprise more than sadness. *David Copperfield* plots the surprises produced by the need to trust others and to attend to "practical ideas of life," a tension that unfolds at the level of the practical material and of the sexual and romantic as the text explores how trust may be nurtured or betrayed. The affective form of David Copperfield, then, binds these manifold relations of trust and its betrayal to a particular style for successfully navigating Victorian economic precarity, a feeling of intensity: earnestness.

Trusted Characters

The problem of trust in Copperfield may give rise to narrative feelings and to affective scenes, but trust is neither a feeling nor an affect. Rather, trust produces affective situations that are especially open to narrativity because it imbricates temporality, agency, and otherness. From a socio-logical view, trust is, as Piotr Sztompka puts it, "a bet about the future contingent actions of others" (25). In other words, it manages one's need to act in the present against the likely actions of others in the (near) fu-ture. From this perspective, trust reduces the complexity of relationships so that one can do something. As a result, trust captures a conjunction of emotional experiences, symbolic complexes, and performative acts because it describes an active relationship between individuals, groups, and institutions. Trust is not an affect in and of itself, but a way of man-aging relationships in order to accomplish something.

Most sociological analyses of trust treat it as ahistoric, but its role in Copperfield is likely best understood as a historically embedded solution to what Adam Seligman calls "a particular type of risk... a decidedly modern phenomenon, linked to the nature of the division of labor in modern, market economies" (8). Such a view helps to histori-cize trust's demand that one learns how to interpret people, institutions, and systems based on how they present themselves, and to consider how one chooses to present oneself to others. Because trust is effectively an estimation of the degree to which one's actions, in Niklas Luhmann's words, are the "expression and reaffirmation of personality" (45), it is effectively a way to ensure that one's partners in market exchange and cooperative work relations act in foreseeable ways. Self-presentation is central to the production of trust because how one presents oneself pro-vides social, symbolic, affective, haptic, and other information which others may use to estimate trustworthiness. As a historical turn, trust's production of the self is a story about the market-based, trustable self, one that is haunted by the risk that one's self-presentation may not match one's actions. In other words, it is a story of character's precar-ity. This precarity is the historically embedded reason why sociologists insist that trust exists only to the extent that it can be betrayed. Hence ahistorical sociological readings routinely describe trust as a hazard, "a bet" (Sztompka 25), or a "risky advance" (Luhmann 46). For Luhmann, risk reveals why relationships of trust are most readily formed in "easily interpretable situations" (47): when all agents understand their roles in a situation, trust is easier to establish. Seligman argues that it is precisely this limitation of the self to a social role that indicates trust's historical specificity: the division of labor and the atomization of society creates the roles and social structures that make trust necessary.

The rise of market society also reframes why sociologists insist that trust cannot be reduced to formalizable ethical norms. The chaos of the marketplace ensures that no stable rules can guide the creation of trust beyond the ease of interpretation made possible by reliable data. This poses a problem. Because trust cannot be formalized, its relationships are highly particularized, offered to and accepted by individuals or particular systems. Here affect returns. If any generalization informs trust, it is a generalization of prior affective connections. As Luhmann notes, "the emotional attachment of the child to his family is... the foundation for the learning of all trust" (90). Emotional attachment provides a model for the particularization of trust in later relationships between individuals. Personal connection was central to Victorian business. As economic historian Pat Hudson notes,

> in a climate of unlimited liability and ubiquitous credit, confidence and trust were pivotal.... The vital ingredients in business success... [were] face to face and personalized transactions through networks of families and friends, and by trade and information centred upon clearly defined, often localised and self-conscious business communities. (49)

Yet the role of personal connections in business was also being offset by the mid-nineteenth century with the rise of impersonal market forces, most especially in the credit markets. Luhmann explains that trust in impersonal systems depends upon agents learning to navigate distinctions within their own identities and between their different relationships to different systems. For impersonal systems such as courts of law, financial markets, and so on, trust creates a seeming paradox. To generate trust, Luhmann argues, impersonal systems must "institutionalize distrust"— that is, create distinctions that offer individuals "structured *alternatives* of trust and distrust" (98). According to Luhmann, distrust's institutionalization effectively reduces complexity and uncertainty in much the same way as trust and thus allows distrust to become "a functional equivalent for trust" (79). Trust, then, grounds the modern self in the affective patterns of early trusting relationships while that self is forced to navigate impersonal systems where distrust is central and affect seems a danger.

A novel that used an ahistorical notion of trust to bridge narrative feeling and affective scene would look a great deal like *David Copperfield*.

It would begin with an examination of one's emotional attachment to one's family before considering the ways in which this initial attachment affects subsequent relationships and generates new highly particular affective situations in which trust is risked. The plot would narrate a continuing search for trust through affective encounters that do not elicit feelings of trust in and of themselves but that provide emotional signals for trusting relationships to occur. One would expect to find the main character in such a tale forced to consider how each situation leads him to present himself and how others choose to present themselves, and how, based on his interpretations, he would act in relationships that carry the risk of betrayal, generating relationships of trust and distrust in the process. The novel as a whole would illustrate how trust emerges through experiences with others and attention to self-presentation. It would be a tale that displays how trust and distrust grow and how one becomes the self that one presents. In short, it would be a kind of biography.

To grasp the historically specific aspects of trust in *Copperfield*, we must grapple with the novel's embedding of trust in the peculiarly Victorian discourses of character. As we have seen, character matters to sociological theories trust as a fit between one's words and actions. Victorian notions of character emphasize this aspect of self-presentation alongside a positive normative content that sociological theories of trust lack. As cultural historian Stefan Collini details, to have character meant not merely to act in accordance with one's self-presentation but from a position of personal disinterest. Character made one trustworthy by displaying willpower over one's passions and interests. Habits were the signs of good character. The consistency of personal action reflected self-control and thus disinterest. In Collini's account, this notion of character is bound to the rise of liberalism and the late Victorian era. Britain's increasingly belligerent empire sent young men into uncertain colonial circumstances in which the consistency of character could serve as a guarantee that they would dutifully superintend the interests of others. Character provided an ideological counterweight to the conflict of material interests that led Adam Smith to inveigh against colonial endeavors in *The Wealth of Nations*. This is why the failure of character in an imperial romance such as Joseph Conrad's *Lord Jim* appears as a moral scandal. From this perspective, character imbued the loose structures of imperial domination with the atmosphere of trust necessary for a dominating class of men placed in powerful but uncertain positions and tasked with taking political, economic, and military decisions with little or no direct oversight. *Copperfield* is too early a text for this late imperial mode, but it suggests this aspect of character by insisting that only its most morally resilient minor characters flourish in the imperial world. The louche Jack Maldon returns from India in disgrace while Mr. Pegotty and Mr. Micawber flourish in Australia.

Victorian notions of character long precede its imperial apotheosis. Initially, they took the form of questions of personal character formation, specifically whether impersonal outside forces such as the socioeconomic affected individual character. The utopian socialist Robert Owen introduced the idea that environment shapes the character of workers in *A New View of Society* (1813). Owen's analysis of the development of New Lanark led him to argue that circumstances form communities and that communities form individual character; thus, Owen reasoned, society could and should act on circumstances to improve the characters of workers (he dubbed his plan for universal secular education "a national system for the formation of character" [35]). Owenite became a byword for both an emerging socialism and this sociological notion of structural determination. Such ideas were certainly in the air of the late 1840s when Dickens began *Copperfield*. In *Mary Barton* (1848), which Dickens read during his novel's early composition, Elizabeth Gaskell dramatizes how hunger, impoverishment, and a prolonged labor strike could lead a good workingman to murder his boss's son. The novel's working class voice of reason declares this man "no fool" of a utopian "Owenite" (37:452) but also remarks his material determination as a factor in his crime: "it was a sore time for the hand-loom weavers when power-looms came in: them new-fangled things make a man's life like a lottery" (37:454). The focus of *Copperfield* on questions of character in a period immediately following the tumult of the hungry forties and the high watermark of the Chartist movement makes its engagement with issues of determination and free will inescapably political, if also ambivalent.

Nothing captures this political ambivalence more than the fact that Dickens met Gaskell through Thomas Carlyle during the serialization of *Copperfield*.[4] Where Gaskell apprehends the possible effects of material determination on the character of Owenite radicals, Carlyle offers the period's countervailing conservative argument to material determination, one drawn largely from the discussion of determination and free will in the work of Immanuel Kant. In *The Critique of Pure Reason*, Kant described the problem of necessity and free will as a logical contradiction between the necessary human belief that we are radically free and that we are also clearly materially determined by natural laws.[5] Kant presses this contradiction further in *The Critique of Practical Reason*, arguing that although humans were subject to phenomenal necessity and natural causality they were free to choose ethical norms and make judgments. Material causality affects individuals but they have the ability to reflect on their choice of actions and to make decisions. For Carlyle, like S.T. Coleridge before him, Kant's ethics are not so much a way of navigating phenomenal necessity and the need to make individual moral judgments, however, as the revelation of a shared moral code.[6] In *Sartor Resartus*, Carlyle argues that Kant's transcendental aesthetic revealed space and time to be the "deepest of all illusory Appearances" (2.8:193) and thus provides access to a mystic-ethical encounter with God: "Admit Space and Time to their due rank as Forms of Thought; nay even, if thou wilt, to their quite undue rank of Realities: and consider, then, with thyself how their thin disguises hide from us the brightest God-effulgences!" (2.8:198–99). Later Victorian philosophers such as T.H. Green will offer more nuanced readings of Kant, but Carlyle's loose Kantianism suggests the conservative argument against Owen: one was not formed by out-side forces but instead contained an ineradicable moral character. Such ideas led to a mischaracterization of Owenite material determination as eliminating the ability to change one's own character. Arguments that undermined this notion of an ineradicable character suggested that one had no freedom to act or choose, and without that freedom, one could not make proper and respectable choices.[7]

John Stuart Mill threaded this impasse of necessity and free will in the early 1840s by making character hinge on feeling. Years before Mill directly addressed Kant's rationalist ethics in *On Liberty*, he wrestled with the problem "of liberty and necessity" (6.2:836) in *A System of Logic* (1843) and proposed in turn a new science of character he termed Ethology. For Mill, character could be studied through the insights of analytic psychology and the empirical study of people and their cir-cumstances. Ethology will uncover how people create particular habits based on utilitarian choices until those actions became "purposes ... independent of the feelings of pain or pleasure from which they orig-inally took their rise" (6.2:843). Mill thus accepts that character is materially determined and open to continued change. In what amounts to an extrapolation from Owen's proposed system for the formation of character, Mill suggests that we can change our characters by "[plac-ing] ourselves under the influence of other circumstances" (6.2:840). The problem for Mill is not whether one can alter one's character but whether one has the *desire* to do so. It is "this feeling," Mill writes,

of our being able to modify our own character *if we wish*, [that] is itself the feeling of moral freedom. A person feels morally free who feels that his habits or his temptations are not his masters, but he theirs: who even in yielding to them knows that he could resist; that were he desirous of altogether throwing them off, there would not be required for that purpose a stronger desire than he knows himself to be capable of feeling. (6.2:841)

The feeling of freedom opens one's material determination by habits and circumstances. Mill's later emphasis on individual freedom can threaten to obscure his meaning here. Freedom in this passage is not so much the freedom to change one's character but rather, in a way similar to Kant, the feeling that one is free to change one's character "*if we wish*." One needs the *feeling* of freedom as much as the freedom to change. Mill never specifies how one would know one has the freedom to resist "even in yielding" to habit or circumstance. What matters is the feeling that it is possible to resist one's material determination more than actually resisting it.

David's aspirational narrative of personal success emphasizes his ability to change as a result "of a patient and continuous energy ... which I know to be the strong part of my character" (42:612). To this character-based energy, he attributes "the habits of punctuality, order, and diligence" and "the determination to concentrate myself on one object at a time" (42:613). Success is a result of his will shaping this energy so that "whatever I have devoted myself to, I have devoted myself to completely... in great aims and in small, I have always been thoroughly in earnest" (42:613). David and his successes here capture the high Victorian qualities of character that Oscar Wilde later lampoons in *The Importance of Being Earnest*, here as a feeling of "thorough-going, ardent, and sincere earnestness" (42:613). This sincere earnest power of will to which David attributes his success—in short, his ability to form his own character—cannot be extricated from another problem of feeling, the need not to reveal the effort of working for one's economic responsibilities. David prefaces his account of his character, stating:

> I feel as if it were not for me to record, even though this manuscript is intended for no eyes but mine, how hard I worked at that tremendous short-hand, and all improvement appertaining to it, in my sense of responsibility to Dora and her aunts. (42:612)

David's work relies both on his earnest ability to shape his character and a feeling that he should not record this work.[8]

This hinge, one of the reasons that critics insist David obscures his own interiority, pervades David's discussions of professional work, and turns the few instances in which he discusses his work and success into scenes that elaborate the failures of his wife Dora's character. He describes how

> sometimes, of an evening, when I was at home and at work—for I wrote a good deal now, and was beginning in a small way to be known as a writer—I would lay down my pen, and watch my child-wife trying to be good. (44:652)

Dora's attempts at work revolve around her maintenance of an "immense account-book" and reveal her character to lack the earnestness that David sees as crucial to his character:

> Then she would take up a pen, and begin to write, and find a hair in it. Then she would take up another pen, and begin to write, and find

that it spluttered. Then she would take up another pen, and begin to write, and say in a low voice, 'Oh, it's a talking pen, and will disturb Doady!' And then she would give it up as a bad job, and put the account-book away... (44:652)

For David, Dora's inability to take up the pen and write reveals that she lacks "character and purpose" (44:653). Their marriage comes to seem like that of Annie and Doctor Strong, a marriage between partners with a fundamental "unsuitability of mind and purpose" (45:668). To mitigate this problem, David decides "to form [his wife's] mind" (48:700) through such stratagems as acting "grave" (48:700) or "giving her, as it were quite casually, little scraps of useful information, or sound opinion" (48:701). He eventually gives up this project because he believes Dora lacks the will to change. He reflects, "perhaps Dora's mind was already formed" (48:701). David's thoughts on character exist in an ambivalent space between Mill's belief in the ability to change and Carlyle's conservatism, the radical possibility of character change for men and the conservative insistence on character as set for women.[9] His reflections on character as based in willpower and the feeling that he can and could change, then, raise questions about his work even as they displace those questions into an analysis of his wife's character.

Professional Characters

For scholars, the convergence of David's professional and romantic life has proven a key point of contention. For Mary Poovey, it reveals an ideological manipulation of the feminine domestic sphere for the benefit of the masculine public; for Matthew Titolo, it means to demystify the interrelation of domestic and professional life; and for Andrew Willson, it indicates a need for respectable intellectual and white-collar work to maintain ideological distance from the market even as it operates within it.[10] To read this convergence through character and trust is to uncover the importance of the affective dispositions that constituted the respectable (male) white-collar worker. In this way, my argument reframes Jesse Rosenthal's argument that the novel "is structured around an awareness of, and agreement with, a larger collective judgment...even though it cannot say what, exactly, this judgment contains" (79). This aspiration to collective judgment in my argument is not, as it is for Rosenthal, a question of a Kantian *sensus communis*, but of an affective problem embedded in a historical conjuncture: a conflict between trust and character. The respectable male white-collar worker aspired to a kind of gentlemanliness that needed trust and based itself in ascetic self-discipline. This yields two components of what becomes character: first, its emphasis on self-control gave male intellectual workers a purchase on Victorian masculinity that would otherwise seem blocked by the era's use the muscular body of the workingman as the basis of masculine representation; and second, its reliance on *askesis* or renunciation foregrounds the demand to present oneself as disinterested.[11] David's conflation of the professional and domestic, then, indicates his need to assert his work and his masculinity while maintaining a posture of disinterest in both. The novel's initial conflict between trust and life's practicalities is a conflict embedded in Victorian ideas of masculine professional work.

During the Victorian era, self-control and disinterest were especially important guarantors of the trustworthiness of white-collar workers. As waged employees, such workers saw no profits when a firm or company did well unless or until they were made part of the firm or company. Although such a turn of events could happen in the mid-nineteenth century, it was by no means common and by the late nineteenth century had all but disappeared. At the end of the century, character began to function more clearly as a form of ideological control and clerical workers organized voluntary associations that promoted character as the basis of success, encouraging clerks to develop patience, thrift, and "the time-honoured virtues of punctuality, cheerfulness, respect, and most important, industry" (Anderson 78).[12] In the first half of the century, by contrast, notions of self-control and disinterest exerted their influence in more inchoate ways. The key biographical event for Dickens of *Copperfield*, John Dickens's 1824 imprisonment for debt, illustrates this point. Imprisonment for debt in the nineteenth century was not generally considered a class bar or a strong distinction in character. As historian Margot C. Finn notes,

> Far from serving to distinguish virtuous commercial bankrupts from recklessly insolvent consumers, contemporary [Victorian] understandings of the moral meanings of indebtedness united members of widely divergent social and economic groups under the shared rubric of misfortune and thereby distanced them from the rigid conceptions of personal agency, responsibility and culpability associated with modern economic individualism. (128)

John Dickens's case, however, indicates that clerical employers had stronger views about personal agency. Dickens worked as a clerk in the naval pay office before his imprisonment in the Marshalsea and he retired shortly after his release, ostensibly due to recurring urinary tract issues but in truth because he wanted to quit and the Admiralty wanted him fired. In their eyes, John Dickens had demonstrated a lack of character by availing himself of the Insolvent Debtor's Act. The Act allowed debtors to leave prison if they could prove that they had liquated their assets to repay creditors and retained only £20 worth of possessions, including the value of the family's clothing. Charles Dickens, like all of his family, was called before the court in order to have the clothes he was wearing valued as part of this process (see Ackroyd 83). John Dickens's actions scandalized his employers, but the Admiralty had no policy in place to discharge clerks who used the Act. With his retirement, however, they instituted a new policy that "hereafter Clerks attempting to take the benefit of the Insolvent Act shall be discharged from their situations" (Kaplan, *Dickens* 41). Much as scholars have noted his son's shame at his father's imprisonment, they have overlooked the extent to which the episode struck John Dickens's contemporaries as disreputable. Debt may have been widely understood as a misfortune, but in his case, it constituted something more compromising and shameful than it would have had he not been a member of the lower ranks of intellectual work.

For these workers, it was important to act in accordance with their employers' expectations of character and to maintain proper appearance. Victorian respectability for all classes hinged on a certain level of cleanliness in personal appearance and home, but professional work made the maintenance of respectable self-presentation especially fraught. Although not well paid, clerical workers were expected to signal their respectability and trustworthiness by maintaining more genteel households than those of their wage peers engaged in physical labor.[13] During the 1840s and into the 1850s, the costs of respectable presentation made clerks seem especially open to corruption. Financial historian George Robb notes, "clerical embezzlements were the subject of concern for the mid-Victorian era, at which time economic expansion and the proliferation of joint-stock companies increased the opportunities for such crimes" (132). Dickens dramatized the problem of interested subordinate clerical workers the year before in *Dombey and Son* with the "smiling urbanity" (17:233) of Dombey's corrupt office manager, James Carker, who dies like so many of the fraudulent companies of the 1840s, smashed up by a train. Dickens took up the issue again in *Copperfield* with Uriah Heep, whose machinations in Mr. Wickfield's office bankrupt David's aunt and nearly destroys Wickfield. For Heep and Carker, the failure of professional disinterest is also a failure of masculine askesis. Both men press their pursuit of economic self-interest into sexual interest: Carker tries to coerce Edith, and Heep Agnes.[14] As a clerical worker, Heep's defining feature is a hypocritical veiling of interestedness, which nonetheless leaks from his sweaty hands and "snaky twistings of his throat and body" (*DC* 16:245) and undermines his declarations to be "a very umble person" (16:244). In the novel's conclusion, Heep has been imprisoned for bank fraud, yet continues to present himself as a model of humbleness in the guise of a reformed prisoner. Heep uses his penitent reform to wish imprisonment on David: "The best wish I could give you Mr. Copperfield, and give all of you gentlemen, is, that you could be took up and brought here" (61:860). The crimes that land Heep in prison emphasize the discursive articulation of trust, character, and economic command: Heep committed "fraud on the Bank of England" by "[setting] others on" and he was found guilty of "fraud, forgery, and conspiracy" after the Bank "was just able to put salt upon his tail – and only just" (61:860). Financial fraud was rampant in the 1840s and 1850s, but the majority of these cases were savings bank frauds, not frauds on the Bank of England. The century's best-known frauds, the cases of Strahan, Paul, and Bates, and of John Sadleir, who inspired Mr. Merdle in *Little Dorrit*, both occurred in 1855, well after the publication of *Copperfield* (see Robb 58–61). As a fraud on the Bank, the nearest model for Heep's crimes may be those of Francis Wakefield, a well-known stockbroker and City banker remembered for fleeing the country in 1841 after stealing £5,000 from the London Stock Exchange's Fund for the Relief of Decayed Members (Kynaston 125). In addition to this "flagrant breach of trust," Wakefield, the *Times* wrote, "had misconducted himself in every conceivable way" ("Money-Market"): he was found to have debts somewhere between £30,000 and £40,000 ("Consistory Court"), and immediately before his flight, he had "pawned" ("Money-Market") the dividend warrants for payments from the Bank of England which he held for one of his clients, a move that allowed him to defer repaying a loan from his personal banker (*Jurist* 805). Wakefield did not so much commit fraud on the Bank as fraud via Bank instruments—the money he stole from the relief fund was in Exchequer bills ("Money Market and City News")—and the Bank's customary reliance on the character of City bankers. Wakefield's defrauded client sued the Bank for Wakefield's transactions, arguing that dividend warrants should be endorsed before transfer rather than allowing trusted merchants and bankers like Wakefield to use them as ready cash to secure other deals. The Bank countered that professional reputations made such endorsements unnecessary (*Jurist* 806).[15] The judge agreed.

In the mid-century financial world, character counts. Heep's crimes and Wakefield's case indicate the importance of character and personal trust to secure the transactions of the mid-century financial world and the vulnerabilities of this confidence to hypocrisy and self-dealing. The London discount market between 1830 and 1858 reveals the threat that the centrality of character and trust posed at this historical conjuncture to the stability of the economic systems as a whole. As Wakefield's case illustrates, this threat was a result of the Bank of England's confidence in the character of particular agents, bill brokers, to ensure the functioning of the credit markets after the resumption of currency convertibility after the Napoleonic wars. During the wars, the Bank assumed an informal policy of loose discounting for competing banks—that is, they bought bills of exchange from these institutions before the bills had come due, a process known as "discounting" because the buyer deducts a percentage from the full value of the bill at sale. The Bank's loose discounting policy during this period meant they effectively set interest rates for the country and their discounting gave them the power to intercede during financial crises by acting as a lender of last resort. Nonetheless, with the resumption of convertibility, the Bank did not understand its role as a central bank but rather considered itself to be simply one bank among many, a view supported by Parliament's willingness to allow country banks to continue to issue notes under £5 (King 35). Speculative activity by country banks spurred the financial crisis of 1825, and, as they had for almost twenty years previously, these institutions turned to the Bank of England for discounting facilities only to be turned away. Over ninety English and Welsh banks suspended payments (Murphy 339) before the Bank relented and restored market liquidity (King 36). As financial historian WTC King notes, the crisis had myriad effects on the financial system in Britain, including a loosening of the restrictions on joint-stock banking, the creation of bank branches by the Bank of England, its assumption of some central banking roles, and, perhaps most importantly, the end of banks using the Bank to discount bills (37–39).

The Bank then limited its facilities to discount houses of established character, most importantly Overend, Gurney, and Company, which would become the largest bill-brokerage in London. In the early nineteenth century, bill brokers were understood not as speculators but as intermediaries who bought and sold bills to the facilitate movement of capital from London to production elsewhere in the country. As King details, brokers became crucial intermediaries during as the credit market's expansion, driven in part by the rise of joint-stock banks which relied on rediscounted bills to maintain liquidity. The Bank's reliance on personal trust thus perversely drove an impersonalization of the credit market: When these joint-stock banks rediscounted their bills, they endorsed them (that is, assumed the debt if the prior payors were insolvent), and brokers viewed these endorsements as authorizing the discounting of bills from people they knew little about. Samuel Gurney, one of the principals of Overend, Gurney, and Company, explained to Parliament:

> There has been paper discounted in the London market that would not have been current without the endorsement of the joint-stock banks; this arises from parties to the bill residing in the country, and not being known in London. The paper may be of equal character. (qtd. in King 46)

The Bank's privileging of institutional character thus allowed a more impersonal system to emerge alongside the highly personalized systems of trust that had long undergirded the City.

The effects of this imbrication of personal trust and a subterranean impersonalization of trust can be seen in the ways that discount houses affected bank reserves during this period. After the 1825 crisis, banks began to maintain cash reserves. The increased volume of activity in the discount market, however, led them to search for ways to earn interest on their reserves. Trusted brokers again proved key. Bankers began to deposit substantial portions of their cash reserves with discount houses to earn interest with the understanding these reserves would be available at call. Discount houses invested these deposits in securities and bills of exchange that could be almost immediately discounted when necessary, with the Bank as a line of last resort. Importantly, the easy convertibility of securities meant brokers held no cash reserves. Known as the call loan system, this arrangement spread through the British credit markets by the early 1850s even though observers had understood for over a decade the systemic threat it posed to the financial system. Alexander Bair, the Treasurer of the Bank of Scotland, told Parliament that this way of maintaining bank reserves "would be secure only because the system is not general" (qtd. in King 50). The issue, as Bair saw it, was an over-reliance on individual character and credit rather than on more impersonal systems. King notes that Bair "argued that in lending to brokers a banker trusted to an individual rather than the public credit of the country, which he would be doing if he bought Exchequer bills" (50). In 1857, Bair was proved right. The call loan system generated a system-wide crisis as the reserves of the entire financial system were caught in the grips of a speculative credit market crash.

David Copperfield precedes this crisis but captures the coming dominance of impersonal trust to British credit markets. At the turn of the decade, this dominance was understood to be a problem, but it is one that Dickens plays for comedic effect via the Micawbers. Dickens's most direct representation of his father in the novel, Mr. Micawber avails himself of the Insolvent Act (*DC* 11:179), yet like so many of Dickens's imprisoned debtors, he retains his respectability. This reflects in part the continued internal division of debtors' prisons by class, something Dickens witnessed with his father and dramatized. In *Little Dorrit*, Mr. Dorrit patronizingly lords over other debtors in the Marshalsea with his assumption of the title "father of the Marshalsea" (1.6:76), and in *Bleak House*, Skimpole uses sponging houses typical of well-heeled debtors. This continued respectability also reflects Micawber's inability to think of his own interests. This absentminded disinterestedness means Micawber pays no attention to his finances or professional advancement and undertakes a variety of acts of kindness toward David as a child and adult. Micawber thus possesses an innately gentlemanly character worthy of trust in spite of appearances.[16] This absentminded disinterest allows semes of finance and feeling to cluster around Micawber for comic turns. Even during the dismal scene of David dining with Mr. Micawber in debtor's prison, he calls a "loin of mutton ... our joint-stock repast" (11:177). When Micawber searches for a new position, Mrs. Micawber opines that his "manners peculiarly qualify him for the Banking business" because they "would inspire confidence and must extend the connexion" (28:426). She suggests that he should advertise for such a position by "[raising] a certain sum of money – on a bill" (28:427), and they hope to find someone "of sufficient natural feeling to negotiate that bill" or they will be forced "to discount that bill" and take it "into the Money Market" (28:428). Tommy Traddles proves to be such a one, even as the Micawbers' speculative discounting almost immediately smashes up when a "broker" (28:436) takes possession of their rooms and Traddles'. Traddles will sign another bill for the Micawbers, he explains to David, because it is "delightful ... to my feelings, Copperfield, to see the matter settled" (34:499), though he also makes "a solemn resolution to grant no more loans of his name, or anything else, to Mr. Micawber" (34:500). Bills cluster around Micawber, so much so that his wife recounts how "there are members of my family who have been apprehensive that Mr. Micawber would solicit them for their names... to be inscribe on Bills of Exchange, and negotiated in the Money Market" (54:779). Bills are the legal mechanism by which Uriah Heep exercises control over Micawber (54:785)—as well as Mr. Wickfield, including "a relinquishment of [Wickfield's] share in the partnership, and even a bill of sale on the very furniture of his house, in consideration of a certain annuity" (52:761). For Micawber, these associations turn positive when Aunt Trotwood agrees to assist his family's relocation to Australia with money. Micawber suggests she pay him with

> bills—a convenience to the mercantile world, for which, I believe, we are originally indebted to the Jews, who appear to me to have had a devilish deal too much to do with them ever since—because they are negotiable. (54:777)

Personal character and disinterest may help individuals entering unknown colonial circumstances, but Micawber's final turn to bills and anti-Semitism indicates such character to be hemmed in by a financial world increasingly dehumanizing and "devilish"—in a word, impersonal.

Firm and Feeling Characters

Yet on its face, *David Copperfield* seems a story of personal rather than impersonal trust.[17] David's character is central to his success and the basis for the shame and humiliation of the novel's pivotal affective sequence, David's trial of laboring at Murdstone and Grinby. In this section, David laments being sent to work at such a young age because it meant that no one recognized "any promise I had given" (10:161), a phrase that captures the interrelation of assurance and personality that marks the novel's interconnection of character and trust. In effect, David laments that no one thinks of him as a good bet and this makes his experience at Murdstone's bottleworks "the secret agony of my soul" (11:66):

> [I] felt my hopes of growing up to be a learned and distinguished man, crushed in my bosom. The deep remembrance of the sense I had, of being utterly without hope now; of the shame I felt in my position; of the misery it was to my young heart to believe that day by day what I had learned, and thought, and delighted in, and raised my fancy and my emulation up by, would pass away from me, little by little, never to be brought back any more; cannot be written. (11:166)

For David, the failure of the world to recognize him as worthy of trust generates his shame and binds it to an experience of class. David's shame is one for the work he must perform, the company he must keep in doing it, and the character he must assume as a result. This shame is corporeal and spatial, a "position" (11:166) that he captures through tropes of vertical space and hierarchical movements, the upward movement of "raised" fancies and his "deep" recollection of "crushed" hopes.

Yet as David narrates his becoming "a learned and distinguished man," his sense of self is more tightly bound to the feeling of interruption. David's emotional experience is the result of manifold interruptions and their effects: the interruption of the enjoyment that he discovered in learning, the interruption of his learning, which will diminish his current knowledge and his ability to learn in the future, and the interruption of his social position, which may make any further learning impossible even as his desire to learn remains unabated. While these interruptions may yield shame, it is interruption—of enjoyment, desire, and social position—that the text emphasizes:

> I know enough of the world now, to have almost lost the capacity of being much surprised by anything; but it is matter of some surprise to me, even now, that I can have been so easily thrown away at such an age. A child of excellent abilities, and with strong powers of observation, quick, eager, delicate, and soon hurt bodily or mentally, it seems wonderful to me that nobody should have made any sign in my behalf. But none was made; and I became, at ten years old, a little labouring hind in the service of Murdstone and Grinby. (11:164–5)

Interruption thus takes us toward an affect, surprise. For psychologist Silvan Tomkins, surprise is an affect that "momentarily renders the individual incapable of either continuing what he was doing before the startle or of initiating new activity so long as the startle response is emitted" (107). In other words, surprise is the affect of interruption, an affect of break that alters attention.[18] For David, surprise halts his narrative and provides one of the few moments in which his experience as a character is yoked to his experience as a narrator: the wonder of being "so easily thrown away" occurs during and "even now" as he writes, disrupting the flow of story time as the narrator ponders society's willingness to neglect him and his promise. This shock of vulnerability is a particularly physical and embodied question of precarity, what Judith Butler describes as a confrontation with the body's fragility and apparent disposability by others. The interruption of surprise, this jolt of precarity, then, resonates with the shame David experiences due to interruption itself. The resulting intensity suggests that much as David's character seems stable, it is shot through with the interrupted and discontinuous.

The text's deployments of feeling underscore the role of discontinuity in David's character. As Mill's discussion of character indicates, feeling offered a way to introduce free will and contingency into the material and social determination of character, effectively inserting a space of potential dislocation into one's determination by impersonal exterior forces. In *Copperfield*, feeling maps David's relations to others. Of the four hundred sixty-seven instances of the words *felt, feeling*, and *feel*, three hundred and one cases refer to David's feeling. D.A. Miller claims that David's feelings are omnipresent but lack specificity and treats this lack as a ruse to displace narrative attention. The omnipresence of bare feeling in the text, however, might be better understood to articulate the impersonality of the social forces that impinge upon David. What matters is his affective receptivity, not the density of description this receptivity might generate in a different text. The apparent impersonality of David's feelings conveys the possibility that his character *could* be different, that the social world which impinges on his development makes his character almost impersonal. David's persistent turns to feeling map his social relations: he feels "quite uncomfortable" when he thinks about someone owning the caul he was born with (1:14) or when Mrs. Micawber imagines he thinks she would desert Mr. Micawber (12:182), "very brave" when left at Mr. Pegotty's house (10:159), and "friendly to everybody" (15:235) his first night at Mr. Wickfield's. At times, this social articulation of feeling takes on the language of sentiment, largely as feelings in David's heart. When he takes leave of his mother before her marriage, he notes, "I felt [my mother's] heart beat against mine" (2:38); before he is sent away to Creakle's school, he describes how "the vacancy in my heart... closed upon [Pegotty], and I felt toward her something I have never felt for any other human being" (4:72); and the final happy evening at home with his mother and Pegotty leads him to write, "I wish I had died with that feeling in my heart!" (8:121). Even when words of feeling do not belong to David, they articulate sociality: Mrs. Micawber wants her husband "to feel his position" when they leave for Australia (57:814)—a locution that she repeats five times—and when

Micawber upends Heep's schemes, Heep "felt his power over [Agnes] slipping away" (52:754). Mrs. Gummidge's repeated complaint "I feel it more" is emphatically relational, a point she makes early on: "I feel it more than other people" (3:50). Moreover, when these feelings are given the detail of emotion, the emotions map felt relations between people: shame, embarrassment, jealousy, and gratitude.[19] These felt relations to what is external and other make impersonal forces and the possibility of difference central to David's character.

The importance of exterior forces for David's character is most clear when David tries to extricate his life from necessity. Without impersonal forces and the possibility of felt differences, David could never have escaped his life at Murdstone and Grinby. David's interruptions and discontinuities give him an affective permeability in contrast to the impermeable characters of Mr. Murdstone and his sister. For the Murdstones, character is "firmness" (4:56), a view that captures the certainties of personal character and a demand that one control one's desires and interests against the passions. David's mother gestures toward this notion of character after his attack on Mr. Murdstone when she laments the "bad passions in [David's] heart" (4:72). David insists that Murdstone's is a "miscalled firmness" (4:63), "another name for tyranny; and for a certain gloomy, arrogant, devil's humour" (4:60). Firm character camouflages dishonest character, one in which the interior and exterior are at odds:

> The creed, as I should state it now, was this. Mr. Murdstone was firm; nobody in his world was to be so firm as Mr. Murdstone; nobody else in his world was to be firm at all, for everybody was to be bent to his firmness. Miss Murdstone was an exception. She might be firm, but only by relationship, and in an inferior and tributary degree. My mother was another exception. She might be firm, and must be; but only in bearing their firmness, and firmly believing there was no other firmness upon earth. (4:60)

Firmness is the demand of patriarchy, a performance of masculine socioeconomic command. Others may reflect this rigidity "only by relationship" to the firmness of the male head of household. Murdstone's insistence that David's mother must take and defer to his firmness makes this an assertion of phallic potency and a murderous psychosexual project of character formation. Murdstone describes this work as "forming her character, and infusing into it some amount of that firmness and decision of which it stood in need" (4:61). Such firmness, she complains, "is very hard" (4:56). It kills her.

Initially, David's rejection of Murdstonian firmness seems a rejection of Victorian hypocrisy. Walter Houghton identifies three historical bases for Victorian hypocrisy—conformity to social expectations, moral pretensions, and evasion of unpleasant social realities—and Murdstone's firmness can seem in equal parts conformity and moral pretension. As Houghton argues, Victorian hypocrisy was a result of exterior social forces pressuring one to conform, and "the *smart* man was happy to conform and play the game" (399). In *Copperfield*, Heep perhaps more directly captures the performative nature of hypocrisy—he is twice called a "hypocrite" (49:717; 61:861)—but Murdstone's firmness more insidiously reproduces hypocrisy around it. David writes of his first encounter with Murdstone's firmness:

> God help me, I might have been improved for my whole life, I might have been made another creature perhaps, for life, by a kind word at that season. ... [it] might have made me dutiful to him in my heart henceforth, instead of in my hypocritical outside. (4:56)

Firmness breeds hypocrisy, the novel implies, because it blocks emotional expression, not just in the above instance but also when Miss Murdstone "had a choice pleasure in exhibiting what she called her self-command, and her firmness" (9:140). It is this emotional blockage produced by hypocrisy that makes the firmness of personal character, the basis of its claims to trustworthiness, untenable. The problems of such firmness are not limited to the Murdstones. When Aunt Betsey encourages David to develop a firm character, she frames firmness as resistance to emotional influence. She tells him to be "a fine firm fellow, with a will of your own... With determination. With character, Trot—with strength of character that is not to be influenced, except on good reason, by anybody, or by anything" (19:283). To her mind, David's initial profession as a proctor apprenticed to Spenlow and Jorkins means "she confidently trusted that the life I was now to lead would make me firm and self-reliant, which was all I wanted" (23:363). Much as Mr. Spenlow insists to David that proctoring is "the genteelest profession in the world" (26:395), however, it too is marked by hypocrisy, as evidenced by Spenlow's constant invocations of his silent partner's opinion to justify his actions.

David may become a fine fellow, then, but the narrative makes it clear that this has nothing to do with his stepfather, who he runs away from, or his first profession, which he leaves. Indeed, it has nothing to do with the cultivation of resistance to influence. Rather, it is a result of the relationality of feeling, an embrace of exterior influence. Agnes, the chief representative of positive influence, is a "calm, good, self-denying influence" (18:278), an "influence for all good" (16:241), and a pervasive "good influence" (36:532). Agnes does not simply replace Dora, whom David wishes "had had more character and purpose, to sustain and improve me" (44:653), but manages through her influence to make David understand romantic love in properly disinterested terms. He tells her, "there is no alloy of self in what I feel for you" (62:866). For some readers, Agnes and her influence are the text at its most ideological; a ramping turn toward what will become the high Victorian ideology of domesticity and the civilizing influence of the private sphere on the masculine public. This ideological turn, however, also captures a tension within the text between personal character and the impersonal exterior forces that may shape character. As a character, Agnes provides a personal figure able to influence David and mitigate the dangers of impersonality and permeability. Thus David reflects upon meeting Agnes mid-way through the novel in an anaphoric deluge:

> Whatever contradictions and inconsistencies there were within me, as there are within so many of us; whatever might have been so different, and so much better; whatever I had done, in which I had perversely wandered away from the voice of my own heart; I knew nothing of. I only knew that I was fervently in earnest, when I felt the rest and peace of having Agnes near me. (39:574)

Agnes evacuates David's contradictions in the still certainties of the heart. David knows himself to be the sum of his inconsistencies, but he wishes to be this thing that is "fervently in earnest" and yet affectively dead in "the rest and peace" of Agnes's presence. Even in her arrest of external influence, Agnes testifies to the fundamental precarity of David's character, shaped by exterior forces in ways beyond his control. One might read David's later reflections after Agnes accepts his proposal as a celebration of his character as fixed and achieved, but they also suggest the ways in which his character is haunted by difference, a reflection of the interruptions, surprises, and exterior forces that shaped him: "Long miles of road then opened out before my mind; and, toiling on, I saw a ragged way-worn boy, forsaken and neglected, who should come to call even the heart now beating against mine, his own" (62:868).

Feeling with Others

Feeling's address to an impersonal social exterior becomes more pronounced when the narrative searches for ways to make readers share a feeling with David. To conjure feeling with David, the text turns to the uncanny, making its strangest feelings those most familiar. Throughout, David uses "strange" whenever he encounters something that is unfamiliar or resists interpretation; for instance, "strange lady" (1:16), "strange public house" (11:171), and "strange foot" (61:850). When he notes feelings as strange, however, this defamiliarization allows for a more detailed account of his emotional experience and for muted appeals to outside experience. No passage better conveys this quality of David's empty yet full narration of feeling than his reflection upon approaching home after his first school term:

Ah, what a strange feeling it was to be going home when it was not home, and to find that every object I looked at, reminded me of the happy old home, which was like a dream I could never dream again! (8:119)

Fifty years before Freud, *Copperfield* proposes that to feel with David is to feel the *unheimlich*, the simultaneous feelings of home as familiar and unfamiliar. Elsewhere, David pairs strange feeling with parenthetical asides that more directly evoke the possibility of a shared affective experience that demands yet evades description. When he discovers Heep's plan to marry Agnes, David finds himself in the midst of a murderous rage before suddenly experiencing "the strange feeling (to which, perhaps, no one is quite a stranger) that all this had occurred before, at some indefinite time, and that I knew what he was going to say next, took possession of me" (25:389). The feeling of déjà vu is of less import than the fact that it is at once an unusual sensation and yet one "to which, perhaps, no one is quite a stranger." This pairing of strangeness and the parenthetical aside appears when David accepts a ride to his mother's funeral with the cheerful mortician Mr. Omer and his family; he reflects "I do not think I have ever experienced so strange a feeling in my life (I am wiser now, perhaps) as that of being with them, remembering how they had been employed, and seeing them enjoy the ride" (9:139). The shared use of "perhaps" in these passages underscores the uncertainty of the familiar unfamiliar. It is not that affective experiences are shared or familiar but that they are not unfamiliar.

The novel's climactic scene of shared feeling is Steerforth's death, an undoubted point of intensity for the novel as a whole. The affective power of this section led Dickens to make it the climax of his readings from the novel. As Philip Collins notes, audiences considered it "the most sublime moment in all the Readings" (136). An anecdote from Kate Douglas Wiggin conveys the scene's effects even without Dickens's performance. Wiggins met Dickens on a train during his second visit to America in 1867–68 when she was no more than twelve years old and told him of her love for *Copperfield*, a book she had already read six times. Dickens asked if she wanted to hear him read, and she replied yes, explaining, "I know how I feel when I read one of the books, but I wanted to hear how it sounded" (41). This response, Wiggin writes, brought tears to Dickens's eyes:

"Do you cry when you read out loud, too?" I asked curiously. "We all do in our family. And we never read about Tiny Tim, or about Steerforth when his body is washed up on the beach, on Saturday nights, for fear our eyes will be too swollen to go to Sunday School."

"Yes, I cry when I read about Steerforth," he answered quietly, and I felt no astonishment. "I cried when I wrote it, too! That is still more foolish!" (41–42)

Steerforth's death is inextricably bound to the evocation of readers' (and the writer's) tears. By the time Dickens composed the scene, he was well versed in crafting melodramatically staged deaths. Paul Dombey's death was widely hailed as the high point of *Dombey and Son* when it appeared. Thackeray told Mark Lemon of *Punch*, "There's no writing against this [*Dombey*], one hasn't an atom of a chance; it's stupendous" (Churchill 74). Yet Paul's death stylistically more closely resembles the pathetic death of Little Nell more than that of Steerforth as Dickens's contemporaries noted. Francis Jeffries wrote him in 1847 "since the divine Nell was found dead on her humble couch, beneath the snow and the ivy, there has been nothing like the actual dying of that sweet Paul, in the summer sunshine of that lofty room" (Churchill 74). The narration of both scenes is ripe with sentimental language and direct narratorial appeals to reader's sympathies, both of which are lacking in *Copperfield*. David offers one brief pathetic appeal for Steerforth in the first sentence of the subsequent chapter, but this piece stands divorced from the scene's reportage.

The difference in approach is due in part to the complex role that Steerforth plays in the novel. Unlike Paul or Nell, Steerforth is no innocent child. From a structural perspective, he is the class obverse of Uriah Heep and his clerical untrustworthiness, a figure for the untrustworthiness of the dominant upper class. Where Heep plays up his repulsive subservience to the class hierarchy, Steerforth assumes his dominance in it, and his handsome appearance allows his character to appear "very generous and noble" (20:304). His self-presentation inspires trust in everyone he meets, from David and his schoolmates to Ham, Mr. Pegotty, and Emily, as well as Steerforth's mother. Yet like Heep, Steerforth is a hypocrite, seizing and spending David's pocket money at Creakles' school under the guise of taking care of him. This early sequence echoes David's encounter with a friendly waiter who cheerfully protects David from his supper by eating it. David describes that episode as a result of what he calls "the natural reliance of a child upon superior years ... I had no serious mistrust of him on the whole, even then" (5:81). David's relationship with Steerforth throughout the novel evinces this same childish reliance on a protecting superior, someone who he describes as "very good-looking, and at least half-a dozen years my senior" (6:97). When Steerforth betrays David by using his account of Mr. Mell's mother against Mr. Mell—thus losing Mr. Mell his place and David his only supportive teacher—David contrasts "what a noble fellow [Steerforth] was in appearance, and how homely and plain Mr. Mell looked opposed to him" (7:109). Gentlemanly appearance and manner are the basis of

Steerforth's seeming trustworthiness just as humbleness is that of Heep. Much as Heep resents those above him in the hierarchy, Steerforth disdains those below him. Such people, he tells Rosa Dartle, "have not very fine natures, and they may be thankful that, like their coarse rough skins, they are not easily wounded" (20:303).

Even if he is a "bad angel" (25:374), from an affective perspective, Steerforth is an ineradicable influence upon David and remains, as David once drunkenly exclaims, "you'retheguidingstarofmyexistence" (24:368). David's continued attachment to Steerforth can suggest David as a character is too desirous of his class status to recognize Steerforth's perfidiousness. As a narrator, however, his continued recognition of this attachment—indeed, his refusal to reject or frame Steerforth as an evil character, unlike Heep—indicates an awareness of Steerforth's influence on his character for good or ill. Steerforth is the first to encourage David to tell stories, and thus inseparable from his development as a writer. More than that, his influence allows David to practice a particular kind of character-based attachment. He describes his relationship with Steerforth as

> moved by no interested or selfish motive, nor was I moved by fear of him. I admired and loved him, and his approval was return enough. It was so precious to me that I look back on these trifles, now, with an aching heart. (7:104)

Steerforth allows David an early attempt at a relationship of proper influence and romantic love that he subsequently achieves with Agnes, a situation intimated by Steerforth's nickname for David, "Daisy," and David's reaction to Steerforth's steps on the stairs—"I felt my heart beat high, and the blood rush to my face" (28:431). Once Steerforth is understood as a figure for untrustworthiness and for the influence of exterior forces on character, his betrayal and death makes sense of David's reaction to that death: he reflects on his "undisciplined heart" (58:819) and how "my first trust, my first affection, the whole airy castle of my life" had been "shattered" (58:819).

Steerforth's death thus captures the novel's pervasive grappling with the problem of trust and character and does so as the culmination to the novel's major plots. In this sense, as the compact expression of multiple narrative strands and ways of feeling, the scene exemplifies a literary instance of affective intensity. At this stage, Dora has died, Heep has been thwarted, and Mr. Pegotty has found Emily after Steerforth seduced and abandoned her to the mercy of his manservant, Mr. Littimer. David means to deliver a final message to Ham from Emily before she departs for Australia, but he arrives only to witness a fierce storm battering and wrecking a small boat against the coast. Ham tries to rescue the men on-board, unaware that one is the man who seduced his fiancé. Ham is killed in the attempt and the boat destroyed before Steerforth's body washes ashore in the chapter's closing paragraph. Throughout the novel, storms and shipwrecks serve as leitmotifs for class precarity, beginning with Emily's wish for her family to "all be gentlefolks together" so that "we wouldn't mind then, when there comes stormy weather" (3:47), a reasonable thought for a child who has lost her family to storms and wrecks. Such language also appears after Mr. Micawber's release from debtor's prison when the Micawbers are "quite shipwrecked" (12:183), and later when Ham worries about the fallen Martha tainting Emily's reputation he says he "couldn't, kind-natur'd, tender-hearted as he is, see them two together, side by side, for all the treasures that's wrecked in the sea" (22:345), and David uses this phrase when he encounters Martha again (40:588). Wrecks, then, are largely motifs for downward mobility, though David also describes sleeping in his old room at Mr. Wickfield's after Heep's expulsion in positive terms as feeling "like a shipwrecked wanderer come home" (54:787). Steerforth's death connects these elements and indicates why Victorian readers like Wiggin viewed the scene as Steerforth's more than Ham's. Steerforth's end is climactic. It gestures to the novel's opening pages and the problem of trust captured by the "ragged old rooks'-nests [that] swung like wrecks upon a stormy sea" (1:17). Those wrecks of trust become in this sequence the wreck of trusted character premised upon appearance.

The resulting scene contrasts the flatly reported sequence of Ham's death as the punctual end to a series of actions and the unfolding narrativity of Steerforth's as memory-laden but unsentimental account. With Ham, a character who is precisely what he appears to be, the narration focuses on movement: the body dragged to David's feet, the body carried inside, David motionless by the body, the beating of the waves, the stillness of the heart. Ham's death consists of one striking image, his body drawn "to my very feet" (55:800). The narrative reduces the process of discovery, attempted restoration, and failure as a contracted intensity, two words captured between two em-dashes as though typographically sapping the movement from Ham's body, the narrative, and finally David himself: "—insensible—dead" (55:800). By contrast, the narration of Steerforth's death focuses on recollection and scene:

> But [the fisherman] led me to the shore. And on that part of it where she and I had looked for shells, two children—on that part of it where some lighter fragments of the old boat, blown down last night, had been scattered by the wind—among the ruins of the home he had wronged—I saw him lying with his head upon his arm, as I had often seen him lie at school. (55:801)

Unlike Dickens's typical scenes of pathos, this paragraph lacks a coherent rhetorical organization. At first, it seems poised to become another of the novel's extended anaphoras, a rhetorical turn that David relies on throughout to underscore the details of a particular memory, as in his account of the days after he bit Mr. Murdstone: "What irksome constraint…what intolerable dullness… What walks… What meals… What evenings… What yawns and dozes" (8:131–32). Here, however, surprise seems to have made the narrative drop its apparent anaphoric stem ("on that part of it where") after the first repetition. Similarly, while Dickens's prose tends to drift into blank verse during climactic scenes, in this paragraph he creates an unusual set of stuttered rhythms around an understated repetition of the word *had*. This rhetorical emphasis of the past perfect seems to enact the past *now*, with Steerforth becoming well and truly *past*: the clauses move from David's recollection of the beach with Emily to its present state covered in the debris of her abandoned ship-home, to the relation of the body to the wreckage itself ("among the ruins of the home he had wronged"), and finally, to David's memory of Steerforth's posture. The penultimate clause—"I saw him lying with his head on his arm"—briefly opens this past perfect rhythm to a moment of temporal possibility before the final clause returns to recollection—"as I had often seen him lie at school." The concluding line thus withholds Steerforth's name and his death and replaces it with the high Victorian trope of death as a sleep, one that he often applies to children and that David has earlier used to describe his mother in death. Throughout this passage, names are excised. David does not name Steerforth at all in this chapter. Everything happens instead to a series of impersonal pronouns, *I, she,* and *he.* At this moment of narrational intensity, David renders his history as an impersonal series of affective encounters created by the radiating lines of memory. Rachel Ablow is thus right that at this moment David discovers a unity between Steerforth's presentation of self and his reality but it is a more critical unity of presentation and reality: Steerforth is a boy lying unwitting in the midst of the home he has thoughtlessly wrecked. The emotive power signaled by this passage is inextricable from Steerforth's proximity to David and David's narrative command, but it means also to operate beyond David, to affect his readers.

This passage thus deepens and problematizes a point made by Alex Woloch about Dickens's protagonists. For Dickens, Woloch argues,

the protagonist's interiority is overwhelmed by the very exterior content that it attempts to process, and this condition also underlies the structure of the character system, motivating the strong minor characters who are, in one sense, the distorted consequence of the protagonist's incomplete processes of consciousness and perception. (133)

Woloch engages with *Copperfield* through Heep and his resentments, but Steerforth offers a more intense and unresolvable social demand that could not be overcome by David, Dickens, or his Victorian audience, the demands of character and of the gentlemanly which provided the cultural bulwark for the construction of relations of trust. The threat of clerical malfeasance or even of resistant exploited labor could be overcome in the world and is overcome in the world of the novel: David eliminates Heep and subjects him to excoriation, much as he does to the tale's other villain, Murdstone. By contrast, David cannot excise Steerforth or what Steerforth represents from himself. In the scene of Steerforth's death, David's interior processes nearly unravel to capture the overwhelming influence of Steerforth on David's interiority. In *The Old Curiosity Shop*, such an experience of interiorization gave rise to anxiety. In *Copperfield*, such interiorization ceases to be a threat and becomes part of process of self-production, one in which the seeming interminability of mourning and its processes of interiorization can be recognized and accepted, if only as the bits and pieces of an untrustworthy exterior whole.

Toward the Dividual

As a controlling theme, trust suggests that *David Copperfield* is the text in which Dickens pioneers his later more explicit syntheses of narrative and social critique in *Bleak House, Little Dorrit*, and *Our Mutual Friend*. Here the more diffuse affective forms of his earlier works become more directly shaped and controlled by authorial interest, an apparent subordination of the scenes of affective intensity in his works of the 1840s, most especially the Christmas books and *The Old Curiosity Shop*, to a more encompassing temporal narrative organization, one able to fold together affective scene and social critique into the narrative of a life. Where *Oliver Twist* and *The Old Curiosity Shop* turned to contemporary material events of political and economic import to ground their affective scenes in a shared historical experience of struggle and contestation, *David Copperfield* relies instead on a more ameliorative framework to ground its narrative and affective scenes. Trust offers an implicit social critique but one so deeply embedded in the events of David's life that its multiple threads can be readily overlooked. Later novels divide and multiply the thematic line in an apparent attempt to disembed social critique from this too deep burial. The next stage of this narrative development for Dickens is the bifurcation of *Bleak House*, half a biographical account from Esther and half the narrator of Dickensian social critique, a shift that forces the biographical open to another narratorial voice and other character perspectives. In the end, the problem of *David Copperfield* may be that for an exploration of the social and material problems raised by trust, it is too much about David.

Yet when read through the lens of trust, the novel offers two apparently contrary solutions to trust's failures: either create a trustworthy character or depersonalize oneself enough to retain the possibility of becoming something *other*. In this way, Dickens intimates Niklas Luhman's analysis of failures of trust with impersonal systems—in short, that failures of trust may lead to a depersonalization of trust throughout a system. In an analysis of Luhmann, Brian Massumi emphasizes that this systemic expansion of distrust "[brings] trust and distrust together into a *zone of indistinction*" (7). For economic relationships, this indistinction has a particular purpose: it obscures the role of the affective in economic exchange. Massumi argues that attention to this aspect of trust and its failure suggests that economic agents are not rational agents of choice but rather agents in which reason and affective states are in constant churn. Trust, whether personal or impersonal, aims to make this churn unconscious and to insist on the reality of the economic individual, the subject, the self. As Massumi emphasizes, though, the self-produced by our conjuncture of trust, modernity, and economic rationality is not one at all but rather that churn of divergent bare activity. For Massumi, this affective self is not an individual but a "dividual," a term that describes the plurality of social roles that a singularity may hold.[20] Those singularities may be primed toward particular tendencies but they contain many possible outcomes, not a single self. Personal and impersonal systems of trust, then, reveal the self to be impersonal, a churn of singularities rather than a coherent subject. Dickens's account of David at once suggests this plurality of the dividual and threatens to obscure it in biography.

David, then, is a character caught between the imagined rationality of trusted personal character and an altogether different kind of *homo economicus*, one susceptible to outside influence and its own earnest energy. A version of *homo economicus*, in short, of churning affects and reasons. This churn is made all the more suggestive by David's story being one about professional work and narrated in in a mode that is at once impersonal and intensely felt. If David at times seems to disappear as a character, his feelings becoming uncanny, it is due to this tension in which he strains toward a different kind of world altogether. At such moments, perhaps it would be better to call him the *davidual*. As the novel's affective if impersonal core, David traces the social situations, including people, that shaped him, not to insist that the outcome of his character is foretold and that his individuality would necessarily come into being but rather to reflect upon the very precarity of this outcome. It is a tale that must be told because, like Mr. Dick's endless retelling of the beheading of Charles I, it contains unnumbered tragedies in *potentia*.

To read the dividual in *Copperfield* is to read the novel in light of its engagement with trust and the centrality of Victorian notions of character to professional work. The credit markets in Britain during the 1850s were caught between personal and impersonal mechanisms for discipline, familial and personal connections on the one hand, and impersonal mechanisms such as Bank rate for bill discounts. Even after the

1857 financial crisis, personal credit remained at the heart of financial analysis through the 1860s. Walter Bagehot immediately blamed the financial panic of 1867 on the extension of credit to new, less connected firms when it in fact stemmed from the collapse of Overend, Gurney, and Company, one of the oldest and most connected firms in the United Kingdom. This deeply personalized and character-based milieu not only pervaded finance but the professions as well. One would expect it to have untrustworthy characters like Uriah Heep and James Steerforth, and trustworthy ones such as Tommy Traddles. David has to learn to navigate this world in which character mattered yet was continually hemmed in by the pressure of more and more impersonal systems of credit and exchange.

The novel's use of affect, then, is not a ruse, a mere strategy to create emotional complicity between readers and David. By emphasizing trust as a central problem for the text's conjuncture, the novel uses David's impersonality and affective sensitivity to suggest an emptiness at the heart of narrative command, the possibility of another way of feeling, though always at some remove, a space that is here and not here, a lost home where we already are. Dickens's earlier novels approach this impersonality as affective receptivity in Oliver and Nell, but with David it becomes a receptivity that grows, develops, and changes. In its alteration, David's is a receptivity that understands itself as fundamentally marked by ruptures and difference. The surprise that makes up the novel's affective form captures this persistent sense of possible rupture and exterior force. Surprise provides the patterning by which David develops his singularity through the continuing loss of figures and places that signal home, from the death of his father before he is born, to the loss of his mother, of the Micawbers (an event that incites him to find Aunt Betsey), of Aunt Betsey's home, of his wife Dora, of Peggoty's home, and so on. The Emily-Steerforth plot reiterates home's loss, destroying the Pegotty household, forcing Steerforth into permanent exile from his mother's house, and ending with the destruction of Pegotty's houseboat. The novel's final pages return to the question of home to offer one last set of surprises, the happiness of Traddles's home and the staid goodness of David and Agnes's.

By attending to the novel's affective form, its attention to surprise and interruption, the novel's contents and feelings suggest a relation to home and self that recalls what Paolo Virno and other autonomist Marxists call "exodus," a continual taking leave of the factory or workplace for an as-yet-to-be-determined elsewhere, a desertion from what is for what could be.[21] For *David Copperfield*, this is the way that home remains a place of leavetaking even as it seems most stable, most at home. The certainty and stability of home and of one's achieved character remains haunted by an otherness, an impersonality that the novel intimates one needs. Such a need can be seen in the expanding world of professional work, of service work, of finance itself. Socioeconomic events in the 1850s solicit an alternate thought of trust and character's becoming, one that is not the becoming of a subject but a singularity, not a sovereign narrative commander but an ad hoc narrator, one readily displaced—indeed, who will be displaced in *Bleak House*. From this perspective, David may be less the narrative's Hobbesian sovereign than its strategic leader, a precarious position from which he can be deposed. Behind the aspirational narrative of character-shaping will, *David Copperfield* gestures toward a model of becoming and social belonging based not on the power of the central subject or the sovereign but on the positive potentiality of permeability and impersonality—that is, on its dividualness. Read this way, the novel suggests that the emergence of the professional subject, a being based on its relationships of trust, brings with it the possibility of another model of being-with, one that is singular rather than subjective. The signal achievement of *David Copperfield*, then, may be Dickens's insistence on the surprise that inheres in the narration of his own becoming. In this fictionalized biography, the possibility of surprise marks the feeling and the knowledge that he and those he knew could have become otherwise.

Notes

1 See Han 41–48.
2 For instance, see Rosemary Bodenheimer's claim that "the silencing enforced by autobiography may well have turned him toward the fiction of *David Copperfield*, where he could re-bury—and in turn effect forget—his story with a context he completely controlled" (72).
3 For similar readings of hypocrisy in the novel, see Poovey 89–125, Ruth 56–82.
4 Chapman and Hall sent Dickens a copy of *Mary Barton* upon publication and met Dickens on 12 May 1849. She wrote for his *Household Words* from the first issue. See Dickens, *Letters* 5, 497 and 532.
5 See Kant, third antinomy.
6 In the *Biographia Literia*, Coleridge notes the influence of Kant on his thought, and theorizes the imagination as a bridging of the human and the infinite: "The primary Imagination I hold to be the living power and prime agent of all human perception, and as a repetition in the finite mind of the eternal act of creation in the infinite I AM" (13:313).
7 The ability to choose was central to Victorian respectability. See Best 258. Throughout his life, Carlyle maintained this view of Kantian ethics as natural supernaturalism, telling William Allingham in 1878:

> It is impossible to believe otherwise than that this world is the work of an Intelligent Mind. The power which has formed us—He (or It—it that appears to any one more suitable) has known how to put into the human an ineradicable love of justice and truth. The best bit for me in Kant is that saying of his, 'Two things strike me dumb wit astonishment—the Starry Heavens and the Sense of Right and Wrong in the Human Soul'.
> (Allingham 264)

8 Intriguingly, Catherine Dickens insisted that her husband's sense of his work as earnest sacrifice was in fact his "pleasure." See Nayder 58.

9 Importantly, Mill refused to follow this conservatism of character in terms of gender and uses character throughout his discussion in *The Subjection of Women*.

10 For more on this line of criticism about *Copperfield*, see Poovey 89–125, Ruth 56–82, Salomon, Titolo 102–34, and Willson.

11 See Adams 42–54, Barringer 81, and Sussman 41.

12 By the end of the century, this path of upward mobility was all but gone, but it had existed, however slightly, through the Victorian era's early decades. See Anderson 41–49.

13 On respectability's costs, see Best 263. On class presentation for clerks, see Anderson 67–68.

14 In *Our Mutual Friend*, Bradley Headstone will offer another instance of this coercive side to respectable intellectual labour in his scenes with Lizzie Hexam, as his gentility is part of the supposed class recompense Lizzie would receive in marrying him.

15 See "Partridge v. The Bank of England."

16 David comes to embody a similar, if more worldly and aware sense of character by the novel's end when he announces to Agnes that "There is no alloy of self in what I feel for you" (62:866) before declaring his love for her.

17 The overtones here of professional work references are more explicit when David receives a "written character" for his servant Paragon (44:641).

18 Tomkins also insists surprise is "neutral… in its milder form" or "somewhat more negative in its more intense form" (107).

19 For shame, see 5:81, 11:166, 22:334, 24:371, 28:421, 32:470, 42:630, 52:750, 55:795; embarrassment 8:132, 14:210, 17:265, 24:367; jealousy 2:33, 24:365, 26:399, 33:489; and gratitude 2:38, 5:85, 7:99, 7:104, 13:210, 19:296, 22:328, 31:453, 38:552, 39:575.

20 Massumi takes the term "dividual" from Gilles Deleuze's late essay "Postscript on a Society of Control," which outlines the negative possibilities of this concept. The term appears as a more neutral descriptor in anthropological work that predates Deleuze's work. See Deleuze, "Postscript" and Strathern 11–15.

21 For a discussion of exodus, see Virno.

References

Ablow, Rachel. "Labors of Love: The Sympathetic Subjects of *David Copperfield*," *Dickens Studies Annual*, vol. 31 (2002), pp. 23–46.

Adams, James Eli. *Dandies and Desert Saints: Styles of Victorian Masculinity*. Ithaca, NY: Cornell University Press, 1995.

Allingham, William. *William Allingham: A Diary*. Edited by H. Allingham and D. Radford. London: Macmillan and Co., 1907.

Barringer, Tim. *Men at Work: Art and Labour in Victorian England*. New Haven: Yale University Press, 2005.

Best, Geoffrey. *Mid-Victorian Britain, 1851–1875*. New York: Schocken Books, 1971.

Bloom, Harold, ed. *Charles Dickens's David Copperfield*. New York: Chelsea House Publishers, 1987.

Bodenheimer, Rosemary. *Knowing Dickens*. Ithaca, NY: Cornell University Press, 2007.

Carlyle, Thomas. *Sartor Resartus*. Edited by Kerry McSweeney and Peter Sabor. Oxford: Oxford World's Classics, 1987.

Churchill, Reginald Churchill. *A Bibliography of Dickensian Criticism 1836–1975*. London: Macmillan Press, 1975.

Coleridge, Samuel Taylor. Biographia Literia in The Major Works. Edited by Heather Jackson. Oxford: Oxford University Press, 2009.

Collini, Stefan. *Public Moralists: Political Thought and Intellectual Life in Britain 1850–1930*. Oxford: Oxford University Press, 1991.

"Consistory Court, Wednesday, April 28." *Times* [London, England] 29 April 1841: 7. *The Times Digital Archive*. Web. 28 July 2018.

Dames, Nicholas. *Amnesiac Selves*. Oxford: Oxford University Press, 2003.

Deleuze, Gilles. "Postscript on Societies of Control," *October*, vol. 59 (Winter 1992), pp. 3–7.

Dickens, Charles. *David Copperfield*. 1850. New York: Penguin, 2004.

———. *Dombey and Son*. 1848. New York: Everyman's Library, 1994.

———. *Great Expectations*. Edited by Charlotte Mitchell. New York: Penguin, 1996.

———. *The Letters of Charles Dickens: The Pilgrim Edition, Volume 5: 1847–1849*. Edited by Graham Storey and Kenneth Fielding. Oxford: Oxford University Press, 1981.

———. *Little Dorrit*. Edited by Harvey Peter Sucksmith. Oxford: Oxford University Press, 2012.

Finn, Margot. *Character of Credit*. Cambridge: Cambridge University Press, 2008.

Flanders, Judith. *Inside the Victorian Home*. New York: W.W. Norton, 2005.

Gaskell, Elizabeth. *Mary Barton*. Edited by Edgar Wright. Oxford: Oxford World's Classics, 1987.

Han, Byung-Chul. *Psychopolitics: Neoliberalism and New Technologies of Power*. Translated by Erik Butler. London: Verso, 2017.

Houghton, Walter. *The Victorian Frame of Mind*. New Haven: Yale University Press, 1957.

Hudson, Pat. "Industrial Organisation and Structure." *The Cambridge Economic History of Modern Britain, Volume 1: Industrisation, 1700–1860*, edited by Roderick Floud and Paul Johnson. Cambridge: Cambridge University Press, 2004, pp. 28–56.

Jaffe, Audrey. *Vanishing Points: Dickens, Narrative, and the Subject of Omniscience*. Berkeley: University of California Press, 1991.

Kaplan, Fred. *Dickens: A Biography*. Baltimore, MD: Johns Hopkins University Press, 1998.

King, WTC. *The History of the London Discount Market*. London: Routledge, 2006.

Litvak, Joseph. "Unctuous: Resentment in *David Copperfield*," *Qui Parle*, vol. 20, no. 2 (Spring/Summer 2012), pp. 127–50.

Luhmann, Niklas. *Trust and Power*. Translated by Howard Davis, John Raffan, and Kathryn Rooney, edited by Christian Morgner and Michael King. Malden, MA: Polity Press, 2017.

Massumi, Brian. *Power at the End of the Economy*. Durham, NC: Duke University Press, 2014.

Mill, John Stuart. *Collected Works of John Stuart Mill*, Volume 8. Edited by John Michael Robson. Toronto: University of Toronto Press, 1974.

Miller, David Allan. *The Novel and the Police*. Berkeley: University of California Press, 1988.

"Money-Market and City Intelligence." *Times* [London, England] 18 December 1841: 5. *The Times Digital Archive*. Web.

"Money Market and City News." *The Morning Post* [London, England] 18 December 1841, p. 2. *The British Newspaper Archive*. Web.

Murphey, Anne L. "The Financial Revolution and Its Consequences." *The Cambridge Economic History of Modern Britain, Vol. 1: 1700–1870*, edited by Roderick Floud, Jane Humphries, and Paul Johnson. Cambridge: Cambridge University Press, 2014, pp. 323–43.

Nayder, Lilian. *The Other Dickens: A Life of Catherine Hogarth*. Ithaca, NY: Cornell University Press, 2010.

Ngai, Sianne. *Ugly Feelings*. Cambridge, MA: Harvard University Press, 2007.

Owen, Robert. *A New View of Society and Other Writings*. Edited by Gregory Claeys, New York: Penguin, 1991.

"Partridge v. The Bank of England," *The Jurist*, vol. 8, part 1, S. Sweet (1845), pp. 803–07.

Pinkard, Terry. *German Philosophy, 1760–1860: The Legacy of Idealism*. Cambridge: Cambridge University Press, 2002.

Poovey, Mary. *Uneven Developments: The Ideological Work of Gender in Mid-Victorian England*. Chicago: University of Chicago Press, 1988.

Robb, George. *White-Collar Crime in Modern England: Financial Fraud and Business Morality, 1845–1929*. Cambridge: Cambridge University Press, 1992.

Rosenthal, Jesse. *Good Form: The Ethical Experience of the Victorian Novel*. Princeton, NJ: Princeton University Press, 2017.

Ruth, Jennifer. *Novel Professions: Interested Disinterest and the Making of the Professional in the Victorian Novel*. Columbus: Ohio State University Press, 2006.

Salmon, Richard. *The Formation of the Victorian Literary Profession*. Cambridge: Cambridge University Press, 2013.

Seligman, Adam B. *The Problem of Trust*. Princeton, NJ: Princeton University Press, 1997.

Strathern, Marilyn. *The Gender of the Gift: Problems with Women and Problems with Society in Melanesia*. Berkeley: University of California Press, 1984.

Sussman, Herbert. *Victorian Masculinities: Manhood and Masculine Poetics in Early Victorian Literature and Art*. Cambridge: Cambridge University Press, 1995.

Sztompka, Piotr. *Trust: A Sociological Theory*. Cambridge: Cambridge University Press, 2000.

Titolo, Matthew. "The Clerks' Tale: Liberalism, Accountability, and Mimesis in David Copperfield," *ELH*, vol. 70 (2003), pp. 171–95.

Virno, Paolo. "Virtuosity and Revolution: The Political Theory of Exodus." *Radical Thought in Italy*, edited by Paolo Virno and Michael Hardt. Minneapolis: University of Minnesota Press, 1996, pp. 189–212.

Wiggin, Kate Douglas. *My Garden of Memory: An Autobiography*. Boston: Houghton Mifflin, 1923.

Willson, Andrew. "Vagrancy and the Fantasy of Unproductive Writing in *David Copperfield*," *Nineteenth-Century Literature*, vol. 72, no. 2 (2017), pp. 192–217.

Woloch, Alex. *The One vs. The Many: Minor Characters and the Space of the Protagonist in the Novel*. Princeton, NJ: Princeton University Press, 2003.

5 Great Expectations
Shame, Suspense, and the Volunteer Forces

The affective form of *David Copperfield*—its surprises and interruptions—reveals the ur-text of aspirational narratives to contain its own processual undoing. A willful cohering of David's character and a grappling with its precarious multiplicity, the interruption of surprise reveals changes in the status of professional workers and the expansion of the role of finance in British culture. One might be forgiven for imagining that Dickens's other gesture toward biography, *Great Expectations*, may suggest similar themes. Certainly, its account of Pip's childhood has long been culled by biographers and used in tandem with David's childhood in their descriptions of Dickens's childhood and his experience of poverty. For critics, the novel can also suggest problems of professional work similar to those of *Copperfield*. For Anna Kornbluh, Pip is a financial subject always waiting for his investments to ripen, an argument in which *Great Expectations* maps the emergence of a corporatized subjectivity and an increasingly financialized economy. From this perspective, Pip seems little different from David Copperfield, another subject caught in the ambivalence between cultural demands for trustworthy personal character and more fluid and impersonal versions of self and trust. Pip too remakes himself, after all. Such an interpretation certainly fits British economic history. Yet it is a problem that the two novels, so stylistically and affectively distinct, can seem from a critical and historical perspective almost interchangeable.

Affective form suggests important differences underlie these apparent similarities. *David Copperfield* is a triumphant narrative deeply marked by David's surprise and shame at the realization of his disposability, and by extension, the disposability of so many human beings in Victorian Britain. This conjunction of surprise and shame resonates with the novel's persistent use of discontinuities and undernarrations of feeling to produce a stylistics of elision and impersonalization. The affective form of *David Copperfield* is about the shock of economic and personal vulnerability. By contrast, *Great Expectations* focuses on the feeling of vulnerability as such. The later novel ironizes *Copperfield*'s aspirational narrative and persistently focuses not on the situational externalities that produce character but on the vulnerabilities of a self-abandoned to the precarious processes of self-making. Where David gradually realizes that the people most important to his character may betray his trust, Pip slowly overcomes his feelings of shame, a process that takes him through the terrors of a hierarchical class structure as he learns to navigate a society organized by feelings of shame and contempt. Between the two novels, emphasis shifts from the problem of the social world writ large to that of will in the face of situational difficulties. Attention to affect in *Great Expectations* reveals a reshaping of the notion of character found in *Copperfield*, one that alters its emphasis from the cultivation of trust and the potential impersonal sociality of the singular person to the mediation and modification of one's vulnerabilities. We move from the presentation of self that is solicited by trust to a more raw encounter with the affective experience of being seen.

In a way, the narrative of *Great Expectations* is a project to mitigate this affective experience. The novel is thus not, as it appears in much of its criticism, focused on questions of interpretation or the drive for meaning but on the persistent exposure of the affective experiences that precede such drives and give shape to what seems to be the self. The novel resembles *Copperfield*, then, insofar as it is not about the creation of a coherent individual subject but about the haunting of subjectivity by its potential unraveling. Yet *Great Expectations* does not engage with this potentiality as surprise or interruption, an experience of something halted. Rather, it explores a primary vulnerability, one that is prior to or separable from coherent subjectivity and self-knowledge, and the ways in which one may navigate this vulnerability. In lieu of surprise, that which abrogates, *Great Expectations* turns to suspense for its affective form, a feeling of waiting that becomes an insistence upon self-renunciation. Only the suspension of desire for whatever saves from vulnerability. In this way, the affective form of *Great Expectations* suggests the discourses of character bound up with imperial administration in its necessary disinterest and concern to protect what is vulnerable at all costs. As we will see, *Great Expectations* offers an affective form geared to the needs of a vulnerable masculine imperial subject.

Personal vulnerability was much on Dickens's mind in the early 1860s. Shortly after finishing the novel, he wrote to John Forster in June 1862:

> I must entreat you, to pause for an instant, and go back to what you know of my childish days, and to ask yourself whether it is natural that something of the character formed in me then, and lost under happier circumstances, should have reappeared in the last five years. The never-to-be-forgotten misery of that old time bred a certain shrinking sensitiveness in a certain ill-clad, ill-fed child, that I have found come back in the never to be forgotten misery of this later time. (*Letters* 10, 97–98)

As Michael Slater notes, "this 'shrinking sensitiveness' is very much one of Pip's characteristics" (492). Slater, like other biographers, connects this feeling to Dickens's situation in the 1860s, most especially the economic drains he experienced as the result of his separation from his wife Catherine (after his unsuccessful attempt to commit her to an insane asylum) and his illicit affair with actress Ellen Ternan, who he met while staging *The Frozen Deep* with Wilkie Collins.[1] By 1862, Dickens was responsible for three households—Gads Hill for himself, Catherine's private residence, and a pied-a-terre for Ellen and her mother—and for establishing his children as they entered adulthood. Dickens's "shrinking sensitiveness" and Pip's vulnerability suggest that the vulnerabilities explored by *Great Expectations* should be treated as inextricable from questions of patriarchy and masculinity, questions in which responsibility and desire may work together or at odds.

This is not, however, to reduce *Great Expectations* to a mediation on Dickens's personal crises but to articulate a more abstract link between the text's formal qualities and a larger historical crisis of white middle and upper-class British masculinity in the late 1850s. For Dickens, this is best be seen in his response to the 1857 Uprising in India. Writing in the aftermath of the Uprising to Miss Burdett Coutts—a woman central to the story of Dickens's separation, including a later attempt to reconcile Charles and Catherine in 1860[2]–Dickens writes

> And I wish I were Commander in Chief in India. The first thing I would do to strike that Oriental race with amazement (not in the least regarding them as if they lived in the Strand, London, or at Camden Town), should be to proclaim to them, in their language, that I considered my holding that appointment by the leave of God, to mean that I should do my utmost to exterminate the Race upon whom the stain of the late cruelties rested; and that I begged them to do me the favor to observe that I was there for that purpose and no other, and was now proceeding, with all convenient dispatch and merciful swiftness of execution, to blot it out of mankind and raze it off the face of the Earth. (*Letters* 8, 459)

Critics such as Grace Moore have used the genocidal call in Dickens's letter to discuss the emergence of Dickens's racism in the 1850s. It is important to note, though, that Dickens's perspective in this letter was widely shared and had real material effects. Dickens and the common man might not have been able to exterminate the Indian race, but their representatives in the British military certainly could. After taking the Raj's Palace in 1857, British soldiers slaughtered everyone inside the Palace, those protecting the City gates, and thousands of others, including "the mass murder of everyone in [Kucha Chelan, a quarter of Delhi]" (Dalrymple 357). One survivor of the British massacre, Qadir Alin, described the scene as "like a Place of Judgment... and prisoners were being shot rather than hanged" (358). The bloodthirstiness of Dickens's proclamation captures a very real and murderous demand for *judgment*. Historian William Dalrymple writes that during the period following the Uprising "daily hangings and murders were the norm rather than the exception, and were looked upon by the British with something approaching boredom" (396). Many of the men in the British military held views similar to those of Dickens. In a letter to Queen Victoria written a month prior Dickens's letter to Miss Coutts, Lord Canning describes

> a rabid and indiscriminate vindictiveness abroad, even amongst many who out to set a better example, which is impossible to contemplate without something like a feeling of shame for one's fellow countrymen. Not one man in ten seems to think that the hanging and shooting of 40 or 50,000 Mutineers beside other rebels can be otherwise than practicable and right. (qtd. in Dalrymple 371–72)

Just as Dickens could intuit and remediate the feelings of precarity, vulnerability, and economic inequality that marked British culture, he also could intuit the violent feelings of a British imperialism forced to confront its power and vulnerability, feelings that could also elicit shame.

The paragraph immediately preceding Dickens's call for genocide reveals that his murderous reflexes were part of a broader desire to construct a particular form of militarized subjectivity for British men:

> When I see people writing letters in the Times day after day, about this class and that class not joining the Army and having no interest in arms—and how we all know that we have suffered a system to go on, which has blighted generous ambition, and put reward out of the common man's reach—and how our gentry have disarmed our Peasantry—and I become Demonaical. (*Letters* 8, 459)

His "Demonaical" concern that the Army has cut off "the common man" from military service is revealing. The common man's distance from the military and a strong sense of duty to Britain, he proposes, is a result of the gentry's decision to disarm a potential unruly underclass. It would be better, in Dickens's view, to rely on hegemony rather than coercion: expanded military service could salvage an otherwise "blighted... generous ambition" in the underclasses. This militarist imagining seems of a piece with Dickens's suggestion in *The Old Curiosity Shop* that a dematerialized, sentimental notion of home could offer a fuller sense of national belonging than one predicated on aristocratic notions of place and property. In the nearly twenty years since *The Old Curiosity Shop*, however, it is no mistake that this imagined domesticity has become directly connected to an aggrieved and racist militarism.

This is not simply because Dickens's son Walter had left for India as an East Indian Company cadet four months prior to Dickens's letter (see Nayder 245). The years following the Uprising reveal that Dickens was not alone in his belief that Britain should arm "the common man." In May 1859, Parliament authorized the creation of a new Volunteer corps, separate and different from the common militia, in response to multiple foreign threats, including an 1858 assassination attempt against Napoleon III which originated in London and increasing tension with the United States in the run-up to the US Civil War. Prince Albert wrote out their first directives, creating what were to be self-funding Volunteer militias—in essence, in the words of historian Ian Beckett, "exclusive middle-class clubs" (Beckett 169). Initially, joining a Volunteer militia was a significant personal expense: Volunteers were expected to purchase their uniforms, rifles, and pay various membership fees, in large part to maintain class boundaries (see Beckett 171). As a result, the early Volunteer rifle corps had little in the way of hierarchy or order. Beckett explains that "discipline was simply expected of gentlemen and would be enforced only by petty fines" (170). Gentry stepped into this vacuum of leadership and effectively recreated the military and social hierarchies which Dickens decries in his letter. Indeed, after the first flush of enthusiasm, the class composition of the Volunteers shifted from gatherings of upper-middle class men to units of tradesmen and artisans commanded by the gentry and supported politically by the Tories.

The rise of the Volunteer forces in the early 1860s, however, indicates the depths of the crisis of imperial masculinity that Dickens's letter suggests, and reveals a deep-seated desire to reshape white British masculinity as a particular form of militarized middle-class maleness. The Volunteers were understood to be a useful mechanism for character formation, a new operator of military order for the common man. This focus on orderliness was not a result of the forces' later class composition but present from the beginning. One famous element in the media push for the creation of Volunteer forces was Alfred Lord Tennyson's poem "The War," published anonymously in *The Times* a month before the signing of the order authorizing the militias. Tennyson later revised the poem and retitled it "Riflemen Form!" as a result of enthusiasm for the Volunteers. The poem's central motif is the role of order:

There is a sound of thunder afar,
Storm in the south that darkens the day,
Storm of battle and thunder of war,
Well, if it do not roll our way.
Form! form! Riflemen form!
Ready, be ready to meet the storm!
Riflemen, riflemen, riflemen form!

Be not deaf to the sound that warns!
Be not gull'd by a despot's plea!
Are figs of thistles or grapes of thorns?
How should a despot set men free?
Form! form! Riflemen form!
Ready, be ready to meet the storm!
Riflemen, riflemen, riflemen form!

Let your Reforms for a moment go,
Look to your butts and make good aims.
Better a rotten borough or so,
Than a rotten fleet or a city of flames!
Form! form! Riflemen form!
Ready, be ready to meet the storm!
Riflemen, riflemen, riflemen form!

Form, be ready to do or die!
Form in freedom's name and the Queen's!
True, that we have a faithful ally,
But only the devil knows what he means!
Form! form! Riflemen form!
Ready, be ready to meet the storm!
Riflemen, riflemen, riflemen form! (T.)

Tennyson's repetitions of "form!" are imperative commands and create rhymed order against the disorder of "storm!", a response to a perceived vulnerability to disorderliness. "Form" can seem a call to interpretation, a demand that one makes sense of an otherwise insensible chaos. Yet the call is situated at an impasse of interpretation, a call to act and not to act. Tennyson uses form to justify the existing political and economic order against demands for reform. Form, not reform, he insists. Tennyson's poem thus indicates that the Volunteers offered a kind of ordering refrain more than a punitive disciplinary regime. Discipline, of which military order is a key example, is a technology of elite rule over other unruly classes. The form of the Volunteer rifle militias was more of an *askesis*, a production of character.[3] The presumption that the Volunteers would promote an orderly character made of them a technology for middle-class character formation, an image of self-directed gentlemanliness engaged in leisurely but orderly outdoor activity. Volunteer training was repetitive, but its repetitions allowed Victorian men to organize their perceived political, economic, and gendered vulnerabilities in acts and displays that assuaged their concerns without challenging or changing any of their actual vulnerabilities. It was a technology of character formation without reformation.

In *David Copperfield* and the early 1850s, the problems posed by early liberal discourses of character appeared as a quandary, caught between the too-firm and personal character of Victorian professional work and a more malleable and impersonal character solicited by an increasingly financialized world. By the time of *Great Expectations*, the contours of liberal notions of character had become more pronounced, in particular a renewed insistence on the firmness of character that *Copperfield* undermines. John Stuart Mill's 1841 discussion of character attempted to nuance the relation of freedom and necessity by focusing on the ability of character to shape circumstances, to bring a force of will on what is exterior. By 1859, character's primary advocate was Samuel Smiles, author of *Self-Help; with illustrations of Character, Conduct, and Perseverance*. Smiles emphasizes the centrality of the individual as a person. Like Mill, Smiles stresses the importance of will to character but rejects any notion that circumstances could affect character, a view he disparagingly calls "the metaphysics of socialism" (qtd. in Briggs 127). For Smiles, "character is not impressed upon [a man] by nature, but formed, out of no peculiarly fine elements, by himself" (*Self-Help* 384). Character, according to Smiles,

is human nature in its best form. It is moral order embodied in the individual. Men of character are not only the conscience of society, but in every well-governed State they are its best motive power; for it is moral qualities in the main which rule the world. (*Self-Help* 383)

This embodying of character in the individual makes Smiles' "men of character" the engines which drive social, political, and economic governance and keeps them autonomous from exterior forces. Character remains untarnished by negative events; instead, "it is in misfortune that the character of the upright man shines forth with the greatest lustre; and when all else fails, he takes his stand upon his integrity and his courage" (*Self-Help* 385). This retreat from determinist readings of character and its implication of social permeability submit that character formation is difficult at the moment that character becomes a key source of success and succor.

Discussions of character thus increasingly focus not on character construction but ways to mitigate character failure. As Stefan Collini explains, mid-century discussions of character saw as an explicitly imperial problem and the solutions it advocated to support character were manly will, habits, and a cynical anti-sentimentalism when "traveling to ... unknown futures" (113). Collini shows that Victorians understood habits as a crucial support for men to maintain "self-restraint, perseverance, strenuous effort, [and] courage in the face of adversity" through any experience of isolation or temptation (100). Walter Bagehot would later argue that this power of habit offers significant national benefits by unifying a culture in what he terms "the cake of custom" (4:445). Character and custom thus helped manage populations in the face of the unknown decisions administrators would have to take. Yet Bagehot understood that such customs could inhibit the development of individuals and of nations. Too heavy a reliance on habits could trap men and nations, to use Bagehot's metaphor, in the cake's "thick crust" (4:474). Partisans of the Volunteer forces, however, insisted the habits of soldiering could shape personal character for the better. Becket writes that popular support for the Volunteers included men such as Smiles, Thomas Hugh, and Matthew Arnold, and was due to their belief that "drill, discipline, and healthy exercise were held to promote habits of order, obedience, cleanliness, and punctuality as well as social harmony" (178). These improved qualities came to be viewed as economically advantageous "to volunteer and employer alike" (178).

Likely the promise of economic advantage as much as the protection against moral failure made the Volunteers appealing to the working-class men who eventually made up the bulk of its ranks in the 1870s and beyond. The initial crop of Volunteers, however, was more likely to come from the professional world, in part because the professions were already well versed in the benefits of character for social and economic advancement, as we saw in Chapter 4. In metropolitan areas, clerical workers dominated Volunteer forces during the 1860s. As historian Gregory Anderson notes, the Volunteers provided clerks with status compensation by allowing them to interact socially with their employers (74). The Volunteers also gave professional workers a point of entry into what Karen Harvey has called the nineteenth century's turn to "rougher, tougher and more taciturn styles of manhood" (69). The entrance of gentlemen and gentlemanly aspirational workers into military garb made the Volunteers targets for ironic commentary, most especially for the Volunteers' fascination with uniforms and their undisciplined behavior. Even publications that supported the Volunteers treated them as figures of fun. Throughout 1860, *Punch* subjected the Volunteers to mockery in cartoons that also often expressed their support. Cartoons focused on the comedic possibilities of drill as soldiers make jokes such as "There's a Ballo....on!" ("Diversions of Drill"). Other cartoons emphasize the steadfastness of the new Volunteers. One, titled "THE VOLUNTEER MOVEMENT," depicts a Frenchman speaking to an Englishman while Volunteers march by, and is captioned with this dialogue: "Foreign Party: Mais, Mosieu Boot, I ave all ways thought you vass great Shopkeepare! Mr Boot: I am, Moosoo—and these are some of the Boys who mind the Shop!—Comprenny?" (24). Another cartoon locates the spectator behind a marching column of Volunteers with the caption: "A view of our Volunteers as they will never be seen by the enemy!" ("A view" 234). During the summer of 1860, *Punch* also featured comic articles advertising "the UMBRELLA RIFLE, which has been introduced by [Mr Punch] expressly to meet the requirements of the present rainy season" ("Umbrella Rifle" 10) and proposing "to get up a Rifle Corps for ladies" ("Ladies' Own" 19).

Dickens's encounters with the Volunteers during this period reflect a similar attitude of irony and enthusiasm. His first contact appears to be when a recruiting march passed near Gad's Hill on 13 June 1859. The Volunteers, Dickens writes, "started off at eleven very spare in numbers, and came back considerably recruited, which looks to me like the difference between going to church and coming to dinner" (*Letters* 9, 77). The chief attractions of Volunteering, Dickens implies, are colorful uniforms and food. He writes:

> They bore no end of bright banners and broad sashes, and had a band with a terrific drum, and are now (at half-past two) dining at The Falstaff, partly in the side room on the ground-floor, and partly in a tent improvised this morning. (*Letters* 9, 77)

Dickens's son Charley joined the Volunteers in 1860, an interesting turn since Dickens had thwarted Charley's earlier desire to join the Army and Walter's service with the East India Company indicates that he was not opposed all such careers. Dickens focuses on Charley's appearance in uniform, writing that he "[distinguished] himself by looking (in his uniform) extremely like an able-bodied pauper" (*Letters* 9, 219). Elsewhere, he writes that he "put the Volunteer mettle to the proof by turning [Charley] out at 3 o'clock this morning on a false alarm of somebody prowling in the garden" (*Letters* 9, 233). Charley's participation seems to have given Dickens's account of the Volunteers an especially ironic edge. In part, this may be a result of continuing tensions with Charley, who is rumored to have encountered his father with Ellen Ternan prior to his parents' separation (see Nayder 260) and is known to have sided with Catherine immediately afterward (see Tomalin 296). It may also be a response to the resemblance that Dickens saw between himself and Charley as his son began to pursue romantic relationships (see Nayder 234). Dickens's ambivalent feelings about his son and youth thus color most of his accounts of the Volunteers. He drops his irony, however, when he writes about them and the threat posed by Napoleon III. To a French correspondent, he writes

> I have not shouldered my rifle yet, but I should do so on more pressing occasion. Every other man in the row of men I know—if they were all put in a row—is a Volunteer though. There is a tendency rather to overdo the wearing of the uniform, but that is natural enough in the case of the youngest men. The turn-out is generally very creditable indeed. (*Letters* 9, 248)

Yet the suggestion of "youngest men" leads to another jab at Charley as Dickens recounts an anecdote he retails to multiple correspondents in his letters:

> At the Ball they had (in a perfectly unventilated building), their new leather belts and pouches smelt so fearfully that it was, as my eldest daughter said, like shoemaking in a great prison. She consequently distinguished herself by fainting away in the most inaccessible place in the whole structure, and being brought out (horizontally) by a file of Volunteers, like some slain daughter of Albion whom they were carrying into the street, to rouse the indignant valour of the populace. (*Letters* 9, 248)

For Dickens, then, the Volunteers were the ambivalent figures they proved for *Punch*, figures to be ironized and embraced as the standard bearers for a defensive masculinity, uncertain of their capacities yet also primed to protect Britain's women against foreign invasion. Yet as Dickens's biography suggests, there is some uncertainty about the worthiness or necessity of this masculine protection of feminine virtue, a resistance and ironizing of masculinity and romantic relations that will also mark *Great Expectations* itself.

This approving if ironical attitude appears throughout the coverage of the Volunteers in the pages of *All the Year Round*. In the year before the novel's serialization, *AYR* ran an essay endorsing a new scheme to recruit naval Volunteers and end impressment ("Royal Naval Volunteers") and one on the creation of a Volunteer cavalry corps ("Volunteer Cavalry"). The issue containing the novel's sixteenth and seventeenth chapters also includes a first-person account of "musketry instruction" for Volunteers—from Charley, perhaps?—that emphasizes the enthusiasm and athleticism of the experience ("Volunteers at Hythe"). Shortly after the novel's serial run concluded *AYR* ran a follow-up piece about a Volunteer's experience of a field day of drills ("A Field Day"). Each piece endorsed the Volunteer movement and evinced concern about whether Volunteers would be as effective as regular soldiers and remain culturally distinct. Its commendations of the Volunteers are often filtered through a light class-based irony that echoes the ironies of Pip's narratorial reflections, particularly in "Volunteers at Hythe." The narrator of this piece begins by stating, "no artist was ever mad enough to paint Hythe" and insists that he was simply

> a volunteer who cares only to seize facts, and has a fancy for exhibiting their skeletons. Would anybody like to see the Skeleton of a Fortnight—the skeleton of a fortnight that I spent in attendance on the course of musketry drill at Hythe? (402)

The narrator proceeds to mock grammatical errors in a dining hall sign and throughout gestures toward the class and educational differences between Volunteers and their soldier-instructors. This insertion of class distinction also appears in the piece about a Volunteer cavalry; the writer insists that Volunteer uniforms should be "workman-like... with a view to their being useful and appropriate in the field, [rather] than handsome, or what young ladies call 'lovely,' in the ball-room" ("Volunteer Cavalry" 331). By denuding military dress of its career connotation, drab uniforms could mitigate class and status concerns between respectable Volunteers and soldiers. With these status distinctions in place, *AYR*'s two first-person narratives suggest, military practice and drills could form useful new masculine habits; the first piece describes the rigmarole of learning to shoot, march, and parade, and the second their application in military field exercises.

The affective ambivalence here will become more apparent in our later discussion of *Great Expectations*, but one can note this ambivalence in the novel simply in its representation of soldiers as figures of fun that suggest both a defensive masculinity and a worrying confusion of social hierarchy. Hence the novel's soldiers police the boundaries of social order yet remain distinct from it. Its most charismatic soldier is the sergeant who captures Magwitch, yet his flattery of Pumblechook and heavy drinking do little to mark his character as orderly. Other soldiers in the novel appear aimless, lazy, and morally lax, whether they

> stood about, as soldiers do; now, with their hands loosely clasped before them; now, resting a knee or a shoulder; now, easing a belt or a pouch; now, opening the door to spit stiffly over their high stocks, out into the yard. (5:31)

Or fall asleep in a disinterested pile like animals "not much interested in us, but just lifted their heads and took a sleepy stare, and then lay down again" (5:39). As if to underline the male soldier's lazy and untrustworthy character, Wemmick introduces Pip to "the Colonel" in Newgate as "a soldier in the line and bought his discharge" before noting his imminent execution for forging coins (32:262). Throughout the novel, soldiers are at best disinterested in the law they enforce and at worst searching for ways to escape it. It is thus telling that when Pip encounters social demands he wants to escape, whether from Joe as a blacksmith's apprentice or from Magwitch as the convict's gentleman, he thinks he might "go for a soldier" (41:342). Soldiers are ambivalent figures in the novel, enforcers of social discipline whose existence on the edge of such discipline affords them the possibility of escape.

This characterological ambivalence allows soldiers to figure psychological ambivalence toward social discipline. Magwitch tells Pip that during his night on the marshes he sees the soldiers, with their red coats lighted up by the torches carried afore, closing in round him. ... Why, if I see one pursuing party last night – coming up in order, Damn 'em, with their tramp, tramp – I see a hundred. (3:20)

Magwitch's horror is as much of the order in the soldiers' "tramp, tramp" as of capture itself. For Pip the soldier is at once the threat and promise of order. When he and Joe eat dinner, "we had our slices served out, as if we were two thousand troops on a forced march instead of a man and boy at home" (4:22). For Pip, to become a solider is to escape into a kind of orderly social nothingness and he only resists this temptation initially out of love for Joe: "It was not because I was faithful, but because Joe was faithful, that I never ran away and went for a soldier or a sailor" (14:108). This fantasy returns once Magwitch reveals his patronage and Pip again turns to the fantasy of the soldier: "Once, I actually did start out of bed in the night, and begin to dress myself in my worst clothes, hurriedly intending to leave him there with everything else I possessed, and enlist for India as a private soldier" (40:338). Importantly, though soldiering remains in the novel a fantasy of escape, when Pip tells Herbert of his plan, he replies, "soldiering won't do" (41:342). Herbert interprets Pip's plan to escape into the Army as a search for another kind of order, economic security and a calling. Pip at this moment is neither a gentleman nor a solider but an agent in search of meaning. Herbert thus suggests that he "would be infinitely better in Clarriker's house, small as it is" (41:343). Yet this work entails a step down in social position, and thus Herbert in "his delicacy was avoiding the right word, so I said, 'A clerk'" (55:450). Like Charley, Pip cannot go for a soldier, but he can volunteer.

In this act of voluntary abasement, *Great Expectations* reveals something crucial about its affective form, something inseparable from the discourses of character that also marked the emergence of the Volunteers. Here and in the final section of the novel, Pip willingly displays his economic and personal vulnerability and confronts the feelings of shame and contempt that have pervaded his life in order to produce a new character. As we will see, this new character is one in which his shame and personal suffering become the basis for a suspension of affectivity, for a character based in disinterest and self-control.

Interpretation, Irony, Affect

As most readers will recognize, Pip's vulnerability is the basis for the novel's irony: the Pip who confronts his vulnerability narrates the character-Pip who is driven by the same "certain shrinking sensitiveness" that Dickens describes in himself. As a character and a narrator, Pip *is* multiple. For critics such as Peter Brooks, Caroline Levine, and Jon

B. Reed, the irony of Pip's multiplicity is based on Pip's overcoming this division. He comes to know himself by remedying the division between what he knows as a narrator and the interpretative mistakes he makes as a character. *Great Expectations* is thus often cast as a novel about interpretation, specifically about the ways that interpretation produces a coherent subject, and affective concerns merely inhibit Pip's achievement of self-knowledge.[4] To engage with the novel's affective form, then, we need to step back from interpretations focused on unified subjectivity, knowledge, and interpretation and to reconsider irony, the style with which Dickens, *AYR*, and *Punch* treated the Volunteers.

Georg Lukács's account of irony would seem dispositive for a reading of *Great Expectations* as a tale of unified subjectivity: the play of irony transmutes the mundane details of daily existence and allows the biographical form of a life to become an aesthetic totality able to rival that of the epic. Irony thus coheres and transmutes a life into art. Paul De Man, however, reveals a fundamental rhetorical incommensurability between the aesthetic totality and lived contingencies in Lukács's analysis.[5] In "The Rhetoric of Temporality," de Man argues that irony is not the coherence of the biographical and aesthetic but their persistent division. Ironic texts remain divided between an empirical self unaware of its ironic situation and a linguistically constituted self aware of its own ironicalness. This division has a particular temporality. Ironic transcendence exists in the present tense of narration and textual uptake and pushes a character's empirical experience into an inaccessible past and future. Irony can thus seem to be the motive force of a Hegelian dialectical struggle, a contestation that produces a new knowing totality. De Man insists, however, that irony refuses the logic of sublation. The two selves of irony do not even compose an intersubjective relation. They are rather what he terms a "reflective disjunction," one that "transfers the self out of the empirical world into a world constituted out of, and in, language" (213). It is thus a "degradation" of irony "for the ironic subject to construe its function as one of assistance to the original self and to act as if it existed for the sake of this world-bound person" (217). Irony means to keep these empirical and linguistic selves distinct and thus to generate a situation in which there is "no end... no totality" (222). To leave the ironic position of narration and language for action in the diegetic world is to fall into an intersubjective relation, one that means to ameliorate an empirical condition rather than reflect on the fraught and unresolvable division between a subject and an impersonal force of narration.[6] To take ironic reflection for a process that produces interpretative knowledge, then, is to undercut a text's irony and direct readers away from its material operations.

De Man's theory of irony suggests that to read *Great Expectations* as a story about interpretation is to miss the point. One might object that the narrative of *Great Expectations* encourages readers to fall into interpretative questions and intersubjectivity rather than to maintain irony and plural subjectivity in an unresolvable present.[7] Critics such as Q.D. Leavis and Brian McFarlane, however, have rightly argued that Pip as a character and Pip as a narrator remain incommensurable.[8] Pip's position at the novel's end—with or without Estella and narrating at one remove from this final episode—reinforces this interpretation and suggests that the novel is more an ironic text than a pedagogical one. Yet if *Great Expectations* is not about interpretation, what is it about? Here, I believe, the affective helps. The novel's irony is one of Pip's vulnerability. For the text, this appears as feelings to be represented in narration and reflected upon by the narrator. Prior critical analyses of feeling in the novel reduce these feelings to a single term, guilt. For Julian Monyahan, Pip's guilt generates Orlick and Drummle as his Gothic doubles, and Q.D. Leavis's perceptive account of the novel highlights guilt's narrative importance. For Leavis, Pip is conditioned by his feelings of guilt and must escape these emotions by

> ordering [his impulses] according to a code he acquires through trial and error and self-examination of an open kind ... that at the crisis of his life... he is able to master his immediate reactions and control them, substituting a 'better' mode of feeling and action, not of course by forcing them on himself as a duty, but by understanding himself and his needs more fully so that his new self is produced of free choice, a choice that is seen to be steadily prepared for, unconscious of it though Pip has been, by undercurrents of feeling since his first association with 'his' convict. (287)

Leavis captures the function of emotion in the novel but treats its emotions as given. Guilt in the novel thus has no texture or form. It is simply an obstacle to be overcome. Pip's tale for Leavis, then, is essentially one of humanist self-construction, a reading that makes the novel's irony one of intersubjective self-construction.

When the novel's irony is foregrounded, however, the division of narrating subject and characterological object in *Great Expectations* reveals the complex operation in the novel of the affects it signals, beginning with guilt.[9] The work of psychologist Silvan Tomkins suggests an analysis of guilt in the novel should be replaced by an analysis of the two affects that guilt encompasses, contempt and shame. These affects are strongly linked by their opposed relationship to objects. Contempt is in some ways closer to guilt. "Much of what has been called guilt we would call internalized contempt," he writes, and acts as "a type of punishment for norm violation" (*Shame* 144). Contempt's primary operation, Tomkins explains, is "a literal pulling away from the object [of disgust]" (*Shame* 135).[10] Shame maps a contrary movement. Where contempt pulls away from a rejected object, shame draws closer to the object that rejects, an affect that connects one to an object and insists on one's separation from it. Where contempt is an affect of exclusion, shame is one of inclusion, making it "the negative affect linked with love and identification" (*Shame* 139).

As we will see, these affects are red threads running through *Great Expectations*, threads that reveal the ways in which the text is constructed, emotions signaled, and scenes produced. To examine shame and contempt, however, is not to restate guilt's importance to the novel. Instead it highlights the fragmented processes of subject production that the irony of the text and Pip's plurality suggest and offers a particular set of mechanisms by which these processes operate. In Tomkins's work, shame is crucial to the construction of the self, the affective experience of self-consciousness as such. One might best understand its operation in conjunction with psychologist Daniel Stern's work on attunement and misattunement. Stern's work focuses on the earliest experiences of love and identification between caregiver and infant. His term attunement describes a transubjective fusion with the beloved object which exceeds the limits of personal identification and offers a process of becoming through which vitality affects—stylistic repetitions of intensity, timing, and shape—bring mother and infant together. Stern also notes misattunements, ways of shaping and manipulating behaviors through mismatches of emotions or vitality affects—a softer pat, a slower repetition, or a larger movement may intensify or dampen a mood.[11] Shame, Tomkins explains, begins as an abrogation of the apparently undivided relationship between infant and caregiver, when infants lose sight of their caregivers' faces. It is a falling out of attunement. Such misattunement also marks the experience of the gazes of strangers. Shame creates identity by foregrounding the looker's implication in the act of looking, drawing the looker into the world while heightening the looker's sense of self as looking. In Tomkins's words, "In shame, I wish to continue to look and to be looked at, but I also do not wish to do so" (*Shame* 137). This fractured quality of shame is one reason why Tomkins argues that shame may skid out of control, a process that he calls "affect promiscuity," "an intensification of any affect [such] that objects for affect investment are sought indiscriminately" (*AIC* 2:270). The imprecise language of guilt underscores an individualization of feeling as felt responsibility. Attention to shame and contempt, by contrast, highlight their intense sociality. Indeed, Tomkins argues shame and contempt have their own politics. Democracies, he writes, rely on "empathic shame" (*Shame* 139). Shame provides "a perfect vehicle for the transmission and preservation of social norms from generation to generation" (*Shame* 156). By contrast, Tomkins argues that contempt, which punishes objects that violate norms, is a key affect for hierarchical societies because it helps to "maintain distance between individuals, classes, and nations" (*Shame* 139).

The plot and themes of *Great Expectations*, the problems of social mobility and class shame, reveal it to be a novel caught in the skein of this affective political tension, torn between a norm-reproducing shame and a hierarch- reinforcing contempt. Guilt is a part of this problem—Pip's guilt for abandoning Joe above all—but Pip's guilt is better understood as an admixture of his shame of and contempt for Joe. It is this mixture of feeling and its different proportions that the novel explores. Shame is of particular importance for the novel's formal construction because its focus on visual relations and the self fundamentally alters the text's use of sentimentality and scenes of sentimental spectatorship. Shame recalls the visual mechanisms and object relations of Smithian sympathy but it shifts its emphasis from moral judgment assumed in theories of drive to sympathetic attunement assumed in theories of affect. The psychological analysis of shame and contempt thus gestures toward a suggestion that Adam Smith makes only in passing, not of a judgmental man in the breast who observes our actions but of a continued modulation of feeling between sufferer and observer. For Smith, this process should produce what he calls "the harmony of society" (*Theory* 1.4.7:27), a kind of affective attunement between sufferer and spectator (see Chapter 1 for further discussion). As Tomkins's analysis of shame and contempt reveals, these modulations of feeling operate through differential relations between observer and observed, the observer's response to the observed and the observed's response to the observer constructing a sociality premised on experiences and losses of attunement and misattunement.[12] This affective analysis has particular ramifications for Pip as a character and a narrator. The ironic Pip-as-narrator is less Smith's superego-like man in the breast than an onlooker in problematic attunement with Pip's continually modulated experiences of wishing to-look-and-be-looked-at and not-to-look-or-be-looked-at, an ironic reduplication of shame as a narrative drive to examine and not to examine one's past.[13] One might take this as Dickens's own multiplied relation to his past, a display without displaying, a looking-at that will and will not be recognized, but it is also something more.

Shame, Contempt, and "The Identity of Things"

Shame's visual operations mark the novel's intensely visual opening pages as Pip discovers his identity through encounters with familial and strange gazes. It is this experience of fundamental vulnerability, vulnerability prior to any constituted subjectivity, that marks the novel's use of shame. Shame is the coming-to-be of a subject in its feelings of abandonment by caregivers and of threat from strangers, and the novel opens with an isolated Pip experiencing the failure of the reassuring attuned gaze of his mother. A signifier of the gaze has replaced the signified, a linguistic relation between Pip and the material inscription of his mother's gravestone. He thus infers his family characteristics and sense of belonging with another "from the character and turn of the inscription" and focuses on the idea that these characters reveal "that my mother was freckled and sickly" (1:3). The displacement of identification allows Pip to gaze and to be gazed at but only through signification. The novel's opening sequence thus captures the text's ironic detachment of diegetic character and character-narrator through this distanced commentary on Pip and his mother in the bonds of signifying attunement. Magwitch's appearance breaks this transsubjective experience and inaugurates his shame. A winding 124-word sentence intimates the appearance of the stranger's gaze, its focus moving across the churchyard like a roving camera eye as it pulls tighter around the visually and graphically minute figure of Pip:

At such a time I found out for certain that this bleak place overgrown with nettles was the churchyard; and that Philip Pirrip, late of this parish, and also Georgiana wife of the above, were dead and buried; and that Alexander, Bartholomew, Abraham, Tobias, and Roger, infant children of the aforesaid, were also dead and buried; and that the dark flat wilderness beyond the churchyard, intersected with dikes and mounds and gates, with scattered cattle feeding on it, was the marshes; and that the low leaden line beyond was the river; and that the distant savage lair from which the wind was rushing was the sea; and that the small bundle of shivers growing afraid of it all and beginning to cry, was Pip. (1:3–4)

The passage presents Pip to readers as an identity prior to his recognition of himself, yet it is Magwitch's appearance that gives Pip his "first most vivid and broad impression of the identity of things" and makes it a "memorable raw afternoon" (1:3). This arresting opening image of signification visually tracking and identifying Pip narrates his coming into being as a temporal torsion: his shame retrospectively identifies him at the nexus of three gazes—the blind gaze of the signifier, the yet-to-come gaze of the stranger, and his retrospective gaze—where he is—as a character—not yet. The fundamental separation of Pip as character and as narrator appears in this initial temporal emptiness, a processual coming into being through the confrontation of gazes and the churn of feelings, a linguistic placeholder rather than an identity.

Magwitch's gaze means to pin Pip into place and it is this demanding gaze that produces Pip's shame and underscores his physical vulnerability, from the threat to "cut your throat" (1:4) to Magwitch turning him upside down. Shame is also caught from Magwitch, a result of his physical vulnerability as an escaped convict and of his domination by Compeyson, a situation that he expresses as one of his racialized subjection: he "made me his black slave" (42:350). Pip's initial experience of shame also reveals its promiscuity as his desire to meet and explore this gaze produces more shame. It is this problem that Pip experiences in the scene of Magwitch's capture. Pip anxiously signals that he is not responsible for the pursuit and receives an indelible look from the convict: "if he had looked at me for an hour or for a day, I could not have remembered his face ever afterwards, as being more attentive" (5:38). Juxtaposed with Compeyson's refusal to look Magwitch in the face—Magwitch shouts, "He never looked at me" (5:37)—this visual recognition forms an intimate connection between the two. Pip's shame—the desire to look and be looked at and not to look or be looked at—thus becomes a kind of attunement: "I looked at him eagerly when he looked at me" (5:38). Pip's subsequent shame is also the result of this desire for and reception of the convict's recognition, in large part because this attunement puts him out of attunement with another stranger and his intimate gaze, Joe. As he later reflects: "it was for the convict, guilty of I knew not what crimes, and liable to be taken out of those rooms where I sat thinking, and hanged at the Old Bailey door, that I had deserted Joe" (39:323). If like Dickens's "certain shrinking sensitiveness" Pip becomes "morally timid and very sensitive" (8:63) after these events, the novel presents this as a result of his fear that his encounter with the convict will cause him to lose Joe's recognition and care. Although Joe makes it clear that he pities the captured convicts, Pip reflects that he never told Joe he had taken the file and food:

> The fear of losing Joe's confidence, and of thenceforth sitting in the chimney corner at night staring drearily at my forever lost companion and friend, tied up my tongue. I morbidly represented to myself that if Joe knew it, I never afterwards could see him at the fireside feeling his fair whisker, without thinking that he was meditating on it. That, if Joe knew it, I never afterwards could see him glance, however casually, at yesterday's meat or pudding when it came on to-day's table, without thinking that he was debating whether I had been in the pantry. That, if Joe knew it, and at any subsequent period of our joint domestic life remarked that his beer was flat or thick, the conviction that he suspected Tar in it, would bring a rush of blood to my face. (6:41)

Pip calls this decision to suppress the truth "cowardly" (6:41) but he comes to it by his feared loss of recognition from the one person who gave him unequivocal love. His shame is inseparable from the discovery that they have fallen out of attunement. Because his shame is a result of how he imagines he would feel *if* Joe knew—a feeling about a potential problem that he replays again and again—it fundamentally alters his habits of mind and feeling. His need to "morbidly" dwell on the physiological expression of shame, "a rush of blood to my face," underscores shame and its promiscuity as a kind of bad emotional habit.

Shame's promiscuity is perhaps most clearly demonstrated in Pip's description of Smithfield market as a "shameful place, being all asmear with filth and fat and blood and foam, [and it] seemed to stick to me" (20:165). Yet shame's promiscuity also draws Pip into the otherwise repellent situation at Satis House and toward people and objects that hold him in contempt. Satis House provides Pip with objects able to produce the shame he conjures alone by the fire. Pip and Estella's first game of beggar-my-neighbor provides the novel's affective situation in miniature: "I had never thought of being ashamed of my hands before; but I began to consider them a very indifferent pair. Her contempt was so strong, that it became infectious and I caught it" (8:60). The infection here is not, however, a simple transmission of feeling.[14] Pip catches the contours and intensities of Estella's contempt, tries to be with her in this feeling and fails. Then he turns to shame. Rather than promoting a *feeling with*, infection manipulates Pip's propensity to feel, working on Pip's desire for shame to produce a kind of misattunement. Here too shame's promiscuity encourages Pip in new habits. He reflects on the day:

> I fell asleep recalling what I 'used to do' when I was at Miss Havisham's; as though I had been there weeks or months, instead of hours; as though it were quite an old subject of remembrance instead of one that had arisen only that day. (9:72)

For *Great Expectations*, shame and contempt are not at odds but a pair. Contempt promotes shame and shame seeks out contempt to experience more shame, to feed the habit of shame.

Much as shame's promiscuity promotes Pip's change in character by altering his habits, his encounter with Estella reveals that his habits may be altered by the work of others, most especially the work of women. Estella and Miss Havisham can produce or encourage Pip to produce shame himself and thus to alter his character. The text's gendering of affective work suggests Estella's story, which often seems parallel to that of Pip, is in fact quite different.[15] It is a story of what Sara Ahmed calls "mood work" ("Not in the Mood" 19), the work of trying to manage the emotions of others in a situation that often falls on the politically and historically excluded or culturally other. For Victorians, the relationship of femininity and mood work was hardly a secret. As Sarah Stickney Ellis wrote in 1843,

> An able and eloquent writer on Woman's Mission has justly observed that woman's strength is in her influence... you are by nature endowed with peculiar faculties with a quickness of perception, facility of adaptation, and acuteness of feeling, which fit you especially for the part you have to act in life and which, at the same time, render you, in a higher degree than men, susceptible both of pain and pleasure. (11–12)

As a character, Estella may reject this notion of the feminine as more feeling, but she retains the sense that women were culturally authorized to "influence" men and exemplifies the concern that women would threaten male domination if they used their felt influence to achieve their own desires. In Satis House, feminine mood work becomes a Gothic nightmare with Estella a figure for the mercenary mood work of the new woman.[16] Her ends are not so much self-interested as class-focused. Her choices, most especially her marriage to Brummle, indicate that her contempt does indeed mean to reinforce and reproduce class hierarchies. The work of contempt reproduces the demands of the Victorian class system, most especially its attendant notions of deference, respectability, and gentlemanliness, and it shames of Pip for his violations of these class norms.[17] Estella's contempt is affective work on Pip, and the work of misattunement since Pip continually imagines becoming one with her.

Shame and contempt thus reveal a vulnerability in male subjectivity to gendered work. Throughout, Pip's narration disavows this work through ironic counterfactual statements, often in the form of "as if."[18] Hence when Estella "threw the cards down on the table... as if she despised them for having been won of me" (8:61), the narration frames her affect as possibility rather than fact. Yet "as if" has limited protective value. After the game, Estella gives Pip his food "as insolently as if I was a dog in disgrace" (8:62). This "as if" cannot ward off her contempt or his feelings of shame and Pip finds himself caught up in an experience that he either cannot narrate or refuses to for its showing of vulnerability: "I was so humiliated, hurt, spurned, offended, angry, sorry,—I cannot hit upon the right name for the smart—God knows what its name was,—that tears started to my eyes" (8:62). Yet Pip's experience does not stop his desire to be attuned with Estella in her contempt. What he confronts is a problem in the structure of contempt: two people may hold the same object in contempt, but one cannot be attuned with another in contempt *and* be the object of that contempt. As a result, Pip teaches himself self-contempt. Even then, however, he remains unable to share in Estella's contempt and finds "self-humiliation" in his admiration for her and learns "it is a most miserable thing to feel ashamed of home" (14:106). When he comes into his expectations, Pip attempts a solution beyond ironic self-disavowal of his vulnerability: he takes mood work upon himself. Objects of prior attachment such as Joe and Biddy become objects of contempt as they move below him in the social hierarchy. Figures who recall Pip's prior position too closely such as Orlick and Trabb's boy must offer him their obeisance or he refuses to recognize them. This disavowal of past attachments and positions has its limits. Trabb's boy bests Pip in a turn of the contemptible screw by refusing to be shamed by someone he holds in contempt. His parody of Pip—"Don't know yah!" (30:246)—makes it clear that Trabb's boy knows him well enough. Miss Havisham offers

Pip another way to frame his experience of vulnerability, intertwining shame, contempt, and mood work as love. She explains to Pip, "love is blind devotion, unquestioning self-humiliation, utter submission, trust and belief against yourself and against the whole world, giving up your whole heart and soul to the smiter" (29:240). In this model, love is a forceful experience of misattunement, a persistent distancing of self from self and a continual grind to reproduce the one who holds you in contempt all the while wallowing in the shame that contempt produces.

In this convergence of character, shame, and recognition, *Great Expectations* is, if not anti-sentimental, not-quite sentimental. On the one hand, Magwitch's attachment to Pip exhibits the moral sentiments; he insists that even after he has "half forgot wot men's and women's faces wos like, I see yourn [Pip's]" (39:320). On the other hand, Magwitch's gift, at least until his arrival in London, does not attempt to foster mutual recognition but rather *abstract recognition* through cash. Pip concedes that Magwitch "had felt affectionately, gratefully, and generously, towards me with great constancy" (54:446) but the narrative frames his reliance on money as an abstract form of recognition that taints this affection. Only once the money has been lost can Pip see Magwitch as "a much better man than I had been to Joe" (54:446). Here the problem of mood work returns. Money in essence becomes an instrument for affect manipulation, an equivocation perhaps clearest when Estella rewards Pip with a kiss for knocking out Herbert Pocket. He recounts that it "was given to the coarse common boy as a piece of money might have been, and that it was worth nothing" (11:93). Estella later admits that she kissed him in "a spirit of contempt for the fawners and plotters" (33:268) before inviting him to kiss her in the same "spirit," and he does though her "tone... gave me pain" (ibid.). Contemptuous acts and the passage of abstract recognition thus operate in the text as equivalents, instituting hierarchical relations, separating object and subject, and producing shame for the object of contempt. They block sentimental recognition, and shame and contempt become the horizon of all experience. As Pip reflects on his time at Satis House:

What could I become with these surroundings? How could my character fail to be influenced by them? Is it to be wondered at if my thoughts were dazed, as my eyes were, when I came out into the natural light from the misty yellow rooms? (12:96)

"Never be Ashamed of Our Tears": Mist, Repetition, Affect

As the affective forces shaping character, shame and contempt would seem to leave little space for Pip's character to change, a view more in line with Samuel Smiles than Robert Owen. A shared element between

Great Expectations and John Stuart Mill's "On Liberty" may offer a solution: the murderous apprentice George Barnwell. Mill uses Barnwell to consider how one might distinguish immoral characters from characters who differ from social norms:

> George Barnwell murdered his uncle to get money for his mistress, but if he had done it to set himself up in business, he would equally have been hanged. Again, in the frequent case of a man who causes grief to his family by addiction to bad habits, he deserves reproach for his unkindness or ingratitude; but so he may for cultivating habits not in themselves vicious, if they are painful to those with whom he passes his life, or who from personal ties are dependent on him for their comfort. Whoever fails in the consideration generally due to the interests and feelings of others, not being compelled by some more imperative duty, or justified by allowable self-preference, is a subject of moral disapprobation for that failure, but not for the cause of it, nor for the errors, merely personal to himself, which may have remotely led to it. (Mill, *Collected Works* XVII, 218)

This view of habits as problematic insofar as "they are painful to those with whom he passes his life" refines the problem of habit and affect in *Great Expectations*. Pip's shame is a persistent habit, but it matters only to the degree that it affects "the interests and feelings of others." The novel's use of Barnwell underscores the importance of activity to character. When Pumblechook insultingly compares Pip to Barnwell, he tells Pip he will "go wrong" (15:117), a phrase repeated later by Jaggers (20:170). The affective may in part shape Pip's character but the text insists that what matters is his activity, not his affect. This is why Pip refuses to turn to Joe for comfort after he realizes that he "deserted" him for a convict: he "could never, never, never undo what [he] had done" (39:323). The going, the doing, the done, these matter. Shame and contempt may produce affective habits but it is only the expression of these habits—the doing—that makes them character. To alter it, Pip must *do* otherwise.

The interrelation of habitual activity and character deepens the connection between Pip and Magwitch. In Australia, Magwitch too finds himself in a character-testing situation, cast into an unknown future, subject to society's contempt and his own feelings of shame, and possessed by the desire to command contempt himself. His success as a rancher, his dedication to others, and his actions in the face of uncertainty suggest traits that Victorians might recognize in a strong and moral character. Nonetheless, these offer no protection from the potential corrosion of bad habits. Consider Magwitch's boast to Pip:

> "I've come to the old country fur to see my gentleman spend his money *like* a gentleman. That'll be *my* pleasure. *My* pleasure 'ull be

fur to see him do it. And blast you all!" he wound up, looking round the room and snapping his fingers once with a loud snap, "blast you every one, from the judge in his wig, to the colonist a stirring up the dust, I'll show a better gentleman than the whole kit on you put together!" (40:332)

Magwitch's scheme has little concern for the interests and feelings of others. Pip is a gentlemanly simulacrum for his visual pleasure, an embodiment of shame reshaped by wealth into a weapon of contempt. Although Magwitch offers a "grimly-ludicrous" apology to Pip for the "lowness" (40:332) of this outburst, it means to protect his class-fantasy-spectacle from his shame. Only his steadfast adherence to Pip, his interest in another, redeems him.

Pip's redemption similarly comes through a short-circuiting of affective habits for the interests of others. The novel presents this experience not as an affective education but as a forced expulsion "into the natural light from the misty yellow rooms." Yet this willing against habit—the assertion of voluntary control or doing as not doing—does not end Pip's vulnerability. It heightens it. In this way, much as shame and contempt map the emotional contours of the novel, suspension, the doing of not doing, is the affect that marks it most deeply and makes up its affective form. Pip is forced to show and to see what he wishes not to see or be seen. The formal presentation of this experience operates through the presentation of distance, an overcoming of shame and contempt through the examination of feelings and reactions as narrative objects rather than feelings that immerse him in their experience. That character-Pip never catches up to narrator-Pip is not a narrative irresolution but a formal solution to this affective vulnerability, a holding of feeling at a distance that allows Pip as a narrator to feel and not feel at once.

The text captures Pip's change of character not in his actions, reflections on positive change, or good works but in the presentation of a recurrent motif, a rising mist. This image appears three times: at the end of the first stage of Pip's expectations, after their failure, and in his final encounter with Estella. Throughout, Pip treats mist as a blockage to vision and aspiration, both inseparable from shame. In describing his state of mind as Joe's apprentice, Pip states that he

used to stand about … comparing my own perspective with the windy marsh view, and making out some likeness between them by thinking how flat and low both were, and how on both there came an unknown way and a dark mist and then the sea. (14:107)

Mist conveys the novel's clinging atmosphere of shame and contempt as much as Pip's desire to misunderstand his social position. No wonder that the novel's villains rise out of and disappear into the enveloping marsh mist. Pip watches as Compeyson "ran into the mist" (3:18), describes "[stopping] in the mist to listen" as Magwitch files at his fetters (3:20), and discovers Orlick in a "heavy mist" the night he attacks Mrs. Joe (15:118). The convict who gives Pip two one-pound notes describes the marshes with four words: "Mudbank, mist, swamp, and work; work, swamp, mist, and mudbank" (28:229). The text embeds its villains and those who society views with contempt in an atmosphere that conjures Gothic threats and obscures its use of Gothic doubling. Mist thus figures the plot's haze of *méconnaissance* and the immersive emotions that attach to misrecognition, from Pip's early ironic experiences of misrecognition as he runs in search of his convict, the accusing faces of livestock rising up before him, to the day of his humiliating encounter with a newly engaged Estella, which he describes as "wrapped in patches of clouds and rags of mist, like a beggar" (43:354). It culminates in Pip's repudiation of Miss Havisham for "the mistake I have so long remained in" (44:360). Mist is a visual figure for the ache of misrecognition.

This metaphoric use of mist returns us to military questions. Fog is the figure most tightly bound to post-Napoleonic warfare. Carl von Clausewitz famously writes in On *War*:

> The general unreliability of all information presents a special problem in war: all action takes place, so to speak, in a kind of twilight which, like fog or moonlight, often tends to make things seem grotesque and larger than they really are. Whatever is hidden from full view in this feeble light has to be guessed at by talent, or simply left to chance. So once again for lack of objective knowledge one has to trust to talent or to luck. (140)

As Jan Mieszkowski notes, Claueswitz's metaphor of fog "does not obscure so much as it provides a form, albeit a hazy, shifting one, for something more abstract that is not directly accessible to the senses" (19–20). Such abstraction is the simultaneous necessity and impossibility of seeing what Clausewitz calls the "full view." Mieszkowski describes this as a tension in post-Napoleonic texts between "the observational authority of the solitary watcher" and "the need to generalize the substance of the experience via the mind's power to envision something that is not or cannot be directly viewed" (69). In other words, fog offers a figure for the simultaneous possibility and impossibility of objective knowledge, a figure for division that recalls de Man's theory of irony, caught between the limits of the empirical observer and the imagined total knowledge of a transcendent observer. For the post-Napoleonic era, war emerges, in Anders Engberg-Pederson's words, as an "empire of chance," a contest of contingencies. Cultural texts from the end of the eighteenth century through the nineteenth treat war in this fashion, turning to irony's suspension between the empirical and transcendent to navigate war's suspensions of the contingent.[19] The rising mist of *Great Expectations* straddles this division, at once suggesting an empirical character-based mistake and its evaporation in the distant and full knowing vision of the narrator. Consider the mist's second appearance as Pip wonders about the extent of Joe's knowledge: "But whether Joe knew how poor I was, and how my great expectations had all dissolved, like our own marsh mists before the sun, I could not understand" (57:469–70). Like "natural light," knowledge threatens to dissolve the mist and reveal Pip's mistakes and shame but Pip cannot know for certain it has.[20] Thus, much as the rising mist implies a clearing away of contingencies and the emergence of an abstract transcendent observer, it also suggests an ironic destabilization of this vision. Such can be seen in this passage where Pip daydreams of Estella and Miss Havisham while observing picturesque sea vistas:

> Whenever I watched the vessels standing out to sea with their white sails spread, I somehow thought of Miss Havisham and Estella; and whenever the light struck aslant, afar off, upon a cloud or sail or green hill-side or water-line, it was just the same—Miss Havisham and Estella and the strange house and the strange life appeared to have something to do with everything that was picturesque. (15:110)

Were the subjects of Pip's fantasy not so willfully misrepresented to the observer, one might argue that this passage suggests the emergence of an aesthetic morality, a Kantian disinterest in the picturesque. Yet open vision in this passage is simply not a power relation available to Pip. It is an aesthetic lure, a fantasy of knowledge in which the pleasure of visual command binds the viewer tighter to his desired object.

The problem of total vision thus suggests another aspect of total vision and nineteenth-century warfare, total war. The open horizon of the sea, as Paul Virillio notes, is the initial field for total war in the nineteenth century, an open battlefield "without obstacles" (78). This vision of the open horizon has intriguing subjective effects. On the one hand, it underscores the increasing vulnerability of all subjects to war, a vulnerability that drove the initial enthusiasm for the Volunteers in middle-class Victorian men. On the other hand, it reveals a curious game of nineteenth-century subject-construction in which men used the open sea to produce travel narratives emphasizing the melancholy yet pleasurable experience of isolation.[21] As Marc Augé argues, these smooth spaces of transit gave men an opportunity to imagine shedding their identities. The open horizon, the space of total vision and total vulnerability, allows one to become, if only briefly, oneself and nobody. It is this modality of the open horizon that Pip uses as a model for his narration, one in which the self dissolves alongside a fantasy of total narratorial vision.

The rising mist, then, is ambivalent, an ironic suspension between total and mystified vision and an undermining of total vision itself.

Nonetheless, its first appearance seems insistently sentimental. Shame leads Pip to walk alone to the coach from his childhood home due to his "sense of the contrast there would be between me and Joe" (19:159), which Joe and Biddy's shoe-throwing further heightens. As he walks, however, he reflects on his weakness of character—his failure to do right in the face of temptation—and the rising mist then confronts him with an unknown world:

> I walked away at a good pace, thinking it was easier to go than I had supposed it would be, and reflecting that it would never have done to have had an old shoe thrown after the coach, in sight of all the High Street. I whistled and made nothing of going. But the village was very peaceful and quiet, and the light mists were solemnly rising, as if to show me the world, and I had been so innocent and little there, and all beyond was so unknown and great, that in a moment with a strong heave and sob I broke into tears. It was by the finger-post at the end of the village, and I laid my hand upon it, and said, "Good-bye, O my dear, dear friend!"
>
> Heaven knows we need never be ashamed of our tears, for they are rain upon the blinding dust of earth, overlying our hard hearts. I was better after I had cried than before,—more sorry, more aware of my own ingratitude, more gentle. If I had cried before, I should have had Joe with me then.
>
> So subdued I was by those tears, and by their breaking out again in the course of the quiet walk, that when I was on the coach, and it was clear of the town, I deliberated with an aching heart whether I would not get down when we changed horses and walk back, and have another evening at home, and a better parting. ...
>
> We changed again, and yet again, and it was now too late and too far to go back, and I went on. And the mists had all solemnly risen now, and the world lay spread before me. (19:160)

As Pip stands at the edge of a new world, the lure of the picturesque turns his traumatic childhood home into a kind of Eden—indeed, the closing phrase of this passage echoing Milton's expulsion of Adam and Eve in *Paradise Lost*.[22] Yet Pip is more like a Volunteer rifleman or an imperial worker, traveling into an unknown future in which his character will be tested and found wanting. His astonishment at "the light mists ... solemnly rising, as if to show me the world" indicates a possible reprieve through sentimental tears. Fred Kaplan notes that in sentimental literature, "tears ... are often the visible sign of rediscovering or returning to our first natures, our best natures, our moral sentiments" (*Sacred Tears* 60). They seem to fulfill that role here. As the one thing of which "we need never be ashamed," Pip's tears suspend his shame in an apparent return to the moral sentiments. His address to the fingerpost suggest that his moral sense has been suppressed; earlier, this post appeared out of the mist as a metaphoric extrusion of his conscience: "as I looked up at [the post], while it dripped, it seemed to my oppressed conscience like a phantom devoting me to the Hulks" (3:16–17). Mist obscured the moral sense, but it reappears as Pip stands in tears on the verge of a new world.

Yet Pip's tears suspend his shame only momentarily. This suspension is in effect an act consubstantial with the mist's "rising," an act bound to a moment—a doing rather than a done. Much as Pip's tears indicate a proper moral response, this moral response does not transform Pip and they do not provide the basis for a new or renewed character. What matters is the *rising*, not the tears or the mist, a figure that suggests the contingency of character and moral judgment. As a narrator, Pip is an observer who insists on the distance between his observation and on his total knowledge, and thus on his ability to move transparently between actual and potential, between the knowledge of the character in the empirical world and of a transcendent knowledge that escapes these empirical limits. By contrast, as a character, Pip must achieve an embodied suspension from empirical experience—a focus on the good of others—without the invulnerability of transcendent ironic narration. Hence the novel's persistent and unresolved tension between character and narrator, a tension that remains held in suspense.[23] The narrator demands an impossible embodied state. Suspense becomes an end in itself. The centrality of the rising mist is a figure for unresolved suspense, the movement of rising from potential to actual and from actual to potential.

Nowhere is this suspension clearer than in Pip's renunciation of his love for Estella which becomes meaningful only once it has been renounced. Initially, Pip's feelings are the result of shame's promiscuity, a promiscuity seen in the lure of the open horizon. Herbert tells Pip that his feelings for Estella are the result of "nature and circumstances" (30:250). Pip later admits that he made her "the embodiment of every graceful fancy that my mind has ever become acquainted with" (44:364). The text hints at another relation when Pip refuses to "detach" himself from Estella (30:250): he falls into a reverie of distant observation and attachment, and recalls "a feeling like that which had subdued me on the morning when I left the forge, when the mists were solemnly rising, and when I laid my hand upon the village finger-post, smote upon my heart again" (30:250). When Pip ostensibly forgives Estella for marrying Drummle, he assumes a similar position. His speech accepts the importance of her mood work to his identity and his shame: "you cannot choose but remain part of my character, part of the little good in me, part of the evil" (44:364). Yet his desire to extricate the good from the evil in her work and to mitigate his own vulnerability leads him to focus on an act of will that separates him from her: "in this separation I associate you only with the good" (44:365). This volunteerism at the heart of character does not triumph over shame so much as try to hold it in abeyance by sheer will. In separation, Pip suspends himself in the midst of shame's relation of looking while enacting contempt's movement away from its object. The unique aspect of the novel's engagement with shame and contempt is its imagining of a tertiary position between the two, one in which shame's attachment and contempt's withdrawal can become the basis for a disinterested and selfless character. Character on this model suspends, withdraws, and views from afar. It is the action of rising, of suspension, of separation—in short, of holding between shame and contempt.

The final image of a rising mist captures this production of character through the active pursuit of affective suspension. For the novel, this is the result of the active pursuit of separation and the embrace of shame and contempt in personal suffering. Pip and Estella thus do not so much exemplify Samuel Smiles claim that "in misfortune ... the character of the upright man shines forth with the greatest lustre," as turn it on its head: the upright pursue misfortune. In the novel's draft ending, these concerns suggest Evangelical notions of atonement:[24] Estella's abuse at the hands of Drummle, Pip reflects, shows that "suffering had been stronger than Miss Havisham's teaching, and had given her a heart to understand what my heart used to be" (509). The published ending retains these words but gives them to Estella: "suffering has been stronger than all other teaching, and has taught me to understand what your heart used to be" (59:484). It also emphasizes separation and suffering, beginning with Pip's eleven-year separation from Joe and Biddy and Estella's separation from Satis House. When she speaks of suffering, he replies with the pain of separation: "the remembrance of our last parting has been ever mournful and painful" (59:484). Separation and pain operate together to answer a question Pip asked of Estella years earlier: "When should I awaken the heart in her?" (29:244). The answer Estella offers is that awakening comes only after separation and suffering. She is now "glad" to think they are friends and "will continue friends apart" (59:484). The final image of a rising mist emphasizes this happiness as a suspension within the midst of suffering:

> I took her hand in mine, and we went out of the ruined place; and, as the morning mists had risen long ago when I first left the forge, so the evening mists were rising now, and in all the broad expanse of tranquil light they showed to me, I saw the shadow of no parting from her. (59:484)

In these final lines, Pip and Estella do not enter a new world out of the rising mist but reenter the world as it is and leave the ruins of the past behind. The rising mist allows a new narrative command of vision—the light shows—and creates a hiatus in what it shows—"the shadow of no parting"—an image of no image, a seeing of not seeing. Is this the reappearance of Pip's mystification, as Peter Brooks suggests, a veiling after the unveiling of the truth of Pip's expectations? Or is it an imagistic capturing of suspension itself? It seems important that in the final proofs Dickens cancelled an additional clause "the shadow of no parting, but one." With a stroke, he removed the suggestion of a final closure for another suspension.

The thematics of suspension and this revision in particular resonate with Dickens's personal life: by deleting "but one," the text eliminates the suggestion that romantic relationships between men and women have one appropriate ending. That Dickens crafted this ending at the urging of Sir Edward Bulwer-Lytton may matter more than we have understood. As John Bowen notes, Dickens took concrete steps to commit his wife Catherine to an insane asylum, a plot that followed closely on Bulwer-Lytton's successful commitment of his wife, Rosina, the same year, 1858 (see "Unmutual Friend."). From a biographical perspective, separation and the suspension of parting become more freighted. Perhaps no parting, perhaps a parting. The decision is emphatically his. Again, this is not to reduce the novel to biography but to unravel some of its affective intensity. Throughout, Pip is subject to the threat of Estella's mood work. Only in the conclusion does decision return to him. Dickens's later revision of the final line in 1862 further obscures the question of what or whether Pip sees or decides. The rising mists now show "no shadow of another parting," another showing of not showing now as an indeterminate event. Another parting like the last or another parting after this one? The suspension reiterates the figure of the rising mist itself, an image that suggests that no shadow can been seen because the evening's "tranquil light" throws them behind Pip and Estella and out of their field of vision. To be suspended between actual and potential is to be free of what falls behind and of what is to come. It is a feeling of suspended openness in their forever unconcluded walk, an openness of possibility narrated to make such possibility the perquisite of a man.

The novel's affective form, its suspensions, reveals problems of Victorian male subjectivity and the possibility of a more plural and open-ended singularity that may be separable from this gendering. This is to insist that the novel's plotting of suspense as mystery and its suggestions of the will to know are secondary to its feelings of irresolution. One might object, following Peter Brooks, that Pip's misreadings drive the novel's narrative and its readers. To read *Great Expectations* for affect turns on its head Brooks's argument that we "read present moments ... as endowed with narrative meaning only because we read them in anticipation of the structuring power of those endings that will retrospectively give them the order and significance of plot" (94). It is not that the novel may not offer readers an opportunity to sift a plot for the satisfaction of knowledge and a return to equilibrium, but that its interleaving of irony, shame, and contempt reveals a crisis in masculine subjectivity and a masculine form of narrative satisfaction. In this way, it is bound up with Dickens's life and the text's conjuncture, a drive to escape a new sense of bodily and emotional vulnerability to foreign threats that enfolds existing fears of social and economic vulnerability. It is this skein of vulnerabilities that makes the Volunteer rifle corps so suggestive to middle-class British men at the turn of the 1860s, first as a way to form oneself against such threats and then for working-class men to gain more social and economic currency by the exhibition of one's orderliness and attachment to Great Britain as a nation. The desire to suspend these emotions is not simply a desire to escape but to reimagine their cultural deployment. Silvan Tomkins's political analysis of shame and contempt places these two affects in political opposition, but the affective form of *Great Expectations* goes beyond Tomkins's political binary. Shame and contempt, Dickens proposes, reciprocally condition one another: the contempt of hierarchies may discipline horizontal relations, and the shame of horizontal relations may mitigate the harshnesses of social hierarchies and their contempt.

Pip's shame and contempt remain but mitigated as long as he holds himself in suspension. In this way, Pip, not David, is perhaps liberalism's ideal earnest (male) subject, one that relies on a voluntarist command of the will alongside a stiff-lipped and sometimes cynical irony. He is a subject who believes he can suspend his desires even if there is little evidence that he does. In broader cultural terms, it indicates the role of these affects to a Victorian notion of character predicated on self-reliance. No wonder, then, that men of Victorian character could be so readily moved from self-pity to aggrieved violence against those they held in imperial contempt. Yet the novel also suggests a more thoroughgoing suspension of subjectivity itself, a pluralism more affectively variegated than the dividualism of *David Copperfield*. In *Copperfield*, pluralism is a persistent strangeness of feeling, a surprising possibility of otherness. In *Great Expectations*, it becomes a plurality of feelings, of humor, of shame, of care and contempt, surveyed from a distance. It is this need to be close to and distant from the objects that generate feeling that the novel captures in its irony and suspension, a demand to expect without expectation.

The suspension of *Great Expectations* thus suggests the recognition of a tendency in liberal subjectivity toward violent, reactionary self-aggrandizement and the possibility, albeit contingent, of its suspension. Much like Pip's tears in the rain, the suspension of violent aggrandizement was something that Victorians may have prized more in *potentia* than in actuality. Suspension, after all, can give imperial hegemony a feeling of deferral and disinterest even it reveals a readiness to fall violently out of balance. The affective qualities of *Great Expectations* thus divulge the power a culture reserves for its most politically fraught emotions, a demand that individuals hold the affective within themselves and at arm's length, to exist within the contradictoriness of a feeling and to act as though it could be different, even if—or perhaps especially because— it was not.

Notes

1 See Bowen, "Unmutual Friend."
2 Miss Coutts, would later try to reconcile Dickens's marriage during the same period in which Dickens writes of Charley in the Volunteer forces. See *Letters* 9, 230, and 234.
3 Foucault's initial analysis of the discipline presents it as a method by which elites reshape what he terms the "popular illegalisms" (140) of the unruly lower classes, an analysis meant to redress E.P. Thompson's argument that nineteenth-century law focuses on the repression of seditious mobs. See Foucault, *Punitive Society* 140–45.
4 For Peter Brooks, the search for meaning that drives the novel's narrative exemplifies the seduction of narration as a biological drive for impossible meaning; for Caroline Levine, the narrative's use of suspense teaches us an experimental ethics of reading for difference; for Jon B. Reed, the interpretative problems of narration enact the surpassing of a hero-narrator for a socially conscious narration; for Anna Kornbluh, the narrative's unfinished and retrospective qualities capture the unfoundedness and subjectivity of the era's fictitious capital. See Brooks, *Reading* 113–42, Levine, *Serious Pleasures* 84–98, Reed, and Kornbluh 45–64.
5 De Man describes Lukács's theory of irony as predicated on a division similar to his division of contingent and transcendent selves: "irony actually provides the means by which the novelist transcends, within the form of the work, the avowed contingency of his condition" (*Blindness* 56).
6 As de Man explains, the temporal division of irony creates "a past that is pure mystification and a future that remains harassed forever by a relapse within the inauthentic" (222).
7 For example, see Caroline Levine's account of the novel as an ethical pedagogy in *Serious Pleasures* 84–98.
8 See Leavis 376 and McFarlane, "David Lean's" 68.
9 I have refrained in prior chapters from drawing extensively on psychology's analysis of the affects because my focus on the historically embedded specifics of the affective put my readings at odds with psychology's desire to limit the affective to a small set of ahistorical biological qualities rather than exploring the mutual conditioning of the affective and the contextual.
10 In later work, Tomkins distinguishes humiliation and contempt, linking humiliation with shame and contempt with disgust. See Tomkins, *Shame* 157.
11 On misattunement, see Stern, *Interpersonal World of the Infant* 213.
12 For Adam Smith's intimation of this mode of social feeling, see chapter one.
13 Subsequent critics who treat questions of shame point out its importance in terms of social identity and link it to feelings of guilt. For example, Julie Anne Levine and Alison Beth Levine offer a Freudian account reading of the novel that treats shame as a negative evaluation of the self and guilt of a thing done and maps a "spectrum" (66) in which Pip exemplifies shame and Miss Havisham guilt, and Staci Floyd uses analysis of shame to interpret Pip's shame as anxiety over class passing.
14 For contemporary theories of affect as contagious, see Brennan. Elspeth Prober similarly argues, "shame is contagious" (88).

15 As Hillary Schor notes, the novel reserves a special place of disgust and contempt for its women, and Shanyn Fiske's reading of Miss Havisham through British notions of sati suggests Dickens's murderous racism turned against one of the novel's central female characters. See Schor 166–70, and Fiske.

16 On the new woman, see Ledger, *The New Woman*, and Richardson and Willis.

17 I follow Ahmed's suggestion here that Tomkins's account of subjective development is situated in an effectively pre-discursive and pre-social space, and thus one must position shame—the visual encounter with the strange and the construction of self-consciousness—within the discursive to determine how the social world constructs the unfamiliar. See Ahmed, *Cultural Politics* 205–29.

18 On the role of counterfactuals in the novel, see Miller.

19 On the connection between contingency and war, including its effects in Conrad's *Heart of Darkness*, see Ford.

20 When Orlick threatens to burn him in a limekiln, he worries that his disappearance would mean Joe and Biddy would not know of his desire to change and he visualizes "the lonely marsh and the white vapour creeping over it, into which I should have dissolved" (53:427), making the kiln's "ghostly" vapor (53:422) a phantasm of his remembered unregenerate self.

21 See Augé 70–83.

22 Dickens, *Great Expectations*, 493, n. 7.

23 Caroline Levine reads this suspense as part of a Victorian ethics of "self-suspension" (*Pleasures of Suspense* 86). For Levine, suspension reveals the novel's "experimental realism" (95) and demands that readers learn to test their interpretative skills against the experiences of alterity offered by fiction.

24 Early in the century, Evangelicals emphasized the pain of reparation in Christ's sacrifice on the cross; by mid-century, however, liberals reframed atonement as part of a less punitive worldview in which the pain of atonement produced, as Boyd Hilton describes, "[energizing]... feelings of self-mortification and self-sacrifice" (345). Liberal notions of character drew in part from this modification of atonement. See Collini 105. Jan-Melissa Schramm also argues that Dickens's religious views do not map a particular Evangelical creed but his use of narrative scapegoats may reveal the influence of arguments about the Atonement during the 1850s. See Schramm 140–80.

References

Ahmed, Sara. *The Cultural Politics of Emotion*, 2nd edition. London: Routledge, 2015.

Anderson, Gregory. *Victorian Clerks*. Manchester: Manchester University Press, 1976.

Augé, Marc. *Non-Places: An Introduction to Supermodernity*. Translated by John Howe. London: Verso, 2008.

Bagehot, Walter. *The Works of Walter Bagehot*. 5 volumes. Edited by Forrest Morgan. Hartford, CT: Traveler's Insurance, 1889.

Beckett, Ian. *The Amateur Military Tradition, 1558–1954*. Manchester: Manchester University Press, 1991.

Bowen, John. "Unmutual Friend." *The Times Literary Supplement*, 19 February 2019. www.the-tls.co.uk/articles/public/charles-catherine-dickens-asylum/.

Brennan, Teresa. *The Transmission of Affect*. Ithaca, NY: Cornell University Press, 2004.

Briggs, Asa. *Victorian People*. Chicago: University of Chicago Press, 1954.

Brooks, Peter. *Reading for the Plot: Design and Intention in Narrative*. Cambridge, MA: Harvard University Press, 1984.

Clausewitz, Carl von. *On War*. Edited and translated by Michael Eliot Howard and Peter Paret. Princeton, NJ: Princeton University Press, 1989.

Collini, Stefan. *Public Moralists: Political Thought and Intellectual Life in Britain 1850–1930*. Clarendon Press, 1991.

Dalrymple, William. *The Last Mughal: The Fall of a Dynasty, Delhi, 1857*. New York: Vintage, 2006.

De Man, Paul. *Blindness and Insight: Essays in the Rhetoric of Contemporary Criticism*. 2nd edition. Minneapolis: University of Minnesota Press, 1983.

Dickens, Charles. *Great Expectations*. Edited by Charlotte Mitchell. New York: Penguin, 1996.

———. *The Letters of Charles Dickens, Pilgrim Edition, Volume 8: 1856–1858*. Edited by Graham Storey and Kathleen Tillotson. Oxford: Clarendon Press, 1995.

———. *The Letters of Charles Dickens, Pilgrim Edition, Volume 9: 1859–1861*. Edited by Graham Storey. Oxford: Clarendon Press, 1997.

———. *The Letters of Charles Dickens: The Pilgrim Edition, Volume 10: 1862–1864*. Edited by Graham Storey and Margaret Brown. Oxford: Oxford University Press, 1998.

"Diversions of Drill," *Punch, or the London Charivari*, 14 July 1860, p. 11.

Ellis, Sarah Stickney. *Daughters of England: Their Position in Society, Character and Responsibilities*. London: Fisher, Son, & Co., 1843.

Engberg-Pederson, Anders. *Empire of Chance*. Cambridge, MA: Harvard University Press, 2015.

"A Field Day." *All the Year Round*, 12 October 1861, pp. 61–65.

Fiske, Shanyn. "*Sati* and *Great Expectations*: Dickens in the Wake of the Indian Mutiny," *Victorians Institute Journal*, 35 (2007), pp. 31–52.

Floyd, Staci. "The Spectre of Class: Revision, Hybrid Identity, and Passing in *Great Expectations*," *Victorians: Journal of Culture and Literature*, 122 (2012), pp. 101–16.

Ford, Thomas H. "Ecohistoricism: Aristotle, Dryden, Montgomery, Conrad," *Romanticism*, vol. 24, no. 3 (2018), pp. 278–93.

Foucault, Michel. The Punitive Society: Lectures at the Collège de France. Edited by Bernard E. Harcourt. Translated by Graham Burchell. New York: Picador, 2015.

Harvey, Karen. "Craftsmen in Common: Skills, Objects and Masculinity in the Eighteenth and Nineteenth Centuries." *Gender and Material Culture c. 1750–1950*, edited by Hannah Greig, Jane Hamlett and Leonie Hannan. London: Palgrave, 2015, pp. 68–89.

Hilton, Boyd. *The Age of Atonement*. Oxford: Oxford University Press, 1986.

Kaplan, Fred. *Sacred Tears: Sentimentality in Victorian Literature*. Princeton, NJ: Princeton University Press, 1987.

Kornbluh, Anna. *Realizing Capital*. New York: Fordham University Press, 2014.

"The Ladies' Own Rifle Corps." *Punch, or the London Charivari*, 14 July 1860, p. 19.

Leavis, Queenie Dorothy. "How We Must Read *Great Expectations.*" *Dickens: The Novelist*, edited by Frank Raymond Leavis and Queenie Dorothy Leavis. New York: Pantheon, 1970, pp. 277–331.

Ledger, Sally. *The New Woman: Fiction and Feminism at the Fin-de-Siècle.* Manchester: Manchester University Press, 1997.

Levine, Caroline. *The Serious Pleasures of Suspense: Victorian Realism and Narrative Doubt.* Charlottesville: University of Virginia Press, 2003.

Levine, Julie Anne, and Alison Beth Levine. "The Psychodynamics of Shame and Guilt in *Great Expectations,*" *International Journal of Applied Psychoanalytic Studies*, vol. 9, no. 1 (2012), pp. 62–66.

McFarlane, Brian. "David Lean's *Great Expectations*—Meeting Two Challenges," *Literature-Film Quarterly*, vol. 30, no. 1 (1992), pp. 68–76.

Mieszkowski, Jan. *Watching War.* Stanford: Stanford University Press, 2012.

Mill, John Stuart. *The Collected Works of John Stuart Mill, Volume XVIII – Essays on Politics and Society Part I.* Edited by John M. Robson. Toronto: University of Toronto Press, 1977.

Miller, Andrew H. "A Case of Metaphysics: Counterfactuals, Realism, *Great Expectations,*" *ELH*, 79 (2012), pp. 773–96.

Moore, Grace. *Dickens and Empire: Discourses of Class, Race, and Colonialism in Charles Dickens.* London: Routledge, 2004.

Moynahan, Julian. "The Hero's Guilt: The Case of *Great Expectations,*" *Essays in Criticism*, 10 (1960), pp. 60–79.

Nayder, Lillian. *The Other Dickens: A Life of Catherine Dickens.* Ithaca, NY: Cornell University Press, 2011.

Prober, Elspeth. "Writing Shame." *The Affect Theory Reader*, edited by Melissa Gregg and Gregory J. Seigworth. Durham, NC: Duke University Press, 2010, pp. 71–90.

Richardson, Angelique, and Chris Willis, editors. *The New Woman in Fiction and Fact: Fin de Siècle Feminisms.* London: Palgrave Macmillan, 2002.

Reed, Jon B. "Astrophil and Estella: A Defense of Poesy," *Studies in English Literature, 1500–1900*, vol. 30, no. 4 (1990), pp. 655–78.

"Royal Naval Volunteers," *All the Year Round*, 10 December 1859, pp. 151–53.

Schor, Hillary. *Dickens and the Daughter of the House.* Cambridge: Cambridge University Press, 1999.

Schramm, Jan-Melissa *Atonement and Self-Sacrifice in Nineteenth-Century Narrative.* Cambridge: Cambridge University Press, 2012.

Slater, Michael. *Charles Dickens.* New Haven: Yale University Press, 2009.

Smiles, Samuel. *Self-Help, with Illustrations of Character, Conduct, and Perseverance.* London: John Murray, 1868.

Stern, Daniel N. *The Interpersonal World of the Infant.* New York: Basic, 2000.

T. [Tennyson, Alfred Lord.] "The War." *Times* [London, England], 9 May 1859, p. 10.

Tomalin, Claire. *Charles Dickens: A Life.* New York: Penguin, 2011.

Tomkins, Silvan. *Affect, Imagery, Consciousness*, volume 1. New York: Springer, 2008.

———. *Shame and Its Sisters: A Tomkins Reader.* Edited by Eve Kosofsky Sedgwick and Adam Frank. Durham, NC: Duke University Press, 1995.

"The Umbrella Rifle," *Punch, or the London Charivari*, 7 July 1860, p. 10.

Van Ghent, Dorothy. *The English Novel: Form and Function*. New York: Harper and Row, 1953.

"A View of our Volunteers as They Will Never be Seen by the Enemy!" *Punch, or the London Charivari*, 15 December 1860, p. 234.

Virilio, Paul. *Speed and Politics*. Translated by Mark Polizzotti. Los Angeles: Semiotext(e), 2006.

"Volunteer Cavalry." *All the Year Round*, 14 July 1860, pp. 329–31.

"The Volunteer Movement." *Punch, or the London Charivari*, 24 July 1860, p. 21.

"Volunteers at Hythe." *All the Year Round*, 2 February 1861, pp. 402–04.

Conclusion
Dickensian Affects in the Future Tense

What, then, are Dickensian affects? What affects in Dickens's novels are not the idea of a feeling but a result of the ways that their forms—that is, their arrangement of elements, signifying and asignifying, formal and conjunctural—produce situations able to signal emotional and affective experience. Violence, anxiety, surprise, and suspense are ways of affecting but they do not in their abstraction belong to Dickens alone. Rather, they produce particularly Dickensian effects in the ways that they draw together in patterned arrangement a variety of elements connected to physical, emotional, gendered, racial, social, political, and economic precarity. It is the interaction between form and content, style and meaning, that gives Dickensian affects a qualitative coherence, a unity that we might describe as the persistent movement between experiences and feelings of personal precarity and those of social and economic precariousness. From this perspective, Dickensian affects model ways of feeling that bind situations of material precarity to feelings of personal precarity through the precariousness of feeling itself. The feeling that one could feel otherwise connects the disparate elements that Dickensian affects inflect. Dickensian affects, then, do not reveal convergences of feeling but dissensions. To feel in Dickens's novels is to feel that one could feel *otherwise*. This affective dynamism in Dickens reveals the importance of rhythm.[1] This rhythm is not a patterning that asserts control, as Caroline Levine's analysis of rhythm might suggest. It is rather a production of patterned difference, an engagement with the variable and multi-layered that articulates differences and yokes them in their contradictions and antagonisms.[2]

It is this patterning of felt differences in Dickens's work that resonates. His forms provide patterns for feeling experiences of life's precarity under capitalism. For Dickens, more than any other nineteenth-century novelist, the forces of capitalism provided an aesthetic occasion to explore the feelings of precarity: the violence of its threats against the weak and dependent, the anxiety it raises about one's place in and belonging to a larger community, the surprise of its contradictory demands for personal and impersonal forms of trust, and the suspense it requires of the feelings of shame and contempt produced by precarity. These affects articulate stylistic inflections that can yoke elements of the past to those of a present where the persistence of particular historical elements (or even of historical continuities) may become clearer or more obscure. Attention to Dickensian affects demands an engagement with history, but does not make claims for historical origin stories, and does not mean to produce a history of emotions, affects, or political economy. It produces a conjunctural analysis of the material and social forces in which Dickens's texts were embedded and considers the potential autonomy of the textual transformations of these circumstances into aesthetic machines which signal particular ways of feeling these circumstances whether intended or not.

The transhistorical import of Dickensian affects appears in the ways in which these signals may operate in altered circumstances. A change in situation is a change in affective event. Nowhere is this clearer than in twentieth- and twenty-first-century film adaptations of *Great Expectations*. Consider David Lean's influential 1946 adaptation. Brian McFarlane, perhaps the foremost expert on adaptations of *Great Expectations*, insists that Lean's film is the most properly Dickensian of all film adaptations of Dickens's work. McFarlane bases this claim on his insistence that Lean's film best captures what he terms the novel's "cardinal functions," a list of fifty-four key plot events (*Charles Dickens's* 148) and that Lean uses film form to represent these functions in ways that replicate the novel's style, including its use of subjective perception and ironic narration, the visual details and comic grotesqueness of its characterizations, and its visual remediations of the narrative's symbols and metaphors (see "David Lean's"). McFarlane's formal analysis astutely explains Lean's visual remediation of Dickens's style but it also exemplifies a persistent problem for adaptation studies: it privileges the analysis of story and story elements and thus focuses on cognitive questions of representation and remediation. This focus makes narration a mere function of storytelling and thus limits encounters with what Garrett Stewart calls "the Other Dickens," the textual drift and experience of otherness provided in the textual encounters of Dickens's work. This question of feeling and style is of particular salience for what it means to be *Dickensian*. For McFarlane, the Dickensian is a question of the representation of story events and the visual remediation of narrative metaphors: Does the actor cast as Wemmick closely represent Dickens's description of the character's mouth? Does the camerawork convey Pip's subjective perception of the marshes? Does the mise-en-scène visualize particular metaphors? When McFarlane mentions feeling in passing, he treats it as a discursive concern, explaining that Lean's film uses Pip's voice-over "to articulate what was intensely felt but difficult to express by the young protagonist" ("David Lean's" 70).

It is certainly understandable why McFarlane and adaptation studies ignore affect and the visual and cinematic questions it raises. The visual construction of many film adaptations could be generously described as functional, and Lean's film almost completely lacks the shot most associated with affect by cinema studies, the close up.[3] Yet if we pay close attention to one of the film's few close ups, we uncover unexpected qualities in Lean's film that can tell us a great deal about how a text's affective form may affect the remediation of a novel's story events. In the film's penultimate shot, the camera presents a medium close two-shot of Pip and Estella which ends with their embrace as the strings on the soundtrack swell. The use of an affect image at this point signals that viewers should be caught up in the feeling of the conclusion and encourages them to accept without reflection an important alteration of the story. In the novel, only Pip and Jaggers know that Magwitch is Estella's father. In Lean's film, Jaggers informs Estella of her parentage so that she may take possession of Magwitch's property after his death (the Crown does not confiscate his property in this version). This alteration allows the film to compress its final events into the space of a few days rather than a span of eleven years: When Drummle learns of Estella's parentage, he breaks off their engagement. Estella then takes up residence in Satis House. Pip discovers her there shortly after his illness where she has become a double of Miss Havisham. Thus, he pulls down the house's draperies and tells Estella "to let in the sunlight" and recognize the house's "dust and decay." The close up that follows this revelation bathes their faces in light, banishing the gloom and mist that otherwise defines the film's lighting design and Pip's narrative trajectory. Lean's film conjures affect at its most intense point of narrative adaptation, the moment that brings Pip's expectations to a climax as Pip runs off with Estella, Miss Havisham's fortune, and Magwitch's too.

In this achievement of Pip's expectations, Lean's film uses an affect image to bring its feelings of shame and contempt to an end. At first, Estella looks away from Pip as she voices her desire to escape vulnerability, whispering, "Pip, I'm afraid." In response, Pip tells her, "Look at me. We belong to each other. Let's start again." In these returned gazes, Lean's film offers viewers a reprieve from the broken and withheld gaze of shame. In their held gaze, the precarity of expectation becomes a feeling of the past surpassed, of completion. This climax of achievement in Lean's film offers a template for the adaptations of *Great Expectations* that follow and captures the way that the Dickensian in the twentieth century comes to conjure and evacuate feelings of precarity. If the affective forms of Dickens's novels underscore feelings of precarity and the precarity of feeling that still marks twenty-first-century life under capitalism—an *otherwise* of feeling that haunts even the most seemingly secure moments—twentieth-century adaptations of his work reframe this *otherwise* as a feeling that other feelings will surely come. The Dickensian thus increasingly solicits a plurality of affects in order to evacuate this plurality of threat. Lean's film insistently brings to a close the feelings of *Great Expectations*, shame, guilt, and vulnerability, in expectation's achievement. The Dickensian marks a past that should be well and truly past.

Lean's film, then, shows us something useful about the transhistorical work of a text's affective form. Like Dickens's revisions to *The Chimes*, it wrestles with the affects and effects a story may signal or more inchoately suggest as a result of its altered circumstances. McFarlane notes briefly that it may reflect "the film's production period of postwar hopefulness" (*Charles Dickens's* 153), a period that included the election of the Labour government that would create the British welfare state. It is worth pondering, though, how the film's hopefulness may articulate events in the past rather than events that were to come. First and foremost, the experience of war's physical vulnerability resonates with the novel's feelings of economic precarity and imperial masculine vulnerability. Made with limited resources, the film evinces some desire to reclaim lost British military and economic power: when Magwitch's estate devolves upon Estella, she takes up residence on Miss Havisham's chair, a throne that draws a likeness not only to her and Miss Havisham but also to Queen Victoria. Its conclusion reframes these feelings of precarity as bound up with the past and thus insists on their necessary passing away. Andrew Higson, a film scholar who specializes in English period films, rightly notes that "it is the Victorian period [in Lean's film] that is horrendous and threatening, and against which true modernity can be defined" (*Film England* 229). The film's concluding image makes this plain and, in the process, reveals the film's transposition of the novel's suspense. Pip and Estella leave Satis House and close the gates behind them, but the camera remains positioned just beyond the house's threshold, an image that suggests a desire for change and the necessity of the past. Pip and Estella escape from Satis House but viewers remain firmly behind its gates, suspended between past and present.

The film's simultaneous grounding in and surpassing of the past is part of an industrial push by the British film industry to assert the existence of a British form of cinema, a project to project British cultural hegemony that drew heavily on the cultural significance of British literary history as its imperial power began to wane.[4] McFarlane notes that Lean's film was well-received by British and American critics but does not note the role that literary heritage played in its reception. The rise of a British film industry associated with literary culture was part of a resurgence of interest in British heritage following the Second World War and able to perpetuate itself by penetrating the American market.[5] *Great Expectations* was one of the first postwar productions of the Rank Organisation, Britain's first vertically integrated film studio. Rank films were pivotal to the emergence of a British filmmaking in the mid-twentieth century. Its productions in the immediate postwar years included Lean's *Great Expectations* and *Oliver Twist* (1948) and

Laurence Olivier's *Hamlet* (1948), his follow-up to *Henry V* (1944). At the time of the film's release, influential American critics such as *The New York Times*'s Bosley Crowther and *The Nation*'s James Agee read Lean's film in light of its literary heritage and compared the film favorably to Olivier's *Henry V.*[6] By embracing a film like Lean's *Great Expectations* as a particularly well-made British adaptation of a piece of British literature, American film critics suggest a marketing path followed by British literary adaptations into the twenty-first century. As Higson notes, literary film adaptations are now "frequently sold in export markets... received art house release... or were otherwise promoted to 'discerning' international audiences" (*English Heritage 5*). Crowther and Agee's critical framing of *Great Expectations* in terms of cultural fidelity plays to these desires. The film's hopefulness reflects the aspirations of its audiences and producers, and its affective power result from its adaptation of the feelings in Dickens's novel to reflect a past overcome.

This shift in affective form resonates through subsequent adaptations of *Great Expectations* as a hope for the past to be well and truly past. Yet what is hope—an emotion, an affect, a feeling? Terry Eagleton calls hope a being-toward a situation that may include any number of affects or emotions, whether excitement, expectation, dread, anger, and so on. For Eagleton, hope is predicated on rationality. Unlike the ungrounded sunny disposition of optimism, hope needs (or finds) its reasons.[7] Adaptation brings forward, then, a relation that lurks within the affective dynamism and plurality of Dickens's novels, one that recalls what Peter Brooks describes in *Reading for the Plot* as the libidinal drive toward quiescence and narrative closure which he uncovers in *Great Expectations*. Brook's narrative drive—the search for rational closure—also contains a variety of emotive and affective tonalities. Yet if the hope of *Great Expectations* suggests a Freudian textual libido in search of release, this is due to the inherence and relation of particular feelings in the text. That includes the excitement and expectation that libido would suggest of an urging forward and an encouragement to linger and look back, an urge to sum up before pressing forward and a fear that such a sum might not amount to much. This is the push and hesitation of Pip's first experience of the rising mist, part of the suspended texture of expectation that narrative drive as a rush to completion and knowledge overlooks. It is this hesitation in the face of the future—the suspension of suspense—that the novel's conclusion emphasizes, an affective experience to be salvaged from a past marked by shame and contempt. The hope of Lean's film and subsequent adaptations evinces this hesitation but emphasizes the forward glance of hope.

Alfonso Cuarón's 1998 transformational adaptation of *Great Expectations* turn this future-directed hope into a heightened drive for hope's fulfilment, an expectation of better feelings, better social relations, and better economics without the lingering hint of an *otherwise*. The feelings of precarity in Dickens's novel become instead feelings safely encountered in the past. One might argue this change is due to the film's late twentieth-century conjuncture and Cuarón's professional aspirations. Now recognized as an auteur able to helm big budget pictures such as *Gravity* (2014) and *Children of Men* (2006) and award-winning art house films such as *Roma* (2018) and *Y Tu Mamá También* (2001), Cuarón established himself in the American film market with workman-like literary adaptations marketed to tweens and teens: Frances Hodgson Burnett's *A Little Princess* (1995), Dickens's *Great Expectations* (1998), and J.K. Rowling's *Harry Potter and the Prisoner of Azkaban* (2001). Cuarón's *Great Expectations* appears in the midst of a cycle of literary adaptations and so-called frock flicks that contained a number of Jane Austen adaptations, including *Pride and Prejudice* (1995), *Sense and Sensibility* (1995), and *Mansfield Park* (1999). These films, all set in the nineteenth century, exemplify the heritage film, pictures in which, as Rosalind Galt explains, "high production values fill a mise-en-scène with period detail, representing their national pasts through sumptuous costume, landscape, and adaptations of well-known literary novels" (7). This heritage film cycle occurred almost simultaneous with a cycle of transformational literary adaptations aimed at younger audiences such as *Clueless* (1995), *Romeo + Juliet* (1996), and *10 Things I Hate About You* (1999). These films transposed their tales to the present-day, used young leads, and crammed their soundtracks with pop music for cross-marketing promotions. Cuarón's *Great Expectations* marks an intersection of these cycles and should be understood in part as a product of their commercial demands. It is a film constructed to sell tickets and follows the parameters of the teen transformational literary adaptation: a contemporary setting, attractive young leads, and an overbearing soundtrack of au courant acts such as Pulp, Tori Amos, and Chris Cornell. Its casting of Gwyneth Paltrow, a then-rising star, forms a bridge to the heritage film cycle through Paltrow's recent turn as the lead in Miramax's heavily promoted adaptation of Austen's *Emma* (1996).

What is striking about Cuarón's film is the degree to which its commercial demands are at one with its narrative transformations, most especially of Pip as a character. From an aspirational gentleman, Pip becomes an aspirational artist. This alteration reveals the ways in which Cuarón's film offers a version of hope built into the structure of late twentieth-century capitalism. Whether one terms the capitalism of this period late, post-Fordist, neoliberal, or communicative, it is an economic system that relies less on the physical alienation of exploited labor as a commodity—the backbone of industrial capitalism—than on the direct exploitation of workers' cognitive and affective capacities, often in the provision of services.[8] The late twentieth-century turn in the West from industrial to service-based economies increased the political and economic power of finance, insurance, and real estate.[9] In the United States, the cultural imaginary initially mediated this new service-based economy through representations of finance—for instance, Oliver Stone's film *Wall Street* (1987) and Michael Lewis's book *Liar's Poker* (1989)—but by the 1990s increasingly focused on cognitive and creative work. In this new socioeconomic world, the distinction between work and home blurs if it does not disappear altogether. David Byrne's film *True Stories* (1986) provides one of the earliest cultural representations of this ideology of creativity, technology, and postindustrial society; an extended soliloquy from Spalding Grey, playing the chief architect of a small town's renewal through computer technology, extols the virtues of muddling the lines between work and home and ends with the laudatory exclamation: "There's no concept of weekends anymore!" During this period work is no longer organized by Max Weber's "iron cage" (123) of bureaucracy but is instead flexibilized, from "just-in-time" factory production and highly sensitive distribution mechanisms for retailers to unpredictable work schedules and the continued encroachment of work duties to personal time (e.g., the demand for constant availability via cellphone and email). By the late 1990s, sociologist Richard Sennett titled this shift as *The Corrosion of Character* and insisted that the very qualities that had once helped workers define themselves as good workers and good people were driven out by flexibilization. For post-Fordist theorists like Christian Marazzi and Paolo Virno, workers become cynical and opportunist as they are forced to use their basic communicative and affective capacities for economic gain. Subsequent theorists of post-Fordist work emphasize its perverse affective relations. Employers, Frédéric Lordon argues, tell their workers that they should find "'fulfillment' and 'self-realization' in and through work" (52). If they fail to do so, the fault is theirs. The economic and political rise of Silicon Valley and the cult of the visionary entrepreneur binds this notion of fulfillment in work to the creative production of tech visionaries. Individuals who follow their passions will produce unique intellectual property and reap untold wealth, a story retold through the mythologies surrounding figures like Steve Jobs. In this environment, economic success comes to seem inseparable from self-actualization. Artistic success thus becomes a useful figure for a conjunctural insistence that (creative, cognitive, and affective) workers will be rewarded if they realize their unique capacities.

For Cuarón's film, this situation fundamentally alters the character of Pip, beginning with his rechristening as Finn. The name initially suggests Joe's new occupation of Florida fisherman and Finn's eventual fish-out-of-water experiences in New York City. The film's formal construction, though, indicates that Finn has a more substantive talent lurking below the waterline. Its opening visualizes Finn's talent—his childhood drawings—and the source of the wealth that will support it—the escaped convict—below the waterline. Credits appear over young Finn's drawings, tinged a deep green and covered by a rippling transparency effect that suggests submersion in water. The sequence tracks Finn as he sails through shallows of the Florida Keys and then wades through the surf, sketchpad in hand. Finn observes an orange blur in the water that resolves as the submerged face of an escaped convict, renamed Lustig, who leaps from the water and quiets him. This visual metaphor of what lurks on the other side of the waterline permeates the film and makes waterlines central to its affective work. Its representation of Finn and Estella's relationship relies on waterlines, beginning with Finn and Estella's first kiss across a fountain stream on Miss Havisham's ramshackle estate. The film presents this crossing of bodies and streams of water in extreme close ups of open mouths and wet tongues and returns to this visualization of a kiss across a water stream in extreme close up when the two meet in New York City as adults. These sequences consist of affect images distinct from those of Lean's film. Where Lean's images meant to create emotion, Cuarón's conjure physical sensation: wetness, lipness, softness. The disarticulation of body parts from characters in these sequences also link the film's use of affect to Finn's career aspirations since his art largely consists of partial representations of Estella. It should be no surprise, then, that the film represents their sexual encounter in Finn's art-strewn apartment after both are wetted through by a rainstorm. Water and its crossings in the film cast artistic aspiration and class aspiration as an eroticism of fragmentation and flow. In effect, the film embraces the fractured subjectivity of postmodernity as the basis of Pip's physical and economic satisfaction. Cuarón's film thus encourages an embrace of the insecurities that define life in postmodern risk society. To have great expectations, the film tells its viewers, one must accept the precarity of existence in postmodernity and its fragmentation of subjectivity. Everything and everyone must flow.

Initially, this emphasis on fragmentation may seem of a piece with the dividualism that I argue marks Dickens's novels and opens them to the affective before the discourse of affect itself was available. The dividualism of Cuarón's film, however, is more regressive than pluralistic, a sense of the dividual as negative fragmentation. In 1992, Gilles Deleuze argued that such dividualism was the basis of the then-emerging "societies of control" ("Postscript" 3). For Deleuze, this negative fragmentation offers the basis for more supple and discrete modes of surveillance and control than disciplinary regimes which focused on the control of individual bodies. By disarticulating the individual into discrete units of data, societies of control affect behaviors and reinforce disciplinary mechanisms at a more granular level than the relatively coarse mechanisms of the barracks or the schoolroom. In the fully formed societies of control of the 2010s, such mechanisms appear in the pervasive surveillance of domestic electronic communication by law enforcement in the United States and the sophisticated use of electronic and physical surveillance of the Uighur population in China. Cuarón's film embraces this negative dividualism in its embrace of fragmentation as the basis for overcoming economic insecurity. As in Lean's film, this shift hinges on a difference in narrative closure between adapted text and film. In Dickens's novel, Pip's openness to difference and the dividual appears in the anguish generated by the revelation of Magwitch as his benefactor. Pip realizes he has abandoned Joe and his occupation for a criminal and has no subsequent "calling" in life (41:342). In Cuarón's film, this revelation creates only momentary confusion. Lustig purchases all of Finn's work at his first show, effectively transferring his wealth to Finn before revealing himself as his benefactor. Lustig and his wealth form no bar to Finn's continued success because, unlike Pip, Finn is what he claims to be, an artist. Lustig has no need to disavow lowness because he is not attempting to remake Finn into something he is not. His money is a selfless gift that supports a deserving talent, even if, in a striking reversal, it is the result of criminal enterprise (Magwitch's was earned by hard labor). Professional self-realization in the late twentieth century, Cuarón's film suggests, is indifferent to the source of its material support. In a postindustrial economy where wealth seems to accrue to fully realized creative and cognitive workers, Finn's success is his just reward for creative production. What led Pip to change on his own—his shame at abandoning Joe and his subsequent decision not to abandon Magwitch—is for Finn his recompense for becoming what he wished to be.

This achievement of the self as it should be produces the film's conclusion. Finn, now a successful artist who splits his time between Paris and the United States, returns to Miss Havisham's estate where he discovers Estella and her daughter. He and Estella look at the setting sun over a bright, flat expanse of ocean, a scene that recalls Pip's fantasies of Estella and wealth through his gaze at the open horizon of the sea. Here these fantasies are reality and the visual command suggests the coming rapprochement between Finn and Estella and Finn's economic and creative power. The final lines of Finn's voice-over empties the film's title of its irony: "And the rest of it, it didn't matter. It was past. It was as if it had never been. There was just my memory of it." The cutthroat self-interestedness of the late twentieth and early twenty-first century appears here. Who cares how you achieve your expectations? Just achieve them. The how, the past, doesn't matter. Finn's closing lines effectively disavow Pip's description of the past's influence on the present, that "long chain of iron or gold, of thorns or flowers, that would never have bound you, but for the formation of the first link on one memorable day" (9:72). Cuarón's Finn is unchained, a self-composed from fragments to suit current demands in an opportunist dividualism, a fragmentation to match a society of financial flows and technologized forms of social control. In Cuarón's film, affect's potentiality has become the drive for affect's end, the evacuation of the potentialities of the past for a past well and truly passed.

The most recent studio adaptation of the novel, Mike Newell's *Great Expectations* (2012), appears in a world much like that of Cuarón's but in which the promises of upward mobility offered by a financialized and technologized world have collapsed. One could attribute this to the 2008 global financial crisis and resulting austerity in the United States and the United Kingdom but the problems of this conjuncture are more wide ranging. As Lawrence Grossberg details in *Under the Cover of Chaos*, the unwillingness of the state to address its population's material problems—something discernible in state responses to economic, financial, and climatic crises—should be understood alongside the economic transformations of the late twentieth century described above, a shift in the West toward service-centered economies predicated on an educated workforce where social mobility is promised but rarely achieved and worker pay has stagnated. In addition to these material economic problems, demographic shifts, political polarization, and the return of far right nationalist and racist organizations have brought forward social contradictions that 1990s cultural production ignored or camouflaged.[10] The political events of 2016 made these issues more apparent, but the trajectory of the last decade and its cultural productions are best understood through a conjunctural analysis that takes on the affects of its attacks on human expectation.

Grossberg argues that the affective landscape of this conjuncture is one of "passive nihilism" (*Under* 93) and encompasses four structures of feelings: affective autonomy, anxiety and hyperactivism, narcissistic sociality, and temporal alienation. The first, affective autonomy, easily slides into fanaticism and cruelty and is marked by "a demand for affective exaggeration" which makes everything "the best... or the worst" (95). The connection between exaggeration and cruelty, Grossberg argues, is due to "the dangers of failure and even worse, of humiliation" (96). Humiliation is perhaps the crucial affect of the 2010s and reveals the source of a new cruelty in a culture that threatens to refuse empathy and thwart human ability to communicate and bond. Humiliation, Grossberg explains, "is the beginning of the increasing violence of contemporary life, for it is always in the eye of the beholder (as opposed, e.g., to shame)" (98). Paired with humiliation and its violence is anxiety, a dreadful waiting for crises that leads people to search for release in aimless activities, activities that often become forms of performative narcissism, a presentation of self without concern for the differences between the public and private. In this new anxious narcissism, "character," Grossberg writes, "becomes a matter of 'personal branding,' creating a sense of credibility as an image without content, in a kind of affective literalism" (104). This image of self recalls Cuarón's Finn, a present self without reference to future or past, "perpetually stuck in an inescapable immediacy" (106). This presentness is not simply another form of the endless present that Fredric Jameson attributed to postmodernity almost thirty years ago.[11] As Grossberg explains, it emphasizes "a new sense of the anxious immediacy of the now... [that] the very notion of change itself is changing" (107). The now is everywhere and always yet also always not-now, a slipping away of the present in uncontrollable change.

Like its affective landscape, Newell's film is "perpetually stuck in an inescapable immediacy." This is in part because Newell eschews the use of voiceover to capture the novel's doubling of Pip as narrator and character. As a result, his film contains no suggestion of multiple temporalities. For viewers, Pip's present is ours and the film's heritage film mise-en-scéne encloses them in this inescapable immediacy. The result is strange. As Higson describes, the heritage film presents a "[rendering of] history as spectacle, as *separate* from the viewer in the present, as something over and done with, complete, achieved" ("Re-presenting" 113). The enclosure and detailed specificity of the film's historical recreation insists at once that the past is passed and yet in its filmic presentation wholly present. Indeed, the visual presentation of Newell's *Great Expectations* enfolds viewers in the landscape of the past. When Pip runs across the marshes to find Magwitch, the camera begins with an idyllic framing, hovering above a creek in the center of the frame as the sun sets before it glides across as a young Pip enters the frame and traverses it along the creek's visual diagonal. The graphic vastness of the film world emphasizes Pip's size and vulnerability, a strategy that recurs in high angle shots of Pip exploring Satis House. These images underscore how Pip is physically, socially, and emotionally overwhelmed by the place and presented in an all-encompassing diegetic world, a particular kind of realist past in the filmic present.

Presentness is the basis for the film's most significant affects and returns us to the novel's affects of suspense, albeit with altered mechanisms.[12] By removing Pip's narration, Newell's film removes his ironic self-commentary. In its stead, the film offers ironic responses from its female characters, from the wide-eyed sarcasm of Miss Havisham telling a frightened Pip "Then come closer!" to the mocking tone of Biddy after Pip demands she teach him everything. "Everything?" she replies. "Goodness. Well, that will take a little time." Irony makes the film's women more coherent as characters and reshapes Pip into a less introspective and more awkward, humiliated, and shamed character. The present tense presentation of Pip signals a kind of perpetual anxious immediacy organized by his fear that his empty self-image will falter and lead to his humiliation. Throughout the film Pip is in a state of barely repressed rage, a result the film implies of his situation as an awkward and unreflective young man more concerned with fitting in than with the effects of his behavior on others. His rivalry with Bentley Drummle is thus a point of focus. The film includes multiple scenes of near-violent confrontation between the two and tracks Pip's adjustment of his garments and hair to resemble Drummle's appearance, complete with tousled hair and popped jacket collar. Rage and humiliation are central to its presentation of Pip during Joe's visit to London, a scene transposed from Pip's apartment to a public house. There, Pip aggressively reiterates Herbert Pocket's lessons in table manners to Joe and explodes in anger when Joe pays for his own meal. Similarly, Pip's encounter with Miss Havisham and Estella after he has learned that Magwitch is his benefactor focuses on his rage at being misled. Without the irony of narration to temper Pip's experiences, he becomes a character overrun by his emotions, trapped in a perpetual present without reflection or escape to a safer future.

For this reason, Estella becomes a crucial emotional and affective pivot for Newell's film, a subject able to view an unreflecting, rage-filled, and humiliated Pip with irony and understanding. In this way, Newell's film solves a recurring problem for film adaptations of *Great Expectations*. In the novel, Estella is little more than the image that Pip has crafted for himself. Like the narrator of ETA Hoffman's "The Sandman," Pip trades eyes with himself, a vision of love as a fantasy of self-recognition. Narratively, Pip's doubling as character and narrator allows him to present this experience with nuance, at times suggesting the possibility of an Estella who exists beyond his understanding and representational capacities. For Lean and Cuarón, voiceover allows Pip to ironize himself but leaves Estella untouched. Indeed, voiceover gives Pip an increased sense of narrative agency as the man who controls the presentation of his story. Pip's vision of Estella as the object of desire thus readily coincides with the fetishistic demands of the male gaze, and Estella serves in both Lean and Cuarón's films as the object of visual pleasure. Although Newell's film is not free from the suggestion of visual pleasure in its presentation of Estella, its rejection of voiceover frees her from Pip's narratorial control and thus provides her with some narrative autonomy. This representational choice may be due to marketing demands. Higson notes that since the 1990s, British heritage films have used strong female leads to drive crossover between art house and mainstream cinema audiences, producing films that may act simultaneously "as mainstream romantic dramas and as tasteful and 'authentic' adaptations" ("English Heritage" 47). Nevertheless, this remaking of Estella for market demands allows the film to imagine, however fleetingly, an escape from the affective landscape of its conjuncture. With Estella, the film finds escape from exaggeration and humiliation, from fears of failed self-image, and from the perpetual present from which there is no escape.

This line of flight appears in Estella's use of irony to undermine and rewrite the icy denotations of her dialogue from the novel. The film's adaptation of a scene in which Pip decries Drummle to Estella as they wait for her escort to take her home from a party is instructional. In the novel, Pip pleads his desires before she responds:

> "Do you want me then," said Estella, turning suddenly with a fixed and serious, if not angry, look, "to deceive and entrap you?"
> "Do you deceive and entrap him, Estella?"
> "Yes, and many others—all of them but you. Here is Mrs. Brandley. I'll say no more." (38:311–12)

The film resituates this dialogue and alters its characters' affects. Rather than a discussion after a party, Pip angrily storms out of a party after Estella acknowledges Drummle and dances with him for the first time. Estella follows him. There being no Mrs. Brandley, the scene continues. Pip asks, "Why am I to be spared?" and Estella replies, "Why do you think?" In the ensuing pause, the camera pulls back to frame Pip and Estella in the ur-landscape of the English heritage film, the manicured landscape of the British estate house, before they awkwardly clasp hands and draw closer to kiss. Only an interruption by Jaggers prevents them.

The relationship between the two is one guided less by Pip's desire than by Estella's emotional uncertainty, an effect of Miss Havisham's teaching and of Estella's reading of the men in the film as indistinguishable rage peacocks. Throughout the film, Estella seems to have more agency than Pip. Though the narrative continues to revolve around Pip, any drama of motivation, action, and character in the film belongs to Estella. The film's conclusion underscores her role as the chief agent of its romance plot: she sends Pip a note to arrange their meeting, she tells Pip of her husband's death, and she calls Pip "my only friend" and recites his speech back to him. Only then does Pip grasp the situation and stutteringly reply: "I love you, Estella." The tears that show a moral change in this film are Estella's not Pip's and she grasps his hand to indicate that if there is no shadow of another parting in Newell's film, this is a result of her decision. On this image of their clasped hands, the film ends.

What is curious and suggestive in Newell's film is that escape from an endless present, the idea that one may imagine a future, is a decision not available to the character whose experiences organize its narrative. To imagine an escape from the present, an activity that would break through the lack of futurity and pastness, the anxiety of self-presentation and the threat of humiliation, someone who is not centerstage must act. By holding still on their clasped hands, the film does not escape from the present but, much like Lean's film, leaves its viewers trapped in it for perpetuity. The future may be imagined but it cannot be pictured. The gendering of this agent of futurity also seems important. The inability to imagine a masculine future places the onus of futurity on the feminine, a move that relies on a gendering of fecundity and a too easy vision of politics that believes positive political change will come simply by empowering women. (And why would an empowered Estella want Pip?) The ending is equivocal. Its gendering is of a piece with its tidy resolution of the romance plot, a unification of the narrative in much the same way the film presents the past as whole and complete. Yet its need to find an exterior agent to subvert the tale's ways of feeling— anger, anxiety, shame, and humiliation—suggest that they have hardly passed at all.

Are these still Dickensian affects, then, or something different? After all, adaptations are not simple translations of story from one medium to another but revisions of form, content, and feeling to new conjunctural demands. These films share certain patterns and rhythms with their adapted text but differ in crucial ways. Are Dickensian affects simply the felt wake of story elements in Dickens's texts? That would seem to be the sense of an adaptation like the BBC's short-lived series *Dickensian*, which drew together characters from various novels to produce a new narrative. Yet Dickens's story elements are not enough in and of themselves to produce Dickensian affects. What affects in Dickens's novels is the result of their form, the intricate patterning of story elements, narrative forms, and historical resonances. Different conjunctures produce different demands and these demands do more or less violence to the affective form of an adapted text. Adaptations of *Great Expectations* rely extensively on the adapted text's story elements, their narrative organization, and their textual presentation yet produce what are in essence new texts. The results draw on the novel's representations of shame, contempt, vulnerability, and humiliation but inflect the rhythm of their presentation in fundamentally different ways. These differences suggest an affective negotiation much like that between sufferer and spectator in Adam Smith, one in which the adapted text provides the melody and the adapting text the rhythm and timbre, a negotiation in which both strive for compositional and performative control. The resulting affects are if not uniquely Dickensian then in a complex negotiation with the Dickensian, one that suggests Dickensian affects are ways of feeling capitalism's precarity and readily mistaken for the return of a nineteenth-century repressed.

This transhistorical analysis of affect and affective form means to put to rest the charge that literary criticism which engages with affect has no interest in critique. It takes seriously Walter Benjamin's insistence that "To articulate what is past does not mean to recognize 'how it really was.' It means to take control of a memory, as it flashes in a moment of danger" (391). The field of literary studies is in its own moment of danger. "Why do we exist?" we are asked, though often the question is more properly, "Why should you be allowed to continue to exist?" Thus, we return to the question: Why study nineteenth-century British literature, especially if one's interest is the present in its political, economic, or material concerns? The historical precedents for the present moment are more likely to be unearthed in historical research rather than literature with its limited canon and available sources. To look to cultural texts to discover answers to current predicaments can seem akin to looking under a streetlight to find one's keys. Yet cultural texts offer historical evidence and something more. Their uses of a culture's manifold discourses and their representations of material economic forces reveal how that culture felt and represented particular situations. Adaptations suggest that the persistence of Dickensian affects is also the persistence of Dickensian situations. Their imbrications of affect and historical situation demand that we wrestle with the meaning and purpose of presentations of and solicitations to feel. This is the critical political contribution of affect studies to literary criticism: to analyze and critique constructions of feeling, intended and contingent, as they are rather than as we think they should be. The should-be may only follow from what is.[13] Why study the past, the nineteenth century, or cultural texts in general? To understand how the ways we feel with and about others and ourselves have been, are, and can be shaped in relation to our conjuncture. To engage with culture and cultural texts is not to go out looking for good feelings. It is to grapple with the problems of how cultures produce feelings. This is why feelings matter. Fascism, as Deleuze and Guattari argue, is simply a particular form and shape of feeling, one in which the drift of meaning becomes a desire for death (cf. *Thousand Plateaus* 215). By understanding the forms and conjunctural forces that shape them, we may remake them.

To analyze this play of cultural texts, discourses, and feelings, one is better served by thinking in musical terms rather than visual ones. In *A Critique of Hegel's Philosophy of Right*, Karl Marx decries the "spectacle" of

> a society infinitely divided into the most diverse races which confront one another with their petty antipathies, their bad consciences and their brutal mediocrity and which, precisely because of their ambivalent and suspicious attitudes towards one another, are dealt with by their *masters* without distinction (246).

A "criticism" (246) suited to the conflicts and diversity of a such a society, Marx insists, must itself be dynamic, vital, affective. "[Society's] petrified conditions must be made to dance by having their own tune sung to them!" Marx exclaims. "The people must be put in *terror* of themselves in order to give them *courage*" (247). If we are to grasp our moment, we need an analytic that teaches us how to sing society's tune, atonalities, arrhythmias, and all.

Notes

1 Levine's account of rhythm in *Forms* treats it as historical pattern and as a question of prosody. See Levine 49–81.
2 This notion of rhythm runs throughout Deleuze and Guattari's *A Thousand Plateaus*, including their discussion of becoming-animal and the refrain but also appears in their discussion of stratas, e.g., 502.
3 For an account of the close-up as an image of affect, see Deleuze, *Cinema I*, 70. It is important to note that this distinction is not limited to Deleuze scholars but is also accepted by narratology more widely. See Schneider 137.
4 I draw here on arguments about film adaptations of Shakespeare made by Richard Halpern and Jared Scott Johnson. It is also worth noting that the film's opening famously emphasizes its literary basis: Pip speaks the opening lines in voice-over as a breeze begins to turn the pages of Dickens's novel, linking the space of the reader with the image of Pip running across the windswept marshes.
5 See Trimm 94–124.
6 See McFarlane, *Charles Dickens's* 170–71.
7 On hope as a relation to possibility and futurity, see Eagleton, *Hope without Optimism* 52.
8 On late capitalism, see Mandel. On neoliberalism, see Harvey. On post-Fordism, see Marazzi. On communicative capitalism (and the related term "cognitive capitalism"), see Dean.
9 See Harvey, *Brief History* 1–38.
10 See Grossberg, *Under the Cover* 35–39.
11 For Jameson on postmodern temporality, see "Antinomies of Postmodernism" in *The Cultural Turn*, esp. 57.
12 Some critics suggest that spectacle in the heritage film may at times offer a more dialectical engagement with history, in particular via its use of landscape. For Rosalind Galt, landscape in heritage films may operate in a "distinct semiotic register in which visual pleasure and affect produce meaning differently than does the narrative discourse" (61). When produced in tandem with narratives of romantic and historical loss, such spectacles can fall out of the narrative register, Galt insists, and thus "interpellate the spectator... as a subject in mourning" (68), in effect catching the spectator between "masochistic pleasure in the distance of the historical other" and a "mapping of [contemporary] political space" (239). In short, the heritage film may allow viewers to produce dialectical images a la Benjamin, seizing images of the past as they rise up to their own political experience.
13 See Sedgewick, *Touching Feeling* 12–13, and Grossberg and Behrenhausen 1004.

References

Benjamin, Walter. "On the Concept of History." *Selected Writings, Volume 4, 1938–1940*. Translated by Edmund Jephcott and others, edited by Howard Eiland and Michael W. Jennings, Cambridge: The Belknap Press of Harvard, pp. 389–411.

Dean, Jodi. *Democracy and Other Neoliberal Fantasies: Communicative Capitalism and Left Politics*. Durham, NC: Duke University Press, 2009.

Deleuze, Gilles. *Cinema 1: The Movement Image*. Translated by Hugh Tomalinson and Barbara Habberjam. Minneapolis: University of Minnesota Press, 1986.

Deleuze, Gilles, and Felix Guattari. *A Thousand Plateaus*. Translated by Brian Massumi. Minneapolis: University of Minnesota Press, 1987.

Dickens, Charles. *Great Expectations*. Edited by Charlotte Mitchell. New York: Penguin, 1996.

Eagleton, Terry. *Hope without Optimism*. Charlottesville: University of Virginia Press, 2015.

Galt, Rosalind. *The New European Cinema: Redrawing the Map*. New York: Columbia University Press, 2006.

Great Expectations. Directed by Alfonso Cuarón. Twentieth Century Fox, 1998.

Great Expectations. Directed by David Lean. Cineguild, 1946.

Great Expectations. Directed by Mike Newell. BBC Films, 2012.

Grossberg, Lawrence. *Under the Cover of Chaos: Trump and the Battle for the American Right*. London: Pluto Press, 2018.

Halpern, Richard. *Shakespeare among the Moderns*. Ithaca, NY: Cornell University Press, 1997.

Harvey, David. *A Brief History of Neoliberalism*. Oxford: Oxford University Press, 2005.

Higson, Andrew. *English Heritage, English Cinema: Costume Drama since 1980*. Oxford: Oxford University Press, 2003.

———. *Film England: Culturally English Filmmaking since the 1990s*. London: I.B. Tauris, 2010.

———. "Re-Presenting the National Past: Nostalgia and Pastiche in Heritage Film." *Fires Were Started: British Cinema and Thatcherism*, edited by Lester Friedman. Minneapolis: University of Minnesota Press, 1993, pp. 109–29.

Hutcheon, Linda. *A Theory of Adaptation*. 2nd Edition. London: Routledge, 2012.

Jaffe, Audrey. *Scenes of Sympathy: Identity and Representation in Victorian Fiction*. Ithaca, NY: Cornell University Press, 2000.

Jameson, Fredric. *The Cultural Turn: Selected Writings on Postmodernism, 1983–1998*. London: Verso, 1998.

Johnson, Jared Scott. "The Propaganda Imperative: Challenging Mass Media Representations in McKellen's *Richard III*," *College Literature*, vol. 31, no. 4 (Fall 2004), pp. 44–59.

Levine, Caroline. *Forms: Whole, Rhythm, Hierarchy, Network*. Princeton, NJ: Princeton University Press, 2015.

Lordon, Frédéric. *Willing Slaves of Capital: Spinoza and Marx on Capital*. London: Verso, 2014.

Mandel, Ernest. *Late Capitalism*. London: Verso, 1999.

Marazzi, Christian. *Capital and Language*. Cambridge, MA: MIT Press, 2008.

Marx, Karl. *Early Writings*. Translated by Rodney Livingstone. New York: Penguin, 1992.

McFarlane, Brian. *Charles Dickens's Great Expectations: The Relationship between Text and Film*. London: Methuen Press, 2008.

———. "David Lean's *Great Expectations*—Meeting Two Challenges," *Literature-Film Quarterly*, vol. 30, no. 1 (1992), pp. 68–76.

Schneider, Ralf. "Emotion and Narrative." *Routledge Encyclopaedia of Narrative*, edited by David Herman, Manfred John, and Marie-Laure Ryan. London: Routledge, 2005, pp. 136–37.

Sedgwick, Eve Kosofsky. *Touching Feeling*. Durham, NC: Duke University Press, 2003.

Sennett, Richard. *The Corrosion of Character: The Personal Consequences of Work in the New Capitalism*. New York: WW Norton, 1998.

Trimm, Ryan. *Heritage and the Legacy of the Past in Britain*. London: Routledge, 2018.

Virno, Paolo. *A Grammar of Multitude: For an Analysis of Contemporary Forms of Life*. Los Angeles: Semiotext(e), 2004.

Weber, Max. *The Protestant Ethic and the Spirit of Capitalism*. London: Routledge, 2001.

Index

Lightning Source UK Ltd.
Milton Keynes UK
UKHW022250120321
380273UK00005B/1223